Systemic-Dialogical Therapy with Individuals

'Systemic-Dialogical Therapy with Individuals is a groundbreaking exploration of therapy in today's complex world. Bertrando and Lini seamlessly integrate systemic, dialogical, and feminist perspectives to address the evolving challenges of modern individuals shaped by neoliberalism, digital life, and shifting intimacies. Rich with theoretical insights and clinical examples, the book offers a compassionate, relational approach that is both practical and inspiring. A must-read for therapists, this work redefines individual therapy for our time while honoring the roots of systemic thought.'

Prof. Dr. Peter Rober, author of *Becoming an Effective Family Therapist*
(Routledge 2024)

In this book, Paolo Bertrando and Claudia Lini provide a comprehensive and cutting-edge overview of the systemic-dialogical approach, adapted to the ever-evolving requirements of modern-day therapy with individuals.

Following on from the field-defining work *Systemic Therapy with Individuals*, and easily used as a companion, this book introduces a new dialogical approach which will encourage practising therapists to adopt a collaborative and empowered stance in their work. The authors interweave clinical examples and transcripts of sessions collated from over a decade of work to illustrate the applied benefits of this approach in the contemporary therapeutic space. The case studies include work with those experiencing the oppression of patriarchal relationships, social and emotional isolation, physical abuse and pathological shame, reinvigorating and modernising the therapist's understanding of these lived experiences. Moving from general concepts to practical issues, the book explores queer theory, feminist theory, non-traditional family formats, and the impact of neoliberalism. The holistic and systemic approach will guide the reader to work better with clients from all genders, races and economic situations. Building on the foundations of systemic therapy, the theories develop our understanding of emotions and the body, while Bertrando and Lini introduce the concept of 'finding one's place' as a means of encouraging individual positional responsibility.

Presenting an empathetic and inclusive understanding of contemporary life and psychic experiences, as well as personal, couple and familial relationships, this book provides invaluable techniques on how to conduct sessions, and will benefit students and practitioners of psychotherapy, including systemic family therapists, psychoanalysts, psychiatrists, psychologists, psychiatric nurses, occupational therapists and social workers.

Paolo Bertrando is a psychiatrist and systemic-dialogical therapist based in Milan, Italy. He is the co-director of the Systemic-Dialogical School of Therapy based in Italy and is the co-author, with Luigi Boscolo, of *The Time of Times: A Perspective on Time in Systemic Therapy and Consultation* (2019), and the author of *Emotions and the Therapist: A Systemic-Dialogical Approach* (2015) and *The Dialogical Therapist: Dialogue in Systemic Practice* (2007).

Claudia Lini is a psychologist and systemic-dialogical therapist based in Milan, Italy. She is the co-director of the Systemic-Dialogical School of Therapy. Her main interests are gender issues and creative processes in therapy.

The Systemic Thinking and Practice Series
Series Editors: Charlotte Burck and Gwyn Daniel

This influential series was co-founded in 1989 by series editors David Campbell and Ros Draper to promote innovative applications of systemic theory to psychotherapy, teaching, supervision and organisational consultation. In 2011, Charlotte Burck and Gwyn Daniel became series editors and aim to present new theoretical developments and pioneering practice, to make links with other theoretical approaches, and to promote the relevance of systemic theory to contemporary social and psychological questions.

Recent titles in the series include:

Emotions and the Therapist: A Systemic-Dialogical Approach
Paolo Bertrando

Creative Positions in Adult Mental Health: Outside In-Inside Out
Edited by Sue McNab and Karen Partridge

Ethical and Aesthetic Explorations of Systemic Practice: New Critical Reflections
Pietro Barbetta, Maria Esther Cavagnis, Inga-Britt Krause and Umberta Telfener

Working Systemically with Refugee Couples and Families: Exploring Trauma, Resilience and Culture
Shadi Shahnavaz

Psychotherapeutic Competencies: Techniques, Relationships, and Epistemology in Systemic Practice
Laura Fruggeri, Francesca Balestra, and Elena Venturelli

Systemic Perspectives in Mental Health, Social Work and Youth Care
Anke Savenije, Justine van Lawick, and Ellen Reijmers

Systemic and Narrative Work with Unaccompanied Asylum-Seeking Children: Stories of Relocation
Ana Draper, Elisa Marcellino, and Samantha Thomson

Systemic-Dialogical Therapy with Individuals: Finding One's Place
Paolo Bertrando and Claudia Lini

Systemic-Dialogical Therapy with Individuals

Finding One's Place

Paolo Bertrando and Claudia Lini

Routledge
Taylor & Francis Group
LONDON AND NEW YORK

First published 2026
by Routledge
4 Park Square, Milton Park, Abingdon, Oxon OX14 4RN

and by Routledge
605 Third Avenue, New York, NY 10158

Routledge is an imprint of the Taylor & Francis Group, an informa business

Designed cover image: Getty Images

British Library Cataloguing in Publication Data
A catalogue record for this book is available from the British Library

ISBN: 9781032464558 (hbk)
ISBN: 9781032438559 (pbk)
ISBN: 9781003381754 (ebk)

DOI: 10.4324/9781003381754

Typeset in Times New Roman
by Taylor & Francis Books

Contents

Series editors' foreword

Systemic Therapy with Individuals by Luigi Boscolo and Paolo Bertrando, published in this series in 1996, was a hugely influential book within the systemic field. It formed part of a transition from defining systemic therapy mainly by the relational context within which the therapist worked—i.e. family, couple, wider family or professional systems—towards refining and redefining the approach as primarily embedded in its theoretical and clinical stances. Systemic psychotherapy thus took its place as a valid and valuable form of therapy for individuals, enabling those who, for various reasons, worked mainly in this way to enrich and enlarge the foundations of their practice and reflect on new ways of conceptualising and acting in the therapeutic relationship.

Now, 30 years later, we are absolutely delighted that one of the original authors, Paolo Bertrando, together with his co-author, Claudia Lini, has produced a new volume. Rather than revising the 1996 book they have embarked upon an entirely new volume which reflects the many developments and transformations both within systemic theory as well as in the evolution of their own practice, which they now define as a systemic-dialogical model.

In a major development from the 1996 book, Bertrando and Lini subject the whole idea of the individual to rigorous scrutiny, exploring the many different contexts in which individual subjectivity is constructed and experienced. They have thus produced a compelling reconceptualisation of the individual, not only as located within their relational system but more fundamentally within wider social contexts and ideologies such as neoliberalism or the digital world, all with their accompanying discursive practices. They highlight those many exigencies and expectations for living which act as compelling and often invisible constraints on the people who seek their help. They explore how expectations such as the need to be autonomous and self-sufficient, the need to be constantly available to employers, the requirement to take personal rather than collective responsibility can infiltrate subjectivities and are so often experienced in the emotions of shame, humiliation or a sense of failure. Likewise they show how patriarchal power and ideology shape relationships and expectations and they take an in-depth look at different ways of performing sexuality and gender identity, drawing upon feminist and queer literature.

The authors have located their practice within wider systemic frameworks including dialogic (Bakhtin) positioning (Harré) and the work of other theorists such as Zygmunt Bauman who may be less familiar to systemic therapists. All these frameworks form the background to the authors' argument for the importance of exploring emotions relationally, and for "unpacking" the nuanced ways which social discourses frame and influence our ideas about our selfhood while at the same time never determining them. Above all the book provides a wealth of clinical material and the authors have a wonderful way of exposing their own learning from the emotional dilemmas presented to them and describing how they access and communicate their own emotions as therapists.

They provide a compelling description of the processes within their clinical approach—which uses a dialogical, questioning methodology where therapists advance "micro-hypotheses" which are opened up to responses by the client. This highlighting of the dialogic fits beautifully with their central premise that therapy involves "teasing out" the nuanced ways in which individual experience might be embedded in expectations from the wider sociocultural world and at the same time challenging the belief that any of our identities are inescapably determined by it.

The authors' ability to openly and clearly share the basis of their work and to provide such detail about their thinking, feeling, speaking and acting in therapy is a hugely important resource and a great gift for systemic therapists—and indeed any therapist working with individuals. We are delighted to welcome it into our series.

Charlotte Burck and Gwyn Daniel

Foreword

Halfway into our third decade of the twenty-first century many of us who have been concerned with systemic understandings of therapeutic process have acknowledge the need to consider how macro level systems (institutions, material conditions, etc.) co-exist with micro level interactions. Moreover, there is recognition that our everyday interactions (micro level) are inseparable from the (often unquestioned) macro level systems amongst which we live. Not only do these macro level systems influence how we act and what we believe but our micro level interactions sustain (or change) those unquestioned beliefs and worldviews. How has capitalist competition displaced our sense of a stable, secure world and opened the door to a "liquid world" (Bauman, 2000) where the sense of self is polyphonic?

Systemic-Dialogical Therapy with Individuals provides an overview of cultural/historical shifts and the implications of those shifts for therapy, taking us from early systems work to the evolution of the systemic approach, followed by the postmodern movement in therapy. The systemic-dialogical approach introduced in this volume is an attempt to reconsider Boscolo and Bertrando's 1996 *Systemic Therapy with Individuals*, positioned as it was amongst systemic ideas of the 1990s. That volume, published in 1996, was an attempt to bring the Milan systemic approach to family therapy to work with individuals. Here, individuals were, themselves, viewed as systems and systemic therapy with individuals explored how these systems were positioned in relation to other systems in their lives. As the authors of the present volume point out, such explorations were motivated by a search for order (or what we might refer to as pattern). And the search for order, Bauman (1993) claims, is a modernist objective.

In their retrospective look at the early work of the Milan systemic team, Bertrando and Lini now see the systemic view as mechanistic—precisely the movement it was designed to replace! Their attention in this book is placed on *architecture* as opposed to medicine (where medicine serves as the analogy to modernist/mechanistic approaches), citing style as a critical component of architecture. But what is the style (or architecture) presented to us? It is one embracing Bauman's (2000) notion of liquid modernity. This is not only in contrast to modernist ways of being but to the postmodern movement that served as a critique of modernism. To Bertrando and Lini, postmodernism was infused with the privilege of centring discourse and language with disregard for material conditions. Bauman's liquid modernity, on the other hand, places our focus on the consequences of competition spawned by capitalism on our identities, our relationships, and our place in a world that is constantly changing. Concern here is with how material conditions shape how we operate in a world devoid of stability. The shift from modernism to liquid modernity is a shift from viewing the world as stable and fixed (secure jobs, lifelong relationships, and clear and stable social roles) to acknowledging that our world is in constant flux, fragile, unpredictable, and fluid. Such a view offers many potentials and can also invite feelings of instability that create challenges to our sense of self.

The consideration of material conditions—what many of us refer to as the macro systemic level—are united in the present work with the dialogic emphasis on polyvocality. Here, not only the fluidity of material conditions but the movement away from attempts to resolve differences keeps the conversation going and, in so doing, entertains possibility and potential. This embrace of uncertainty, as opposed to our general idea that therapy is about resolving problems, firmly places the therapeutic conversation within our current cultural fluidity. It also, importantly, invites all voices into the arena. This means that the therapist becomes responsible for interrogating his or her positionality and emotions. The therapist is invited to bring him or herself into the therapeutic conversation. This deviates from the therapeutic tradition of—to put it bluntly—conducting therapy the *right way* and as an expert. Where medicine offers clear pathways to diagnosis and treatment, systemic-dialogic therapy invites innovation, creativity, and an integration of diverse modalities. It is a style that departs as well from the iconic style introduced by the architects of systemic therapy, Boscolo and Cecchin. None of us are Boscolo or Cecchin. And the systemic-dialogical approach outlined here reminds us to be present in the therapeutic encounter rather than strive to mimic the masters. In this regard, systemic-dialogical therapy is less about adherence to specific theories and methods and more about "finding one's place." Thankfully, several excellent case illustrations are offered to walk us through what this might look like.

While holding on to much of the systemic approach, the authors develop four pillars that orient their model: dialogue, emotions, finding one's place, and responsibility. From this orientation, the well-known practices of the systemic model (e.g., circularity) become optional and certainly dependent upon the current therapeutic conversation. This echoes the collaborative and participatory nature of dialogue where the patient and therapist—together— engage in examining the interplay of macro level conditions and the multiple—yet incomplete—stories circulating. Introducing patients to a multiplicity of views yields incompleteness which fosters respect for the uniqueness of others. Note, such a focus departs radically from any form of definitive resolution.

This volume is situated within the complex and incomplete moment within which we are living. There are no definitive answers to individuals' problems. There is no "all knowing" therapist to intervene, resolve, or transform an individual's dilemmas. What we have instead is a refreshing realisation that when therapist and individual meet, attention to the four pillars invites patient and therapist into a dialogue as opposed to an expert/client relationship. This underscores the consensual nature of therapy.

Systemic-Dialogical Therapy with Individuals invites us to pay attention to the individual and to wider systems and context. In so doing, we invite those we work with to do the same. When therapists' and patients' attention is thus focused, examination of our individual positions within our relational networks is possible, generating a sense of place and responsibility in the lives we create for ourselves and others.

Sheila McNamee
Professor Emerita, University of New Hampshire, USA

References

Bauman, Z. (2000). *Liquid Modernity*. Polity Press.
Bauman, Z. (1993). *Postmodern Ethics*. Blackwell Publishing.

Introduction

If two people write a dialogical book, the least they can do is to write a dialogical introduction, since it would be hard to write the whole book in dialogical form. Besides being influenced by dialogical ideas, the book is also the—provisionally—final outcome of an ongoing dialogical process. A dialogue between the two of us, and between us and our patients, our colleagues, and other people who influenced us, both directly and through articles, books, conferences, workshops, and works of art. This is why we are shaping the remainder of this introduction in the form of a dialogue.

PAOLO: This book was born out of the idea of updating the original book, *Systemic Therapy with Individuals*, that I wrote together with Luigi Boscolo thirty years ago. I quickly realised that it was impossible for me to modify a book in the absence of its co-author, and when I disclosed my perplexity to editors and publisher, I received the proposal to write a new book instead. At this point, it was inevitable to call you in, and to emphasise the novelties of our systemic-dialogical approach. And we decided to do it together.

CLAUDIA: We had with that first book quite a different relationship: you were a co-author, I had been a reader and a trainee. I always felt that *Systemic Therapy with Individuals* was a child of its time, imbued with the inherent—sometimes short-sighted—postmodernism of the 1990s. When reading and applying it, anyway, we both accepted unquestioningly its basic views, including its view of the individual.

PAOLO: In that book, there is no theory of the subject. I can remember that Boscolo and I decided to skip that part, because the very idea of theorising the subject was at odds with the Milan systemic approach of the time, centred on an external view of relationships. We thought that adopting a theory of the individual was a way of reifying something that, in Batesonian terms, could only be seen as a knot in a network of relationships. So we put in it one of Bateson's famous quotes, about a man cutting a tree, where the system does not involve an "I", but the man is

DOI: 10.4324/9781003381754-1

forced to say "I", although this is simply a version of a severe epistemological error.

CLAUDIA: Your non-theorised individual had another (implicit) pitfall: it was completely out of history. That book obligingly quoted Kenneth Gergen and its theory of the saturated self, but the two of you seemed to consider this condition as the unveiling of some human universal, rather than something whose supposedly postmodern nature was embedded in a transient moment of history.

PAOLO: We lacked that awareness. We had some intuitions, but they never became central in writing that book. Social and historical dimensions were more apparent, and more thoroughly considered in our previous book, *The Times of Time*. The characterisation of the individual in *Systemic Therapy with Individuals* sometimes seems to me schematic, sometimes even shallow.

CLAUDIA: Were those individuals emotional?

PAOLO: They were in practice—I remember Boscolo was very attentive to the patient's emotions—but, paradoxically, not in theory: we simply remembered sometimes that emotions were very important, but we left it there, without any further elaboration. I began to work more systematically on emotions on my own, at least ten years later.

CLAUDIA: Speaking of individuals, our own practice of individual therapy was originally quite close to the one outlined in the original book—also because it was our main source. Slowly, it grew substantially different from it.

PAOLO: That first book was written by two therapists who were attuned to family therapy. To an extent, it was a discovery. Of course, we had been practising individual therapy for some time—in Boscolo's case, quite a long time. But the idea of taking Milan ideas and using them in individual therapy was a new one. This is why that book is so enthusiastic and, at the same time, it appears somewhat provisional, especially in the procedures.

CLAUDIA: In the present book we wanted to describe our current way of doing individual therapy. I think that it was while working on it that we realised the extent of the differences from the previous approach, that we delineated a wholly new practice—or, we can say, a wholly new style. The practice of therapy—of our therapy, at least—is more similar to architecture than medicine, because it involves a style.

PAOLO: There are of course basic principles and techniques, but once a therapist has learned them, they begin to develop their own style, whereas in medicine one tries to make the right diagnosis, then find a way to cure the corresponding disease.

CLAUDIA: In architecture, you couldn't have a Giò Ponti, to name a famous Italian architect, without having had the rationalist movement, with architects like Le Corbusier or Lloyd Wright. I am still grateful to the ones who came before me, because if I hadn't known very well my own roots I couldn't raise my head and develop my own approach. I could develop new branches of the preceding approach, because it had been signed by two previous architects, who were Boscolo and Cecchin. Their style, in turn, was inherent to their personas and their time, exactly like Le Corbusier's or Wright's.

PAOLO: If we go backwards, Boscolo and Cecchin developed their approach out of the original Milan team's, that was quite different. And the original team developed their approach working on Watzlawick's and the MRI's, and Watzlawick in turn developed the MRI brief therapy out of Bateson's and the Bateson group's research.

CLAUDIA: It's a family tree, rather than the evolution of a scientific paradigm, like in physics or biology. Clearly, we train our trainees according to our approach, our style and our signatures. But those who will come after us, if they have taken in the genesis of the approach, will be able to develop something different, albeit starting from our theoretical and practical basis.

PAOLO: When I was (or felt) completely inside the Milan approach, I tried to create something different, but I failed, because it was impossible to renew the Milan approach remaining inside it. Despite Cecchin's emphasis on irreverence, I felt I had to be reverent towards the main tenets of the approach, although I was beginning to feel uncomfortable.

CLAUDIA: It was necessary to get out of it, and to make a fresh start, beginning from ourselves. Even if we had new ideas, those ideas had to be grounded and situated in the different levels of complexity we were inhabiting. The first level of complexity was emotional. I remember that, at first, we had a strong emotional response to the step we were taking. In that liminal phase, when we were kind of defectors, we were wandering: "Where are we? How do we feel, relative to what we have left? And where are we going?" To me, this method implied a feminist practice. I should not speak for others, but first of all for myself: "how do I feel?"

PAOLO: And we added: "where am I?", that was our own contribution...

CLAUDIA: Yes, but with gratitude and appreciation for the women who first outlined this way of thinking, always standing from themselves, refusing to speak for others or create models about the others, how they felt and so on.

PAOLO: When we introduced this kind of discourse, we also introduced the famous statement "The personal is political", and therefore we introduced politics, that was completely absent before. And politics introduces power, that had been all but denied by the Batesonian tradition.

CLAUDIA: If I participate in process of cure, and I am not the one who is cured but the one who cures, I have (some) power. And I must be aware of it. This is why we like the idea that both diagnosis and intervention are shared and consensual with our patients.

PAOLO: This awareness of power has been clear in narrative therapies for years, but I think we add a more thorough refection on economic issues.

CLAUDIA: And of course a reflection on privilege: in our school the majority of trainees are women, but a vast majority of them, in turn, is white, heterosexual and middle class, since they can afford a private post-graduate programme. Psychotherapy is, to quote Foucault again, a technology of the Self that is chiefly reserved for people with a good income. We—and our trainees too—must always remember it.

PAOLO: Yes, in private practice a middle-class therapist sells therapy to middle-class patients. In health services, there is no such peer-to-peer economic transaction: the therapist has a power over the patient, they can make decisions without necessarily getting an agreement, and so the therapist risks to become patronising.

CLAUDIA: To sum up: from the original book *Systemic Therapy with Individuals* we took the emphasis on systems and many concepts derived from Gregory Bateson's thinking, as well as several practices in the Milan systemic tradition. From the following two books you wrote, the dialogical perspective, namely the necessity of consensuality with our patients and a more horizontal approach, and the importance of an analysis of emotions inside and outside the session.

PAOLO: From your feminist practice we took the necessity of starting from ourselves and our position—that, together with emotional awareness, we integrated in the concept of finding one's place, and also the interest toward personal responsibility and expectations. All together, these represent the most innovative aspects of our systemic-dialogical approach. At the same time, they emphasise the individual dimension of our therapy, and they justify the idea to give an account of our individual therapy.

CLAUDIA: All the rest, and the practical aspects of it, we can leave to our readers. Because, as we said above, they are the ones that can use what we have developed. In doing it, they will change it, and lead it to further evolution.

PAOLO: We are, once again, in the hands of our readers.

Milan, January 2025

Note on the text

Language is important to us, and so is the structure of a book. The present book has some peculiarities the reader should get acquainted with. First of all, the way of referring to the people who ask us for help. We debated several terms: the term "client" we don't like anymore, because of its commercial connotations; the term "user" refers specifically to people who seek treatment in the public sector; it was impossible to find a single word that could convey the right meaning avoiding long periphrases that end up sounding awkward. In the end, we agreed on the old term "patient": despite its medical usage, it sounded like the lesser evil.

Then there is the book structure. The book is conceived to be modular, i.e., each chapter should be readable on its own, without requiring perforce to begin from the first chapter and go on. This entailed some repetition, that we tried to reduce to a minimum. We thought that our readers would presumably appreciate the idea of not being obliged to read it consecutively—although, if they so wished, its structure allows it. Moreover, for the sake of clarity, we have also subdivided the text into several sections and subsections.

The reader will find in the book quite a few endnotes. We mostly used them to make specific theoretical points, that we found useful for the reader wanting in-depth information about certain topics, without interrupting the flow of writing with somewhat lengthy digressions. The notes can be skipped without damaging the overall economy of reading.

Finally, we wanted the book to contain many clinical examples, in order to better illustrate the practical aspects of our work. Most of the brief case vignettes presented in the text give minimal information about the people involved. When cases are treated in more detail, we have obtained from the person involved permission for the use of this material. Some are "composite" cases, containing descriptions drawn from more than one situation. In all cases, we have disguised names and modified identifying details, in order to make actual people unrecognisable.

Chapter 1

Individuals

In order to do individual therapy, we must first of all deal with individuals. Here we will consider our view on the individual and its consequences for individual therapy. We will consider first the relationship between individuals and their cultural and social contexts, then their small group and intimate relationships, and finally their relationship with themselves—the inner world of the individual. Finally, we will give some examples of practical clinical work.

The individual and therapy

The individual is not an entity existing outside history and society. The very concept of "individual" is culturally determined: individual agency, the ideas of Ego and Self, are products of a comparatively recent Western culture (see Taylor, 1989). In different cultural contexts, individuals will conceive, perceive and describe themselves differently.

The individual that we will describe in this chapter is deeply embedded in present-day society and culture. Such version of the individual, we feel, may change pretty quickly. The individual of today is already quite different from the individual portrayed in the book *Systemic Therapy with Individuals*, more or less 30 years ago. When we checked how Luigi Boscolo and Paolo had conceived the individual at the time, we found, to our dismay, very little explicit reference to the nature of the individual in the whole book. Paolo even remembered that they deliberately chose not to consider the Self and its determinants in the book, because it did not fit with their Batesonian conception, that devalued any sort of individualistic approach (see Appendix A at the end of the book). They reasoned as if the alternative were between an ahistorical, monolithic individual and Gregory Bateson's radical non-individualistic systemic view. They thus missed the opportunity to investigate the ways in which systemic determinants shape and change individuals—or at least did not develop such perspective in full.

Today we automatically consider the social and cultural context every time we meet a person who asks for therapy. We are aware of our own gender,

DOI: 10.4324/9781003381754-2

social status, class, and race. It is a difference, compared to our past, and it shows better than any other the evolution of our field. This does not mean, though, that we radically change our basic approach every other year. We still maintain our main focus: relationships, relational networks and relational knots. Human systems constantly renew themselves, but they remain human systems. What we do is trying to understand the shape human relationships take in the world we inhabit. Maintaining our focus on relationships, we can adjust to the evolution of the world. A major change in our approach is that today we consider the individual as socially determined (Foucault, 1982), which means that our own "Self" does not simply relate to an ever-changing environment: it is actually created by that environment.

We consider an individual as a small, mobile, intelligent unit (Robert Fripp, in Snowden, 1979), who exists within a tangle of systems and contexts, and from that position acts and takes responsibility for their own actions. Individuals are shaped by all systems, contexts, relationship they are embedded in. At the same time, human systems and contexts exist only because they are defined by the co-existence of a multiplicity of individuals, who act as active participants in the life of those cultural, social, and affective systems.[1] When we talk about individuals, we are talking about what we experience from our own vantage point, in the Italian (European) context of the early twenty-first century—a quite specific cultural, historical, and social position. At the same time, we think our view may be helpful also for colleagues who live and work in different realities, provided they remember that they have to adapt our practices to other contexts and positions.

The individual and the context

Nadia is 28. She is the manager of a co-working space. In the evenings, to make ends meet, she also writes anonymous articles for an online magazine. She works hard for little pay, yet she comes to therapy for a very different problem. She finds it difficult to build an enduring, satisfactory enough relationship with some man and she feels responsible for her own failures. Flora, 35, complains of a lack of sexual intimacy with her husband Leo, 43. She perceives him as always tired and listless; she relates that he, in turn, accuses her of never arousing his desire. She needs appointments for therapy at impossible times, absorbed as she is by her unrelenting job. She hardly realises to what extent her and Leo's life rhythms and work requirements impact on their sexuality. Giorgia is a freelance professional of 36. She is a great user of dating websites, that allow her to find occasional partners whenever she wants. Her issue is her deep longing for a stable relationship, contradicted by her tendency to quickly consume all encounters, getting tired of their very superficiality.

These are just a few examples among many. People today come to therapy with an unprecedented array of discomforts and sufferings, the discontents of postmodern times. Sociologist Zygmunt Bauman (2000) defines the world of today as "liquid modernity", an era when we cannot rely on the support of solid social and cultural structures anymore. Such a condition strongly impacts on individual lives, generating a pervasive sense of bewilderment.

Liquid modernity

Liquid modernity is characterised by a chronic weakening of the relationship between labour and capital, with the unleashing of the latter's power to dissolve social and communal bonds. Precarious and discontinuous jobs, exacting workplaces, the challenge of finding employment, all impact individual lives and family relationships. Work today is a problem for many clients as is impermanence of relationships, with weak connections and frail ties. It is important for us to understand how the very issues our patients bring into therapy are shaped by this economic and cultural context.

The first industrial revolution had liquified means of productions and conditions of work; the new society liquifies the very fabric of human interaction. The failure of governments to act as the principal guarantors of existence pervades contemporary society through "the combined experience of *insecurity* (of position, entitlements and livelihood), of *uncertainty* (as to their continuation and future stability) and of *unsafety* (of one's body, one's self and their extensions: possessions, neighbourhood, community)" (Bauman, 2000, p. 161, italics in the text). The individual bears the burden of remaining afloat in a a precarious, unstable environment:

> It is the patterns of dependency and interaction whose turn to be liquefied has now come. ... Solids are cast once and for all. Keeping fluids in shape requires a lot of attention, constant vigilance and perpetual effort—and even then the success of the effort is anything but a foregone conclusion.
>
> (Bauman, 2000, p. 8)

Neoliberalism

Neoliberalism is the ideology—as well as the practice—of liquid modernity (Dardot & Laval, 2013). In order to understand our patients, we must understand that ideology. Neoliberalism subjects all human transaction to the laws and the rules of the marketplace. Horizontal market dynamics replace the old vertical, hierarchical dynamics of the state. Rather than being connected by rigid power structures, people relate to each other through fluid commercial connections, in an ongoing trading process regulated by the ubiquitous laws of supply and demand. This allows an adaptation of power mechanisms to the growing complexity of modern life, substituting flexibility for rigidity. The price to pay is that everything becomes commerce, and freemarketism overflows from economy to infiltrate all the spheres of community life (Dardot & Laval, 2013).

The basis of neoliberalism is competition, which is privileged in all areas of personal and social, as well as economic, life (Foucault, 2004). Sociologist Luciano Gallino (2011) considers neoliberalism as a constructivist doctrine and power practice, with a definite aim: to create a new form of life—a new subject.[2] It does not posit that humans are inherently economic beings, but that they may become so by stressing continuously the economic aspects of their lives. The notion—or better, the practice—of entrepreneurship infiltrates all areas of life, so that any individual becomes an "entrepreneur of themselves" (de Carolis, 2017). On the one hand, business must become the general form of society. On the other, society itself must be fractioned in a multiplicity of businesses rather than persons. Everybody today lives within this logic, with variable degrees of awareness.[3]

In the neoliberal world view it is taken for granted that anyone has sole responsibility for their own destiny. We have no right to consider any social agency, such as the state we live in, our employers, or any other organised force, as responsible for what is happening to us. As Margaret Thatcher, one of the first and foremost political proponents of neoliberalism, said:

> "I am homeless, the Government must house me!" and so they are casting their problems on society and who is society? There is no such thing! There are individual men and women and there are families and no government can do anything except through people and people look to themselves first.
>
> (Thatcher, in Keay, 1987, p. 9)

If neoliberal ideology purports that only individuals—and families—exist, what actually happens is that social organisation brings us to live and behave as disconnected individuals: we are all subjected to a relentless process of individualisation: "Modern society exists in its incessant activity of 'individualising' as much as the activity of the individuals consist in the daily reshaping and renegotiating of the network of mutual entanglements called 'society'" (Bauman, 2000, p. 31).

Neoliberal individuals are free and consider themselves as such. They are not controlled through traditional means, such as timetables, office buildings or assembly lines. At the same time, they are also extremely sensitive to the environment, and are therefore controllable by manipulating environmental variables. They are governed by accessing their relational habits and their emotions, until work necessities are freely accepted by workers. The control of emotions and behaviour creates value, as much as getting new machineries or modifying the business structure. Motivational coaching strategies standardise emotions, limiting the unpredictable behaviour of workers. Emotional, sentimental, and psychological variables are integrated as much as possible within the production system. This process, in the end, leaks out of the workplace to invest all spheres of life. It began many years ago with advertising and television, and it is brought forth today by that colossal example of environmental manipulation that are social networks.[4]

Philosopher Byung-Chul Han maintains that in neoliberal society projects substitutes obligations. We still are forced to obey, but apparently free to decide how: we exploit ourselves, without a master to complain with. We are our own merciless masters. No more master-slave dialectics, since the slave and the master are the same person. The structure of domination is maintained because we are free: we are free and, at the same time, we are forced to use our freedom to pursue goals that are not ours.

> The ego as a project, which believes it has freed itself from external obligations and constraints imposed by others, now submits to inner obligations and self-imposed constraints forcing itself to performance and optimisation. ... The performing subject who believes herself free is actually a servant, and an absolute servant to the extent that she exploits herself without a master.
>
> (Han, 2017b, pp. 9–10)

Such a growing relevance of economics, such a triumph of free-for-all competition, mobilises resources but, at the same time, marginalises the ones who cannot keep up. Wealth is created, but it is also exposed to speculative bubbles. We are all challenged by economic changes—disadvantaged people more than others. Since state welfare has been dramatically diminished in most countries, families—or any similar intimate system—remain the only entities that provide both the source of reproduction of the human species and the place where we can find care and support. Their role, however, goes unrecognised, thus generating a social double bind: "This regime has ... recruited women into the paid workforce, and promoted state and corporate disinvestment from social welfare. Externalising carework onto families and communities, it has simultaneously diminished their capacity to perform it" (Fraser, 2016, p. 104).

The landscape, in the end, influences therapists too. As professionals, we are subjected to the very same conditions of instability, lack of certainties, undermining of role and position and crisis of recognised and accepted knowledge that characterise the lives of our patients. Just like them, we are requested to perform and to help our patients to perform too.[5]

The neoliberal subject

Neoliberalism subdues individuals both through its ideologies and its micropractices. This led to the emergence of a new subject, the "neoliberal subject".[6] The neoliberal subject is defined by three main characteristics:

competition, performance, and flexibility. Originated in the economical domain, they nevertheless invade all areas of life. We can view neoliberalism, from this point of view, as a technology of the Self in Michel Foucault's (1988) sense. "In other words, neoliberal rationality produces the subjects it needs, using means to govern them so they actually behave as entities in competition, that must maximise their results, expose themselves to risk, and take full responsibility for possible failures" (Dardot & Laval, 2013, p. 421).

Competition, first of all. The neoliberal subject adapts to instability through relentless competition with all other actors on the scene. They accept a life dominated by risk (Beck, 1986). In order to survive, they are always at work, adopting in every moment an entrepreneurial position. "The very need to keep afloat compels all these people to an uncompromising daily self-discipline" (de Carolis, 2017, p. 245). Work invades their life, and they accommodate to it. The borders between business and "non-business" get blurred and confused.

Neoliberal subjects receive an unlimited array of requests, albeit without any (apparent) coercion. They must maintain a high level of performance to answer them. This generates a burnout that comes from the internalised obligation to maintain and increase one's performance. Such imperative generates what Han (2015) defined as the "burnout society":

> The evolution ... transforms not just the body, but the whole of the human being into a *performing machine* that must function unhindered and maximise its performance ... The burnout in the society of performance is a lonely burnout, that operates by separating and isolating ... Such burnout is a violence, because it destroys any union, any commonality, any proximity, even any language.
>
> (Han, 2015, pp. 66–67)

Neoliberal subjects are constantly evaluating both themselves and the others on economic terms: how can we exploit ourselves in order to get more? How can we exploit others? Better to expect the worst from the other—in any kind of relationship

> [t]he present-day uncertainty is a powerful individualising force. It divides instead of uniting, and since there is no telling who will wake up the next day in what division, the idea of "common interest" grows ever more nebulous and loses all pragmatic value.
>
> (Bauman, 2000, p. 148)

In our society, human systems are made of parts that can be deleted and removed, like car spare parts, easier to throw away and substitute than to repair. People are disposable. If future is uncertain and there is little possibility for a common destiny, differing satisfaction and pleasure in other to reach long-term goals becomes more and more difficult. Rather than repairing a tired or damaged relationship, it is much easier to look for a new one. Flexibility, originally adopted as a working position, becomes existential, and leads to the prevalence of weak attachments: the others can be substituted when necessary.

It is hard to imagine such a way of life as really satisfactory. At the same time, refusing it may mean to be cut off from work—and maybe life—possibilities. It is a tragic dilemma. Christine, for example, is a university researcher, 26 years old. After years spent researching in Stockholm, she finally managed to get back home in Italy, under pressure from her boyfriend, who sternly refused to live abroad. Today she works under a time-limited contract, while her boyfriend is jobless after completing his PhD. She cannot help judging him for his lack of initiative. He wallows in his sadness. She feels he is unable to take responsibility for himself and, at the same time, she attributes the couple's problems to his indecision. She chose stability over risk; she is now paying a high price. If she had done the opposite, the price would probably be the end of their relationship.

When interpersonal relationships become fleeting, money becomes the identity mediator, allowing to buy not just objects but also—most of all—experiences that in turn reinforce the person's threatened identity. Yet, neoliberal subjects, active and dynamic as they are, are also strangely devoid of identity, because a proper identity is constructed through the encounter with others.[7] The burnout society is also a society of unhappiness, narcissistic in full Freudian sense: the libido is all invested on the Self, but in this way it can never be satisfactory because only the relationship with others—the proper Eros—can be fully satisfying. Hence the sense of emptiness (borderline disorder, depression, dissociation), the inability to feel oneself (self-harming), the necessity to stuff themselves or to control one's replenishment. Continuing self-imaging, bulimia, compulsive shopping, unrelenting presence on social networks, are all symptoms of the very same emptiness connected with a lacking sense of the other.[8] But even void, dissatisfaction, and lack of self-esteem can be functional to the economy because they lead to fill up oneself with things, on the one hand, and to perform and produce on the other. The problem is: this is not necessarily functional to a good life.

Digital natives

The neoliberal subject is also a digital subject. Since the turn of the twenty-first century, our society has been characterised by a constant increase in information, with the advent first of the Internet, then of social media, associated to the existence of such devices as the ubiquitous smartphones (see Han, 2017a).[9] What we may define as digital life has become a proper form of life, in Rachel Jaeggi's (2018) sense: shared, interrelated sets of practices that exert an informal, subtle form of normative pressure to do things the right or appropriate way—ways of doing things together.

People born after the digital revolution can hardly imagine life as it was in the pre-digital, pre-Internet era. The difference between this latest generation—the so-called "digital natives" (Prensky, 2001)—and all the previous ones lies precisely here. "Digital immigrants" were born in a world where a virtual dimension, if present, was but one of the modes of existence. To them, the digital world is something foreign, an addition to "true" reality; hence the opposition between real and virtual. For digital immigrants, social networks are limited environments that only exist within a phone application: they are separate from real life. There is a constant dissociation between what they experience in real life and what they find on social media. A physical, face-to-face meeting is real, a meeting on a platform is virtual, therefore somehow false, or less authentic, a more or less inadequate substitute for reality.[10]

Digital natives' approach is completely different. For them, the virtual is simply another part of reality. They were born with a smartphone in their hands. At a young age, they use social media to interact with classmates, and then go on as adults in their everyday life. They do not complain about social media on social media: if they do not suit them, they simply avoid using them, or use them in the way they think is right, without much fanfare. The natives' network has everything within it, the futile and the thoughtful, activism and waste of time, spontaneity, lack of planning, the creation of movements that spread like an earthquake. Their Internet has its own code of ethics.

Often digital natives consider digital immigrants ridiculous: they blurt out embarrassing, offensive statements, then they apologise. They spread hoaxes because they do not know how to verify their sources; they believe everything they find on the Internet, because their control anxiety makes them look for increasingly imaginative explanations in a world that changes faster and faster. The worst problem of digital immigrants is that they struggle to properly understand digital logic: they must always translate from analogical to digital languages. If they try to behave like digital natives they always come off as pretenders, like an anthropologist who really wanted to become a native.

A good example of the difference between these two generations is the reaction of digital immigrants and natives to online therapy. When the 2020 lockdown made online sessions compulsory, some older patients decided to interrupt therapy until the lockdown was over; among the ones who accepted, several missed the rituals of reaching the therapist's room and their physical presence. The vast majority of younger patients simply shifted smoothly from one modality to the other. Today, most digital natives choose from time to time whether to see the therapist online or in person, depending on the circumstances.

Digital dimensions have deeply affected our lives, for example creating new ways of spreading knowledge. For digital natives the exchange of information is much more free, immediate and fluid compared to the past. Podcasts are one of the favourite ways of generating and absorbing knowledge for these generations, on the same level as books or articles (Kidd, 2012). This allows them to develop a knowledge that is wider and faster, but also more superficial. As Bauman would say, they glide on the surface (see Bauman et al., 2010). Digital immigrants have to keep in mind both sides of change in order to understand digital natives—and the same caution should digital natives apply in dealing with digital immigrants.

Digital life also led to dramatic changes in the way of being together with others. The romantic encounter often takes place on dating apps (Castro & Barrada, 2020), which have gone from being virtual places for emotionally disadvantaged people to being a way like many others of creating meeting opportunities. Although, for example, both Bauman (Bauman et al., 2010) and Han (2017a) consider this kind of romantic relationship as a downgrade of human intimacy, it is actually quite meaningful for many people. At the same time, digital connections may also foster new kinds of exclusion and powerlessness. Often patients relate that they cannot feel up to the ideal and omnipotent figures that Instagram continually proposes (Lopez & Polletta, 2021). Digital life is extremely connected, yet somewhat lonely: digital natives may often feel "alone together", in Sherry Turkle's (2011) words.[11]

The individual and the others

If we move closer to the individual, we find smaller relational networks. There are two types of them: group relationships and intimate relationships. In the first kind we find formal and informal networks. Formal networks, such as school, workplaces, churches, and so on, have a good degree of organisation, and are socially and culturally quite well defined. The individual usually experiences a feeling of belonging to these groups, although commitment may vary from extremely strong to quite superficial. Informal networks are looser and less regulated, admitting in turn different degrees of belonging: friendships, acquaintances, friend groups, informal groups created around work, sports, hobbies, clubs, peer groups and so on. This may include distant relatives, not closely connected to the more intimate household.

What all these groups have in common is that they allow direct contact between the individual and most or all group members.[12] It is important for the therapist to develop a good enough idea of the relevant groups any individual is involved in. They are an essential part of what we define as the "significant system", that usually comprises

> members of the nuclear family, the extended family (including its most important deceased relatives), the patient's friends and peers, the school,

work, and most importantly, all the "helpers" and health and social services the patient may have had contact with over time. Of course, the
significant system also includes the therapist, as an observer who brings
with her or him all his or her theories and biases.

(Boscolo & Bertrando, 1993, p. 83)

Although the group level can be extremely important in shaping the individual's life, the second kind of relational network is probably the most relevant
for our therapies: intimate relationships—the level that has changed most in
recent years.

Intimacy and the family

According to traditional systemic wisdom, intimacy is an obvious issue: it
belongs first to the family (Wynne & Wynne, 1986), and secondly to the
couple (Snyder & Balderrama-Durbin, 2020). In our approach, however, the
emphasis on the traditional nuclear family tends to wane.[13] It is a pivotal,
albeit unexpected, evolution: after all, the family has been one of the corner-
stones—or *the* cornerstone—of systemic therapy from its origin. Systemic
therapy, actually, was not defined as such in the beginning. Its definition was
simply "family therapy", or, at best, "family systems therapy" (Bertrando &
Toffanetti, 2000). Which implied both that the object of therapy was a family,
and that a family was a definite, self-evident entity. Let us reconsider Margaret Thatcher's famous statement we have already quoted: "There are individual men and women *and there are families*" (our italics). She is saying:
families are as real as individuals, whereas society and societal entities are
abstractions. Our evolution in the past 20 years has been a slow but steady
deconstruction of this prejudice. Everybody knows what a family is, of course;
however, knowing it does not mean that everybody gives the same meaning to
the word "family": we are not always playing the same language game
(Wittgenstein, 1953). Although we think we know what we are talking about
when we speak about families, and we also believe our interlocutors agree
with us, this is not always the case.

The normal family

First, what is a "normal" family like? If we look closely at the archetype we
still bear in mind, we will probably find a kind of nest, intimate and self-
sufficient: mom at home, dealing with the affective life of the family; dad
outside to fulfil his duty as the breadwinner; two or more children and
maybe a dog, all in a beautiful suburban cottage with a good car and a
discreet, but not excessive, economic prosperity. Let us put in parentheses,
for a moment, the actual existence or relevance of families like this. This is
an American middle-class product, dating from the 1950s. In its purest form, it
existed only in the United States in the immediate post-World War II decades.[14] In a looser form, it became ubiquitous in the Western world—minus

the suburbs and dogs—by force of television broadcasts. It resembles the nineteenth-century family, just a little freer from the families of origin, and made more optimistic and dynamic by consumerism and advertising (see for example Lück & Ruckdeschel, 2018). We will refer to this form of family, the Western nuclear family of the twentieth century, as the normative family.

If not exactly in this form, the nuclear family has been considered for a long time as the "natural" form of family, or the family everybody has to regard as the gold standard for conceptualising human intimate relationship. This despite many historians, such as Philippe Ariès (1960), David Herlihy (1985), or Piero Melograni (1988), have argued that the importance of the family for society was greatest in the nineteenth century, and that today it is still greater than it was, for example, in ancient Rome and in the Middle Ages. The family has always existed in our culture, but in weaker, somewhat secondary forms. It was often peripheral. Other ties were more important, such as peer relationships and age groupings, social life, collective games. Intimacy had less value. In other societies the family has different forms and quite another sense—it is not nuclear, to begin with; age groupings were more important in many cultures, even in ancient Greece itself; clans have only superficial similarities with our extended families, and so on (Ariès, 1960). The family as we know it is a relatively recent institution (Herlihy, 1985).

Actually, the notion of a natural essence of the nuclear family was created around the middle of the nineteenth century by a quartet of Victorian—of course male—anthropologists.[15] Amidst long debates about matrilineal and patrilineal original family organisation, a subtler truth was established: the heteronormative nuclear family was either the basic building block of any intimacy, or the final product of our own advanced civilisation—sometimes, both of them at once (Kuper, 2005). Most of all, the family was considered as the basis for the whole of society, and this attitude went on to permeate anthropology for more than a century.

This kind of norm was then projected back in history, creating a normality of the family founded on father, mother, and children, that has never been so clearly defined in actual societies, including Europe and white America. If today the primacy of the family, and the nature of the family itself, are challenged, this means not only that new, alternative views are emerging, but also that we can re-appraise older forms of intimacy that existed and were "naturally" accepted by our society before the present times.

"Wise men see outlines"

"Wise men see outlines and therefore they draw them", wrote William Blake, according to Gregory Bateson. Then Bateson adds: "but in another place he'd written 'Mad men see outlines and therefore they draw them'" (Bateson, 1972, p. 27). We can translate Bateson's somewhat cryptical statements as: any outline that we draw, literal or metaphorical, is arbitrary—in the sense that we are drawing it, that it is not part of nature—but at the same time it tells something about the object we are outlining. The outline of the family surely tells something about intimate relationships, but it does not mean that it is the only possible outline for those relationships. The family is not a "thing". It is more useful to see it a set of processes, that can be seen from various different vantage points. What makes the family so difficult to pinpoint is not just a result of changes or evolution, it is also the result of such differences. Different observers see (produce) different families (Agazzi, 1976).

The fact is, the normative family and couple are no longer the only regulatory principles of togetherness. This is not to say that the normative family, not to mention the couple, is not the standard anymore, since the vast majority of people in Western countries still live in a nuclear family, not to mention the fact that even more people live in a couple, or are striving to form one. At the same time, some novelties are challenging the status quo. First, the outline of the family is stretched, in order to introduce forms of family that are eccentric with respect to the normative family, e.g., traditional families from different cultures, or that are completely new, such as the "rainbow" families created by gender minorities (Gato et al., 2021). Second, there are growing minorities that discuss the very nature of the family and the couple. This is bringing forth the emergence of other forms of intimacy, that are formally non-families, but at the same time can be seen as family-like forms.

Other families

In the fourth edition of her influential book, *Normal Family Processes*, Froma Walsh (2012) argues that today it is quite hard to define the normal family. Let us consider some statistics (we have to rely on USA statistics, since in other countries it is more difficult to find reliable data): according to the Pew Research Center (Aragão et al., 2023), in 1970, 67% of Americans aged 25 to 49 were living with their spouse and one or more children younger than 18. In 2023, that share had dropped to 37%. Correspondingly, there has been an increase in other types of family living arrangements, like unmarried adults raising children.

Several factors have contributed to these changes. First of all, Americans are marrying later in life, and a rising percentage of them have never been married. Moreover, certain types of marriages have become more common over time. Since the 1970s, a growing share of Americans are in interracial or interethnic marriages. In 2015, same-sex marriages became legal nationwide, thus easing the proportional increase of Americans in same-sex marriages. According to the US Census, in 2021 there were over 700,000 same-sex married couples in the United States, accounting for approximately 1% of all married couples. The situation in Europe is not very different, so much that around the turn of the century Italian theorist Laura Fruggeri titled her books on the social psychology of the family *Famiglie* (*Families*, Fruggeri, 1997) and *Diverse normalità* (*Different Normalities*, Fruggeri, 2005), both in the plural, to emphasise the manifold manifestations of family processes.

Non-families

In a future-oriented perspective, the most important (and challenging) change is yet another one: a growing number of people, sometimes consciously, sometimes inadvertently, seek and find forms of intimacy unconnected, or very loosely connected, to the normative family. Italian anthropologist and queer thinker Leo Acquistapace (2022) suggests in the Euro-Mediterranean area and beyond a progressive blurring of the difference between kinship and other affective relationships is taking place (Grilli & Zanotelli, 2010; Jamieson et al., 2006; Spencer & Pahl, 2006): there is no sharp divide between normative and non-normative intimacies, but continuity and cross-fertilisation. Which, of course, makes us wonder about the very nature of intimacy. What are we talking about we when talk about intimacy? Generally speaking, intimacy encompasses several different dimensions: sharing time and space, caring for each other (often understood as a commitment to care), creating a common identity, sense of belonging to each other, commitment, projection of the relationship in the future.[16]

According to Acquistapace (2022), the relationships of affection, intimacy and care that are becoming more and more prominent in our times can be summarised as follows:

- with friends, in the various meanings this term can take;
- with roommates, who may have been friends already before living together, may have been chosen in a circle of friends, or may have become friends as a result of cohabitation;
- with one or more sexual partners, with whom, in addition to sexuality, one can share a more or less large part of their life;
- with persons belonging to one's own self-organised network of political activism;
- with ex-partners, or very close ex-friends with whom one has stopped dating because of conflicts, but with whom one has maintained a relationship;
- with their children, for those who have them, or with other children whom one cares for;
- with other adults caring for these children;
- with members of one's family of origin, of the first- and second-degree kinship network, or with figures who are assimilated to members of the family since they were present from one's early childhood;
- with other figures not covered by any of the above definitions.

Obviously, none of these categories excludes the other: the partner can also be cohabiting, with or without the presence of other roommates, a friend can become such after a love affair, collective partners can also be friends, roommates, ex-roommates, ex-friends or partners and so on. Although this phenomenon is, of course, more easily seen in younger generations, cohabitation of ageing persons is also growing steadily in the Western world (Oldman & Quilgars, 1999). The landscape of the family, far from being motionless, is moving at a growing speed. Therapist should be aware of this, and willing to follow the change rather than resisting it.

Intimacies and couples

As we have seen, intimacy regards several dimensions, and sharing sexual practices is just one of those. Yet quite often our patients, when talking about intimacy, identify it with sex: "lack of intimacy" becomes synonymous with "absence of sexual intercourse". This is why when we think about intimacy we are immediately driven to sexual intimacy, and from there to the couple.

As Gayle Rubin showed in her fundamental "Thinking sex" (1984), by their very nature sexual norms build a permeable and mobile wall between normality and abnormality. Subjects positioned on the side of "normality" are disciplined by the constant fear of ending on the other side. Vice versa, subjects on the side of "abnormality" are governed by the desire and the possibility of being able to shift to the other side. We end up in a continuum from more or less "normal" to more or less "aberrant" sexual behaviour. Yet, for the vast majority of people, sexual intimacy is identified with the couple. The couple too, though, is undergoing major changes, and so is the regulation of sexual relationships.

Scientific literature offers many descriptions of the (perceived) normal way of being in a couple according to different criteria—statistical, legal, social— with different methods of investigating social and cultural dimensions (Abela et al., 2020). Scientific discourse notwithstanding, in everyday life our patients have a more or less normative idea of the couple they live in or they want to live in, exactly as it happens with the family.

According to this (implicit) definition, a normal couple follows a rule of priority, monogamy and projection into the future: the point is not the actual respect of monogamy (betrayal is one of the most frequent motives for couple therapy), but the desire, the effort and the positive value given to monogamy, or at least of the legitimacy of each partner to aspire to some form of exclusivity on the other and to have a say in their sexuality. Other studies that share this criticism of the centrality of the couple in social sciences, in culture and in public policies define their field in a different way: some, for example, include in their field of interest non-cohabiting couples (LAT: living together apart; see Levin, 2004), or polyamorous couples (where polyamory means the practice, or the possibility, of keeping more than one intimate relationship at the time, with the awareness and the consent of all the people involved; see Barker, 2005; Barker & Langdridge, 2010) that, apart from the rule of monogamy, corresponds for the rest to all the other "requirements" of the standard couple. This creates a peculiar duplicity: even if one does not want to identify with the normative family or the normative couple, one still defines oneself by difference from that same standard.

Queer intimacies

A possible way out of this paradox may be found in a queer position (we will not enter here the complex and manifold definition of queer, that we will consider in Chapter 2). Although queer is usually identified with gay, lesbian and related issues, many of the intimacies we have considered may also be called queer relationships (Haraway & Goodeve, 1999). Heterosexual people who at a certain age do not have (yet) a family of their own, not even in the form of a monogamous couple living together, and who do not even strive in this sense, find themselves in a condition that somehow approaches the queer, given the close link that exists between family institution, compulsory heterosexuality, binary structure of genders and age structures (Doty, 1993). Queer intimacy thus becomes an affirmation of non-standard, non-normative intimacies.

Italian writer and activist Michela Murgia fostered a debate on mainstream Italian media about queerness and the family, publicly presenting her own queer family, consisting of four "soul children",[17] none of which was a biological child of Murgia's (although each of them conceived himself as "her only son"), the mother of one of them with her husband, the father of another, and other more or less close friends. As Murgia said:

> It happened. ... The issue of being a family has to do with staying. Remain in my life. The way? We'll find it ... The idea of the queer family is ... to base its relations on the *Ius Voluntatis*, on the right of the will. Why should will count less than blood?
>
> (Murgia, in Marchetti, 2023)

We acknowledge that unconventional intimacies represent today a small minority of intimate relationships—they would not be unconventional, otherwise. At the same time, they also represent a slowly growing trend, more apparent in our younger clients, who show a greater fluidity in their gender identity and object preference, and also in the way they regulate their intimacy. Younger people live their intimacies without considering them as problems or even therapeutic issues in a broad sense. They bring in therapy other problems, and we learn about their intimacies almost by accident. Once again, what we see are mere forms of life. A different, open approach to intimacy is possible, and probably needed today.

Clinical practices

What are the consequences for us as therapists? Here we are helped by our non-normative theory, because it emphasises the primacy of relationship over structure. It is important to understand relationships, independently from the different forms they take. In this way, we are less conditioned by normative expectations about couples and families, and we gain the possibility to explore different ways of being together. We do not judge any kind of intimacy, unless constriction or violence appear in them. We are interested in minority or unconventional intimacies, but of course we appreciate traditional families. All in all, we try to overcome binarism or dichotomies in intimate relationships. Let us consider a few examples.

Deborah is a woman of 38, an Indigenous Australian who lives in North Queensland. She is now in a stable couple relationship, with four children. Joe, her 14-year-old firstborn, though, does not live with them. Deborah had a series of six miscarriages before giving birth to Joe. When she finally succeeded in giving birth, she felt compelled to leave her son in kinship adoption to her older brother: a family tradition imposed to give the firstborn of the firstborn daughter to the firstborn son's family. As a rule transmitted though the generations, it is something obvious and inevitable for Deborah, so that it does not constitute a problem to her—there are many problems she considers as such, including her drug addiction and a story of family violence. It becomes a problem, though, for her (white) therapist, who struggles not to see it as the cause—or at least a contributing factor—of her present distress. Here we act as supervisors, and our main task is to help the therapist to accept Deborah's priorities, rather than look for a presumed distress rooted in her relationship with Joe. This does not mean to overlook the possibility of it. Simply the therapist must learn to stay in dialogue with Deborah and wait: if and when such distress would emerge, they will be able to address it together.

Carola is a 33-year-old employee. She lives with Ivan, 34, a high school teacher. They share the same background, are very attached to each other, and have been together since high school days. During a business trip, Carola encounters Nancy, employed in a branch of the same firm, in another European country. Nancy defines herself as a lesbian, and is married to Nella, with two young daughters. After the customary company dinner and dance, Carola discovers herself unpredictably attracted to Nancy. In the end, they share a night of sex and begin a secret relationship. They both feel guilty: they have never kept any secret from their respective partners. After a few months, guilt becomes untenable. After the disclosure, they choose to involve both partners in a four-way relationship, creating a sort of crossing: besides the original Carola/Ivan and Nancy/Nella erotic and romantic relationships, the new Carola/Nancy and Ivan/Nella relationships now emerge, a complex entanglement similar to the one imagined by anthropological science fiction writer Ursula Le Guin in her short story *Unchosen Love* (Le Guin, 1994): in one of her fictional worlds, every marriage involves four people, two men and two women, with two heterosexual and two homosexual sub-marriages within it.[18] In the end, that solution proves highly unstable, and after a while it collapses. Carola and Nancy decide for a clean break, and try to interrupt their affair, with variable success, leading to a state of suffering. The consequences on Carola last for a long time, and must be worked through in therapy.

Carola's therapy, actually, had been underway some time before these events, for issues mostly related to her family of origin. Carola never questions the consistency of her hetero- or homosexuality, nor does she need to define herself as straight, lesbian, or even fluid: her problem is the state of her relationship with Ivan, and also the loss she experiences due to Nancy's absence. Once again, a person may have a diffuse or fluid identity, but this will not necessarily be the issue they bring to therapy and they want to work on. We must respect their choices and their definition, and work on the areas agreed upon. In this case, the therapist restrains his curiosity about the sexual arrangements of Carola's couples, and chooses to stay with her in what she experiences as her true problem: her long-lasting, yet always complicated, relationship with Ivan. In the end, she decides that their couple must go on as it is, and they consider having a child, a decision he had resisted for a long time. From this moment, the therapy will go on with a completely different focus.

Lorenzo, a 45-year-old manager, comes to therapy in order to be assisted in his exploration of polyamory (see Antalffy & Houston, 2016). In his two previous monogamous relationships, he had felt uncomfortable because of his tendency to be—in his own words—"a serial cheater". He now wants his interest for multiple sexual and affective relationships to become part of the explicit couple contract. He has made clear his decision to his current partner. At the beginning of therapy, they are trying to live their engagement accordingly. Among many one-off encounters, Lorenzo finds Arianna, a woman with a similar past and a similar present. They start a relationship maintaining their previous partners, until, in the end, both Lorenzo's and Arianna's partners feel they are unable to accept polyamory. In therapy, Lorenzo appears well-oriented. What he asks the therapist is to help him in his reflection on his relational situation. The therapist processes both his emotions in his different sexual and affective relationships, and in different contexts, such as his family of origin, which he finds more difficult to face after developing his unconventional (for them) ideas.

Lorenzo remains with Arianna in what outwardly now appears to be a monogamous couple, but it is not, because they maintain the possibility of having sexual encounters with others. Lorenzo also establishes a very good relationship with Arianna's ten-year-old daughter. When he meets his therapist for the last time, Lorenzo comes together with Arianna, who is now pregnant, and both emphasise how they appreciate their "being whole" in this kind of intimate relationship. For the duration of therapy, the therapist maintained a role as a companion, helping Lorenzo to process his changes, without interfering with his choices.

The individual and the self

What about the individual's self? In our view, individuals are defined by the systems and contexts they are embedded in, but at the same time they are not fully determined by them. They hold specific responsibilities. Individuals must take responsibility for their actions, and most of all for the position from which they act (Chapter 7). This is why, by the way, an individual setting is even more relevant than before four our therapeutic approach. It also makes necessary to deal with the individual's self—or, better, the individual's selves.

Manifold selves

Individual selves are manifold, or at least we consider them as such. Developing a theory of the self was not easy for us, since we came from a model created to deal with families in therapy. In family therapy, the session resembles a stage populated by characters that are activated by their in-session interaction, and whom we, as therapists, observe from the outside. In such a frame, the very concept of self is superfluous: all the therapist has to do is to observe people interacting with each other.

In individual therapy the perspective is different: the individual is the only person on the stage. The complex tangle of relationships happening in the person's life must be inferred from what they can say about themselves and the others. In many cases, the individual appears as an unreliable narrator (Booth, 1961)—yet we have to accept their stories as the provisional reality we will work with. We need to understand both how the individual perceives and regards the others, and how they perceive and regard themselves.

We initially focused on the individual's relationships with relevant others. We devised ways to presentify these people as third parties (Boscolo & Bertrando, 1996). Then we considered how ideas, ideologies, cultures, could be presentified in turn, becoming "third parties" with the same relevance as actual people (Bertrando, 2002). If we now focus on the very self of the individual, should we consider it as one, monolithic entity, or can we see it, in turn, as composed and multifaceted? And in this case, what parts—aspects, facets—of it the individual will be presentified in a session? As it usually happens, there is no definitive answer to such a question. But at least, we can hypothesise that such a multiplicity exist.

Dialogical selves

What happens if we renounce the idea of the self as a monolith? We will have something like a complex set of internal relationships. This view is close to the "dialogical self" idea proposed by Hermans, Kempen and Van Loon (1992). Inspired by William James's notions of the self and Mikhail Bakhtin's polyphonic metaphor, these authors conceptualise the self in terms of a dynamic multiplicity of relatively autonomous I-positions. The "I", the subject, moves as in a space, from one position to the other—e.g., from the position of daughter to the position of mother, of professional, and so on. Each position has a voice, "each character has a story to tell about his or her own experiences from its own stance. As different voices these characters exchange information about their respective *Me*s, resulting in a complex, narratively structured self" (Hermans et al., 1992, pp. 28–29). This does not mean that all inner voices are speaking at the same time—which will transform the self in complete chaos: they are activated one at a time and take temporary control of the whole self. Thus, the process happening within the self becomes a form of dialogue.

In this perspective, the "I" is one of the possible positions each person can take both in regard to themselves and the others. From that position, the I can entertain every kind of relationship with the I (i.e., themselves) in another position. This mean that our self exists only in specific positions in space and time, and also that the I in one position may "agree, disagree, understand, misunderstand, oppose, contradict, question, challenge and even ridicule the I in another position" (Hermans et al., 1992, p. 29). In other words, each I-position has its individual, specific beliefs about reality and oneself, thoughts, feelings, reminiscences, moral system, and awareness. The I, therefore, is inseparable from a definite position. No subject which transcends positioning exists.

A dialogical self is fully social: the dialogue does not happen only within the metaphorical space of the self. When the person enters in dialogue with some other person, one of her I-positions is activated. Other I-positions will be activated when the person will enter relationships with somebody else, and so on. All these dialogues take place within the mind's "imaginal space" (Hermans et al., 1992).

For example, during a session Thea, 28, copywriter, tells the story of a complicated shooting for a short commercial video, where she found that the actors arrived unprepared and the director lacked authority.

> I wanted to step in and tell everybody what they had to do, because I knew how to do it! But I also knew that I could not do it. In the past, I would have simply blurted out. Yesterday I was able to tell myself to stop and wait, because there was a part of myself who knew that I would become too assertive, as usual, and I'd be considered aggressive. But, in order not to snap and attack, I need an internal interlocutor who tells me that I must stop!

Here Thea literally shows how a dialogue between two I-positions looks like, with one (assertive) position stopped by another (reflexive) one, both activated by two kinds of interaction with others. (What the therapist adds to her reflections is a question about her being considered as "too aggressive": would it be the same if she were a man? This fosters some conversation about gender and assertiveness: we will further consider that dimension in Chapter 2).

Polyphonic selves

The dialogical self theory has been criticised from many points of view, and its academic acceptance is controversial (see Suszek, 2018). We find it interesting, however, as a loose frame for dealing with the self. The multiple voices that, according to this theory, are active within one's self remind us of Dostojevski's novels, where the characters endlessly discuss with each other from a variety of viewpoints, essential to Bakhtin's (1968) idea of polyphony (see Appendix A). The notion of position is also quite close to Harré and Van Langenhove (1999) positioning theory, that we will reconsider in Chapter 6. It also entails that we are different according to the relationship we are mostly engaged in different moments—and spaces—of our lives. It allows a description of our inner world in terms of a network: we chose to call this domain the "intra-relational" domain, i.e., an inner space where different relational positions are played out. The intra-relations domain, at the same time, constantly relates to outer spaces. The widest of them is what we call the "macro-systemic" domain, and it involves the major contexts that contain, participate in, and shape our lives. This closes the loop that connects the individual to the contexts we have considered at the beginning of this chapter.

The individual and the therapist

This way of considering the individual has had consequences on our way of doing (individual) therapy. They will become more apparent in the next chapters. For the time being, we just want to offer an initial summary, followed by some examples.

First, recognising the multiplicity of the self means to pay attention to different aspects of clients, without necessarily expecting from them an overall consistency. Sometimes their very contradictions may become unpredictable openings toward change. We should also be sensitive to symptoms closely related to the postmodern condition, such as dissociative disorder, borderline personality, depressive traits, and so on. At the same time, we should not take for granted that all features of the neoliberal subject should be considered "negative"—an attitude too easily adopted when we face the many distortions of present-day life: even Bauman and Byung-Chul Han are not spared by it. We should not become nostalgic for the "good old days", not least because they were not really as good as we may remember them.

Second, it is normal for anyone to experience uncertainty as a not particularly pleasant moment; flirting authentically with uncertainty implies accepting that we must remain in the indistinct or in fluidity, postponing or even neglecting the primordial gesture of drawing distinctions. We must develop an awareness of our reactions toward the issues raised by neoliberal subjects, because they will inevitably elicit in us strong emotional reactions that we cannot avoid, and therefore must find a way of processing. We will further our investigation in the following pages, especially in Chapters 2, 4, and 6.

Third, therapists must position themselves in relation to their age and knowledge. Any therapist should be, independently from the culture of their patients, somewhat of an ethnologist, in Clifford Geertz's (1973) understanding of the term: somebody who tries to develop some dialogue with people whose premises they hardly know or guess. Curiosity (Cecchin, 1987) can be really useful in this case, just as the acceptance of uncertainty. When we ask questions, we should imagine ourselves as visiting a new planet, where we are the extraterrestrials, and must ask for consensual understanding. This leads us away from dichotomous and binary thought, and from the temptation to impose order.

Fourth, we should not enter into a judgemental position when we work with digital natives ("they live in a fictitious world"). Therapists should accept the existence of digital forms of life, without trying to describe or explain them according to previous categories. If we are not digital natives, we will never inhabit exactly the same world as them. Even in the future, when all therapists will be digital natives, they will always be one step behind their younger patients. Once again, curiosity can be the state that allows us to maintain a proper therapeutic position.

Therapists must be aware that they are working in a new and different world. In emerging forms of life there is always something new that cannot be reduced to what made sense in the past. At the same time, there are some human characteristics that—if not completely unchangeable—tend to remain the same, and here the therapist can use all of their expertise. We must balance the tension between what remains unchanged (shame is always shame, for example) and what has changed (shame today is not what shame was in the nineteenth century, or even in the twentieth, as we will see in Chapter 5). The issue is to acknowledge novelties without renouncing experience.

Fifth, we need to develop acceptance toward new forms of intimacy, too. To us, every way of being together is legitimate, provided that it does not generate suffering, either in the individual, or the others—or both. The anthropologist's stance we have proposed helps us to let patients explain how their families, new families, non-families or atypical intimacies function, without claims to a normative knowledge of how they should be. The idea of a dialogical self may also help us: we can think that different people evoke different I-positions from the same person, and that therefore there is neither a "right" form of relationship, nor a hierarchy between different forms of relationships that an individual entertains. We are curious to understand what their different intimate relationships are and how they are intertwined.

Finally, we should avoid patronising discourses. We should rather put ourselves at the service of patients who have different abilities, and so we should practise maieutics, personalise the therapeutic action like a tailor-made suit. We take time and show them that we too can live in indeterminacy and liquidity, that we are not afraid because they are there to lend us a hand. We value their skills, because conventional problem-solving exercises or reductionist approaches to problems no longer work.

We will now give a more detailed account of our approach. Rather than going on theorising, we prefer to let clinical examples talk for us. (Remember that, when dealing with our therapeutic choices, we are anticipating methods and techniques that we will deal with in the following chapters. We will refer to each of them in the text, but we recommend to go back to these cases after reading the whole book: they will appear clearer and more interesting.)

Clinical examples: working with neoliberal subjects

The neoliberal subject's characteristics originate in the cultural, social, and economic domain, but in time become personality traits: competition, individualism, acceleration, weak attachments, performance, flexibility, voluntary submission, virtual relationships. From a clinical standpoint, they are not neutral. They produce new difficulties, challenges, suffering, and symptoms. These, in turn, become challenges for the therapist.

Individualism, acceleration, chronophobia

Stefano is 26 years old, from a small city in Northern Italy. He has just earned a bachelor's degree, so his academic career is definitely below average. His life is marked by confrontation and competition, especially with his brothers, but also with a wide network of friends, all showing full academic success and, in many cases, also getting very good jobs.

Comparisons make him ashamed, because he delayed his graduation. He is afraid of having lost time, and therefore of having lost chances: he belongs to a wealthy family, so he can access any type of educational experience, even abroad, but now he lives a veritable delay syndrome: "How can I go abroad to take a master degree, when all my course peers will be much younger than me, and would ridicule me intolerably?"

He is scared of choosing a course of study. All possibilities are open to him, but having all doors open is the same as not having any doors open. Furthermore, he feels an oppressive fear of disappointing everybody—family, friends, the world, himself. He is mired in a swamp. His parents, especially his mother, present themselves as the archetypal good parents: understanding, welcoming, open to fulfil his wishes rather than setting limits. From what he says, they are victims of the myth of responsible parenthood. They tried to control all the controllable, to predict even the unpredictable, in order to guarantee Stefano an ability to be a winner. The possibility of a non-competitive life is out of question.

Such attitude produced a twofold effect. On the one hand, he felt that they did not really trust him, since they needed to take control of his life behind the scenes; on the other, it created for him an excess of possibilities that in turn became a limit: how can he make a choice? Furthermore, there is an untold implication: it is impossible to discuss the basic premise, that competing—and winning—is the core of life.

At the same time, Stefano struggles to develop strong affections for others. Friends are friends, but they are easily replaceable. The same happens with girlfriends, who appear in sessions as pale and evanescent figures: once again, expendable relationships. And the same applies to the therapeutic relationship: Stefano never established a continuity in therapy; he tends to stop and go, often cancelling sessions, forgetting appointments, and giving us—we see him in co-therapy[19]—the impression that he is not fully committed. We wonder whether the same may apply to all other people who get in touch with him.

In Stefano's case, we can see different aspects of the neoliberal subject. His competitive individualism contributes to his feeling of helplessness: he cannot share his frustration with anybody, not even his family, since both his parents and siblings are high achievers: he does not want to be seen as a failure, and thus is left alone, since failure is what he experiences.

Besides, he is haunted by the feeling of losing time. He is experiencing what we call a form of chronophobia.[20] A way of describing it could be: "whatever I try to do, I'm always late". In the past, chronophobia was characteristically found in the elder and in prison inmates, with an existential feeling of slowing down (O'Donnell, 2014); today it is becoming an issue for the youth, with a feeling of unrelenting acceleration. German sociologist Hartmut Rosa has observed that "The powers of acceleration no longer are experienced as a liberating force, but as an actually enslaving pressure instead" (Rosa, 2010, p. 80). In his view, acceleration is the main source of alienation in the (post) modern world:

> Acceleration basically is at the heart of modernisation. … And it is not just on the scale of a small elite; it is very comprehensive. And indeed, it is the same in Korea, Japan, Brazil and other places in Latin America. … the change in temporal structures is modernity's most widespread feature.
> (Rosa, in Lijster & Celikates, 2019, pp. 65–66)

To Stefano, the issue is not (just) acceleration in itself, it is acceleration plus competition. This is true for most of his peers, who are busy trying to find a way of fitting in. Clearly, Stefano does not know how to fit in. He cannot find his place (Chapter 6).

Finally, like most neoliberal subjects, Stefano cannot accept his limits. Partly for idiosyncratic reasons, the apparent inability of his parents to give him limits; partly for reasons deeply embedded in present-day culture. The absence of limits is one of the hallmarks of postmodern philosophy and practice—and the distress of postmodernism is the reaction people show when they have to face the limitations and discomforts of hard reality (Bauman, 1997). According to Italian philosopher Renato Bodei: "In the ancient world, going beyond the boundaries established by the divinity is hybris, and it is punished: the best known example is Icarus" (Bodei, in Marcoaldi, 2013). If we think that our life can be declined through infinite possibilities, any limit is just a bottleneck, a throttling, something not only useless, but harmful. And, when we are forced to see it, the risk is to feel it as inevitable and constrictive, with the result of settling into uncritical adaptation.

The therapeutic work with Stefano begins by working on the therapeutic relationship. We want to establish with him a strong alliance, so first of all we try to thematise his discontinuity in coming to sessions, then we widen our focus to consider his relationship with all significant others: how does he feel with them? And, most of all, how do they feel with him? What happens to the others when he shows his lack of interest? And so on. This requires an extensive use of questioning, especially circular questioning (Chapter 4), and a focus on his and the others' emotions (Chapter 5).

Then we go back to his family of origin and his performance-based relationship with them: were they asking him to perform, was he setting himself the mission to perform and make them happy? Does he feel he got a sort of imprinting to perform—and, together with it, the feeling of being unable to perform properly? What did actually his parents say or do in the past and in the present? This necessitates a presentification of the parents and an accurate inquiry in Stefano's memories (Chapter 3).

Further on, we enter the theme of performance, that we feel makes him blind to the real value of relationships: "I have value for what I do, my identity lies in being successful". To what extent did he internalise those values? We work on these dimensions to help him find his place. At this point, it is possible to face the future: what does he actually mean when he talks of success and failure? And can he take responsibility for his lack of success (Chapter 7)? Why cannot he disobey, put into question the family (social) model he inherited, and look for something different? Most of all, what does really interest him, besides the perceived expectations of his parents and brothers (Chapter 8)? Can he begin to think about his possible goals, beyond winning the race? In our therapeutic work, we think that asking open questions is much more important than trying to give answers to our patients. Stefano will find his answers—or he will discover that he no longer needs them.

Weak attachments

One of Stefano's most serious issues lies in his erratic, precarious relationships: weak affiliations. In his case, the roots of his weak attachment can be, once again, tied back to his family. In his recollection, he had been brought up with a great deal of love, but that love was also conditional: he felt they were expecting a lot from him, in terms of academic, social, and work success. His parents wanted him to be successful—or at least that is what he felt. Now he expects something from the others, and he is ready to dismiss them if he does not get it, or fears that he can lose them. Once again, though, his problems, individual as they are, also speak about a situation that is common to many.

Italian writer Chiara Gamberale speaks of "the untied", meaning individuals who prefer to have weak bonds and weak loves, avoiding the very idea of being bound to somebody. In an era when it is extremely easy to be abandoned, they prevent abandonment by avoiding close ties: "'Solid' modernity was an era of mutual engagement. 'Fluid' modernity is the epoch of disengagement, elusiveness, facile escape and hopeless chase. In 'liquid' modernity, it is the most elusive, those free to move without notice, who rule" (Bauman, 2000, p. 120).

Today communities flourish—as always happened. Unlike other periods, though, communities are easily fictitious and, in any case, not lasting. The individual participates in an array of social groups that tend to be quite mutable and unstable. Social media make extremely easy to construct virtual groups, that can thrive for a very brief period, then disappear as easily as they were created. As a "virtual square" emerges on a platform, people can access it to share an experience, such as a claim or a grief, make comments on it, and so on; then visits to the square thin out and it finally vanishes. Belonging to a virtual square is weak, because engagement can be pretty intense as it lasts, but it tends not to last for long. People can get easily—and very intensively—together for a specific goal. Once it has been reached, the whole community that had been created simply disappears.

The same happens to friendships or romantic engagements. On the one hand, the neoliberal subject wishes relationships that grant them a solid anchor in an unstable world in continuous—and uncontrollable—evolution. On the other, such binding relationships generate obligations, constraints, and above all limit the possibility of establishing new relationships. This concerns in particular love relationships, that in solid, post-romantic modernity were supposed to be the strongest and more durable (Bauman, 2003). Today, such binds are easily felt as burdens and limitations. This is why romantic relationships, besides being one of the main preoccupations of this age, are also characterised by a maximum of ambivalence.

(We could say that polyamory, besides being a challenge to established family form, and a rediscovery of forgotten family geometries, is also a way to reconcile two opposite ways of relating to each other, the solid and the liquid. An attempt to get out of ambivalence without being imprisoned by a clear choice.)

Bauman (2003) even proposes that the most important quality of relationships today is their instability, the easiness to get rid of a relationship when it does not fulfil our desires and presumed needs anymore. Many people, ranging from adolescents to full-grown adults, easily prefer ghosting to argument or disagreement:

> Internet dating agencies have a tremendous advantage over singles bars. The internet has available this key on the keyboard, called "delete". So it's just pushing your finger on the button and the most traumatic aspect of all that occurs "I've made a mistake, I don't like her", or "she's not what I expected, somewhere else the grass is greener, so why should I stick to it?", all this rigmarole is put paid to. You stop sending text messages, you stop answering them, when you get a message you just push "delete", and that's the end of the story.
>
> (Bauman, in Bauman et al., 2010, pp. 50–51)

Our patients often are on the opposite side to Stefano's in this process: a person may be excluded from a common chat through the creation of a new chat which excludes her. The person will often suffer tremendously for losing their friends, but at the same time their loss will be ambiguous (see Boss, 1999), because it is not quite clear whether or not there was a loss, if the relationship ever existed, whether it is really over.

Competition and its discontents

Tiziano, 30 years old, left his small village to study economics in Milan, the most dynamic and affluent city in Italy. He is very determined. After receiving his master's degree, an important firm notices him and hires him as a consultant. He is always ready to work after hours and to accept excess duties, such as flying throughout Europe without notice. He is the favourite of his boss, of course. Sometimes he criticises the system, but at the same time he chooses to stay in it, because "that's the way you do things" (the therapist sometimes feels that his criticism is little more than window-dressing).

To complete his geometry of perfection he should find a woman of his age, competitive and assertive as he is. During his studies he had a long relationship with a young woman of his village. Afterwards, he found Wilma, a colleague of his age, that he immediately introduced to all his friends. But, soon afterwards, he found also Judith, a woman ten years his senior, who already reached the job position she wanted, and fell head over heels for her. Which completely messes up his life, because Tiziano never planned to fall in love with an older woman, further on in her career to boot. His relationship with Judith, therefore, must remain parallel and hidden. Tiziano is now torn between an official relationship that is "right" for the public, whereas the other is socially "wrong", but much more intense and intriguing.

He is stuck, and comes into therapy because he no longer understands who he is, how he feels and where he is: he cannot find his place (Chapter 6). He feels lonely, inadequate in informal contexts. He tries keep in touch with his old friends from the village, but every time he returns there he finds himself lost, because they do not recognise him anymore: his appearance, his way of dressing, have changed; all the codes he had in common with them are lost. When he is there, he wishes to be one of them, but in their eyes now he is a Milanese, a stranger—which generates ambivalence on both sides. Similarly, in his official relationship he gets bored, because his clandestine girlfriend has accustomed him to more adult exchanges, often centred on work issues that he finds extremely interesting.

Tiziano had a clear idea of what he wanted to do and who he wanted to be: a character perfectly adapted to the competitive context that he has partly found and partly chosen. But this now creates a discrepancy with his other feelings. He is still connected to a past emotional life he does not understand anymore, but that is part of him, and fosters nostalgia. He wants to be fully adapted to the competitive city context, and at the same he wishes to remain the same boy that left his village years ago. For better or worse, he cannot.

The therapist's task is to help him understand where he is and how he feels, in order to understand how he would like to feel and where he may decide to stay. As a first step, she tries to determine his dominant and tacit emotions in the relationships and contexts he inhabits (Chapter 5). For example, in his workplace his dominant emotions are satisfaction, enthusiasm, challenge; the tacit ones anxiety, competition, envy. The process is repeated for all of his significant relationships: colleagues, Wilma, Judith, friends, family of origin.

Then his emotions are turned into emotional informations: why is he feeling those specific emotions rather than others? Through emotional questions and emotional micro-hypotheses, the therapist shares with Tiziano her analysis of his conditioning premises and prejudices (Chapter 4). For example, about the couple: "If you feel so good with Judith, why don't you want to share your joy for her with your other loved ones?"

This allows a deeper analysis of his premises, such as:

- the woman in the couple must be the same age or younger because she must guarantee offspring (patriarchal premise: Chapter 2).

And also of his prejudices:

- my parents would not approve of it;
- My old friends in the village would think that I'm just having a good time but the relationship cannot be serious: they would think that I'm exploiting her, because she is affluent and has money;
- My colleagues would think that I'm being a toy boy to further my career (patriarchal prejudice);
- I cannot be the one that explains things to her, as a real man should do, I couldn't protect her because she can protect herself: he has a good income and all the necessary relational competences (another patriarchal prejudice).

The overall hypothesis that the therapist can now propose is that Tiziano's notion of a couple is strongly influenced by patriarchal order. His position with Judith contrasts his patriarchal premises and prejudices, and is at odds with his competitiveness: he could not compete as a "real man" if he discussed his clandestine girlfriend. Here a new round of questions begins: does he recognise himself in this description? Does it make sense to him? If so, where does it come from? What are the actual values of his family of origin? Is it organised around these principles? If so, how does he react to them? And so on.

In subsequent sessions, the emphasis shifts many times. About the family of origin: how did his parents meet? What are their occupations? Who manages the money in the family? Who chooses, money-wise? About the relationship: an older woman, who may be a "teacher" to him, becomes less desirable? Less erotically stimulant? Or is a woman his own age more reassuring and less challenging, emotionally and relationally? And so on: such procedure is applied to friends, colleagues, work, values and expectations.

Hypotheses now can be reformulated: why is his comfort zone not enough for him? Maybe he needs to position himself on the contour, neither in comfort nor outside of it. Maybe he needs to think himself outside of binary definitions of inside and outside, a fluid condition. Maybe he is evolving, maybe not. But maybe this is the best option for the time being: he is exploring. When one explores, one decides to renounce predictability, one stays with an array of emotions, renouncing to a predefined order: one is in the present.

Generally speaking, how does a systemic-dialogical therapist deal with competition? First of all, we must put away all of our moralistic punctuations about competition. Today's world is as excruciating as the world of the twentieth century, only in a different way. In the past century, people easily felt restrained and deprived of opportunities, forced to stand still in situations with little or no stimuli (see Riesman et al., 2001). Present-day society gives us a possibility of unlimited change; only, for most people such possibility is all but illusory.

Compared to earlier generations, liquid generations—people born within the past four decades—take for granted that they will have a harder life compared to their parents. This is new and unfamiliar to the industrialised West, since standard of living got better and better from the mid-nineteenth century up to the 1980s, thus creating the positivistic myth of endless progress (Rossi, 1995). The (quite justified) perception of scarcity and impoverishment necessarily draws to compete for limited resources, a competition which is also enhanced by the dominant ideology we outlined in the previous pages, and also by life practices, such as school or work, that have become more and more competitive.[21]

Emotionally, this creates an urgency to reach goals: the feeling of staying behind generates anxiety, or depression if one fails to reach their prescribed goals. Such goals do not necessarily concern (only) possessions, as it was the case in the past. Today people tend to accumulate experiences: the more the experiences, the more a point in competition has been reached: a course or a master's degree overseas, several work experiences in prestigious placements, many travels, friends, and so on. This is in turn is related to the tendency toward quantification: experiences, abilities, attitudes, intelligence, friends, are all quantified. Everything can be counted. Friendships turn into a definite number of friends, work attitudes in numbers on a test, even anxiety or depression in points on a rating scale.

Competition can be merciless, but a therapist has to develop some tenderness towards those patients who feel they need to overgrow some of their aspects at the expense of others, hypertrophying their most competitive parts. Our task is to enable them to listen to all the different parts of their selves, including the ones that usually remain unheard. Liquid society tends to dismember the self, saving only the parts of it that can be made profitable. Technical rationality requires the individual to overspecialise in some field, leaving out all the rest. Therapy should take the different chops of the patients' selves and aim at re-integrating them in the whole.

Flexibility and (voluntary) submission

Giovanna is a 26-year-old manager. She has been in the same company for two and a half years. She cannot find any actual problem in being where she is; at the same time, she knows that, with her professional profile, she is expected to change her work position approximately every two years. She feels stuck, as if she were missing out on opportunities. She fled from Florence to Milan, that seemed to offer more possibilities. Now she is offered a good position in Florence. What should she do? For her too, having all doors open means the impossibility of stopping.

Lara, 23 years old, is a dietician in training. She came from a small town to study in the big city, and she proved to be a good student. All the same, she cannot stop thinking that she must be more successful: it is something she owes her mother, who made sacrifices to make her study. This could create the temptation for the therapist to find causes for her present distress in her family history and her emotional past. Working with her, though, the therapist can feel that the heart of the matter, despite having some roots in her past, lies mostly in her relentless comparison with her peers and in her need to achieve successful goals. If we weigh different factors, the social condition of the younger generations is probably the main determinant in generating her malaise.

Philosopher Byung-Chul Han (2017b) speaks of a voluntary participation of the subject in her own submission. Liquid, neoliberal society does not suppress freedom, on the contrary it maximises it, but accompanying it with a series of constraints: one must produce, promote oneself, exploit one's potential to the full.[22] Today many young people do not aim at the "steady job" that was the dream of the post-World War II generations. They mostly prefer not to be frozen in a job, a position, a network, that they find constraining. Which implies that, although the liquid state of life allows us to "become anyone", the process never ends, because once we become someone, there will always be the possibility (or necessity) of becoming someone else again. The alternative will be between continuing to move incessantly in anxiety, or remaining stuck in a depressive state. We can make mistakes at will, but nothing ever guarantees that we have done the right thing:

> We live in a world of universal flexibility, under conditions of acute and prospectless *Unsicherheit*, penetrating all aspects of individual life—the sources of livelihood as much as the partnerships of love and common interests, parameters of professional as much as cultural identity, modes of presentation of self in public as much as patterns of health and fitness, values worth pursuing as much as the ways to pursue them.
>
> (Bauman, 2000, p. 135)

Dealing with work issues in therapy is challenging. As we have seen, many patients feel that work requests are mandatory, and cannot be escaped. If we try to introduce different values, we risk trespassing on the boundaries between therapy and political activism. On the other hand, taking the work environment for granted immobilises the therapy, and the therapist gets exactly as stuck as their patients. Here a subtle activity of deconstruction is probably necessary: more than ever, we should ask questions rather than hypothesising too much. With these two patients, most questions regarded their perceived necessities: how it happened that excelling became a necessity? Have there been instances where they came second, or even last (a sort of reversed unique outcome: Chapter 4)? If so, what were the consequences?

What if the same happened tomorrow? What would have happened if they had slowed down rather than accelerated? And so on. The answers were sometimes hard to phrase, sometimes resentful, but in time different—albeit vague—perspectives emerged.

Technical remarks

To us, working with neoliberal subjects means, on the one side, maintaining some traditional tenets of systemic individual therapy, such as understanding the relational network and the significant system(s) of the patient, asking many questions, developing systemic hypotheses, and presentifying third parties (see Boscolo & Bertrando, 1996)—although part of this technical repertoire has been extended and modified, as we will see in detail in Chapter 3. On the other, we added to our practice what we define as the "pillars" of our approach: dialogue (Chapter 4), emotions (Chapter 5), finding one's place (Chapter 6), and responsibility (Chapter 7), plus expectations (Chapter 8). We have made several references to those chapters, because in all cases we have exposed here we felt necessary to resort to them. It may be interesting for the reader to get back to this section after reading the rest of the book.

Here we want to emphasise one specific dimension of our therapeutic work. In all these cases—in all of our cases—we use a micro-analysis of the patient's current practices of life. We try to understand the minimal details of what happens in the patient's relational world, and this means using questions to understand and deconstruct actual episodes, that may shed some light on general processes. We always ask for examples, and then try to enter in their structure. Only after such reconstruction of events do we begin to propose alternative views and hypotheses, that we feed into the dialogue, submitting them to the approval, refusal, or, better, to the patient's reformulation. What usually happens is that the patient, in time, participates in this kind of dialogue, becoming able to see themselves from the outside, and from that position they may find the change they need in order to face the issues brought to therapy.

Of course, for this to happen, a variable amount of time is necessary. Some patients immediately feel at ease in the process, others need a longer span to adjust. We will deal with the different ways to get there in the next chapters. But first, we have to deal with the bodily reality of people.

Notes

1 According to Bateson (1942), individuals deutero-learn the context, i.e., they develop personal characteristics through second-order learning. In this way, we can say, they are created by contexts and at the same time contribute in creating them.

2 Neoliberal theorists maintain, instead, that economic modes of production, the regulation of exchanges, the commercial way of dealing with each other, emerge

spontaneously from relationships and reveal a world that is as close as possible to a "natural" state of affairs. Neoliberalism, according to its proponents, gives a positive answer to the crisis and discomforts of modernity identified by most thinkers of the twentieth century—Nietzsche, Heidegger, Freud, Arendt, Bauman, and so on (see de Carolis, 2017).

3 Not all societies are subjected to the neoliberal condition we experience in the West. Asian countries, for example, are developing their own version of modern economy, linked to neoliberalism in complex and sometimes unpredictable ways (Kyung-Sup, Fine, & Weiss, 2012), and often affected by neocolonialism (Halperin, 2024). Apparently common to all contemporary societies are the emphasis on growth, production and consumption (Røpke, 2008), and the unrelenting acceleration of social change processes (Rosa, 2010).

4 All Internet prophets were originally what Foucault (2004) defined as anarcho-liberal capitalist. Such anarchy, of course, waned when they became virtual monopolists.

5 As Smoliak et al. (2024) observe, the emphasis on emotional regulation in therapy may (also) be considered as a way to adapt patients to social or working conditions they would otherwise reject: in this way, the therapist becomes a tool for the neoliberal emotional standardisation we described above.

6 Also defined as the "neoliberal self" (see McGuigan, 2014).

7 This brings forth the issue of authenticity (see Tagliapietra, 2003): to be authentic, in a neoliberal society, means to create a performance of ourselves that conforms to the prevailing values: "The imperative of authenticity forces the I to *produce itself*. Authenticity is ultimately the neoliberal production of the Self, because makes everyone the producer of themselves" (Han, 2015, p. 30).

8 From a psychopathological point of view, some psychiatric diagnoses appear to have significantly increased at least from 1990: depression (Liu et al., 2020), borderline personality disorder in adults (Clemmensen et al., 2013) and adolescents (Guilé et al., 2018), dissociative disorders (Steinberg & Schnall, 2000). Although some of this research may be biased due to shifting diagnostic criteria, and some diagnostic enthusiasm, all the same the phenomenon shows an increase of social—and psychiatric—attention toward these disorders.

9 The evolution of digital society has been studied by American sociologist Sherry Turkle in a series of seminal books. In *The Second Self* (1984) she studied computers as a part of our everyday personal and psychological lives, with a general optimistic attitude. In *Life on the Screen* (1995) she began to see the computer-generated virtual worlds as more problematic. Finally, in *Alone Together* (2011)—meaningfully subtitled *Why We Expect More from Technology and Less from Each Other*—she addressed the increasing alienation between people paradoxically fostered by the hyperbolic increase of digital (virtual) connection.

10 A century earlier, Sigmund Freud had installed a telephone in his home, but continued to communicate with his Viennese friends by letter: talking on the telephone was a fake, an imperfect copy of a real conversation (see Roazen, 1975).

11 There has been a wide-ranging debate about the effects of digital media and social networks on the socialisation of children and adolescents. Popular books like Jonathan Haidt's (2024) *The Anxious Generation* maintain that digital platforms have an adverse effect on youngsters' "brain rewiring", recommending age-based restrictions and bans on mobile devices among possible remedies. Candice Odgers (2024) criticised this view on *Nature*, arguing that existing data in no way support it: the correlation between digital and social media use and mental illness in adolescence show a mix of no, small and mixed associations. For a meta-analysis regarding Facebook use, see Vuorre & Przybylski (2023); for an umbrella review

of studies about social media use and its impact on adolescent mental health, see Valkenburg et al. (2021).

12 This is often expressed by the so-called Dunbar's number, that identifies the number of meaningful enough relationships any person can have—around 150, according to British anthropologist Robin Dunbar (1992).

13 This evolution actually began with the first generation of postmodern therapies, especially the so-called "post-Milan" models. Salvador Minuchin famously reported the "disappearance" of the family from narrative therapy (Minuchin, 1998): both theories and case examples in narrative, conversational, and solution-focused therapies are less focused on family structures and instead give relevance to individuals (see Anderson, 2016).

14 "Many mistake this model for an ancient, essential, and now endangered institution, when it was actually peculiar to its time. Current social analysis ... view the postwar decade as an aberrant historical period, largely a delayed reaction to the traumas of the Great Depression and World War II. Fueled by the country's strong postwar economy and government benefits, families prospered and bought homes in the suburbs. ... the 1950s reversed the century's steady decline in the birth rate, and couples married at an earlier age and in greater numbers than at any other time before or since" (Walsh, 1993, p. 13).

15 Johannes Jakob Bachofen, Lewis Henry Morgan, Henry Sumner Maine, and J. F. McLellan (Kuper, 2005). The work of Bronislaw Malinowski (1956) was also extremely influential in anthropology, and greatly contributed in shaping the understanding of kinship around the (western nuclear) family (Knight, 2008).

16 See Acquistapace (2022). Anthropologist Janet Carsten (2000) proposes to substitute the term "relatedness" to the standard anthropological term "kinship", in order to go beyond commonplace ideas and prejudices about intimate relationships. She states: "It is a truism that people are always conscious of connections to other people. It is equally a truism that some of these connections carry a particular weight—socially, materially, affectively. And, often but not always, these connections can be described in genealogical terms, but they can also be described in other ways" (Carsten, 2000, p. 1).

17 *Fillus de anima*—literally "son of the soul"—is an expression of the Sardinian language that in the past indicated a rather widespread practice in traditional rural Sardinia: spontaneously entrusting one's biological child to other, generally childless adults, belonging to the same community, but not necessarily to the same family network. It is an example of what today we would call social parenting.

18 "I am a Morning man: I marry an Evening woman and an Evening man, with both of whom I have a sexual relationship, and a Morning woman, with whom I have no sexual relationship. Her sexual relationships are with the Evening man and the Evening woman. ... The two heterosexual pairs are called Morning and Evening, according to the woman's moiety [*clan*]; the male homosexual pair is called the Night marriage, and the female homosexual pair is called the Day" (Le Guin, 1994, p. 208).

19 We chose co-therapy for some individual therapies because we wanted to practise our approach together; in Stefano's case, having two therapists quickly became a need, as if he could not accept to be an ordinary patient with just one therapist, as any other.

20 Chronophobia, a term originally coined by art historian Pamela Lee (2006), "captures the sense of temporal compression and its emotional load of anxiety, fear, and hyperstimulation" (Bussey, 2017, p. 239).

21 The vicissitudes of the Italian school system offer a paramount example of this. Up to a point, Italian schools—at least, the schools that catered for the upper

classes—offered an Italian renaissance-type of teaching, aimed at developing an harmonious personality with wide cultural interests. Apart from the relative success of such a programme, today school offers specialised teaching for people that have to "do things": we teach you to do, rather than to think. Personal fragmentation is thus encouraged by the whole school system.

22 In Australia a campaign was launched to be "aspirational Australians", dynamic people who want to succeed, rather than "leaners", people who settle on the old (Christine Hunt, personal communication, 2019).

References

Abela, A., Vella, S., & Piscopo, S. (Eds) (2020). *Couple Relationships in a Global Context*. European Family Therapy Association Series. Springer. DOI:10.1007/978-973-030-37712-0_1.

Acquistapace, A. (2022). *Tenetevi il matrimonio e dateci la dote. Il lavoro riproduttivo nelle relazioni di intimità, solidarietà e cura oltre la coppia nell'Italia urbana contemporanea*. Mimesis.

Agazzi, E. (1976). Criteri epistemologici fondamentali delle discipline psicologiche. In G. Siri (Ed.), *Problemi epistemologici della psicologia* (pp. 3–35). Vita e Pensiero.

Anderson, H. (2016). Postmodern-Poststructural-Social Construction Therapies: Collaborative, Narrative, and Solution-Focused. In: T.L. Sexton & J. Lebow (Eds.), *Handbook of Family Therapy: The Science and Practice of Working with Families and Couples* (pp. 182–204). Routledge.

Antalffy, N. & Houston, L.D. (2016). Polyamory. In A. Wong, M. Wickramasinghe, R. Hoogland & N.A. Naples (Eds), *The Wiley-Blackwell Encyclopedia of Gender and Sexuality Studies*. Wiley-Blackwell. DOI:10.1002/9781118663219.wbegss136.

Aragão, C., Parker, K., Greenwood, S., Baronavski, C., & Mandata, J.C. (2023). The Modern American Family. Key trends in marriage and family life. *Pew Research Center*. Retrieved from: www.pewresearch.org/social-trends/2023/09/14/the-modern-american-family.

Ariès, P. (1960). *L'enfant et la vie familiale sous l'ancient régime*. Plon.

Bakhtin, M. M. (1968). *Problems of Dostoevsky's Poetics*. C. Emerson (Ed. and Trans.). University of Minnesota Press, 1984.

Barker, M. (2005). 'This is my partner, and this is my… partner's partner: Constructing a Polyamorous Identity in a Monogamous World', *Journal of Constructivist Psychology* 18 (1): 75–88. DOI:10.1080/10720530590523107.

Barker, M. & Langridge, D. (Eds.) (2010). *Understanding Non-Monogamies*. Routledge.

Bateson, G. (1942). Social planning and the concept of deutero-learning. In: *Steps to an Ecology of Mind* (pp. 159–176). Chandler Publishing Company, 1972.

Bateson, G. (1972). *Steps to an Ecology of Mind*. Chandler Publishing Company.

Bauman, Z. (1997). *Postmodernity and its Discontents*. Polity Press.

Bauman, Z. (2000). *Liquid Modernity*. Polity Press.

Bauman, Z. (2003). *Liquid Love: On the Frailty of Human Bonds*. Polity Press.

Bauman, Z., Bertrando, P., & Hanks, H. (2010). Liquid Ethics – psychotherapy in a time of uncertainty. *Human Systems*, 20 (1): 42–56.

Beck, U. (1986). *Risikogesellschaft. Auf dem Weg in eine andere Moderne*. Suhrkamp.

Bertrando, P. (2002). The presence of the third party. Systemic therapy and transference analysis. *Journal of Family Therapy*, 24 (3): 351–368. DOI:10.1111/1467–6427.00224.

Bertrando, P., Toffanetti, D. (2000). *Storia della terapia familiare. Le persone, le idee.* Raffaello Cortina Editore.

Booth, W. C. (1961). *The Rhetoric of Fiction.* University of Chicago Press.

Boscolo, L. & Bertrando, P. (1993). *The Times of Time: A Perspective on Time in Systemic Therapy and Consultation.* 2nd edition. Routledge, 2020.

Boscolo, L., Bertrando, P. (1996). *Systemic Therapy with Individuals.* Karnac.

Boss, P. (1999). *Ambiguous Loss: Learning to Live with Unresolved Grief.* Harvard University Press.

Bussey, M. (2017). Time's Calling: Time, Timing, and Transformation in Futures Work. *World Futures Review,* 9 (4): 236–247. DOI:10.1177/1946756717697335.

Carsten, J. (Ed.) (2000). *Cultures of Relatedness: New Approaches to the Study of Kinship.* Cambridge University Press.

Castro, Á. & Barrada, J.R. (2020). Dating Apps and Their Sociodemographic and Psychosocial Correlates: A Systematic Review. *International Journal of Environmental Research and Public Health,* 17 (18): 6500. DOI:10.3390/ijerph17186500.

Cecchin, G. (1987). Hypothesizing-circularity-neutrality Revisited: An Invitation to Curiosity, *Family Process,* 26: 405–413. DOI:10.1111/j.1545-5300.1987.00405.x.

Clemmensen, L.M.Ø., Jensen, S.O.W., Zanarini, M.C., Skadhede, S., & Munk-Jørgensen, P. (2013). Changes in Treated Incidence of Borderline Personality Disorder in Denmark: 1970–2009. *The Canadian Journal of Psychiatry,* 58 (9): 522–528. DOI:10.1177/070674371305800907.

Dardot, P. & Laval, C. (2013). *The New Way of the World: On Neo-Liberal Society* (translated by Gregory Elliott). Verso (original edition 2009).

De Carolis, M. (2017). *Il rovescio della libertà. Tramonto del neoliberalismo e disagio della civiltà.* Quodlibet.

Doty, A. (1993). *Making Things Perfectly Queer: Interpreting Mass Culture.* Minneapolis: University of Minnesota Press.

Dunbar, R.I.M. (1992). Neocortex size as a constraint on group size in primates. *Journal of Human Evolution,* 22 (6): 469–493. DOI:10.1016/0047-2484(92)90081-J.

Foucault, M. (1982). The subject and power. In: H. L. Dreyfus & F. Rabinow, *Michel Foucault: Beyond Structuralism and Hermeneutics.* Chicago: University of Chicago Press.

Foucault, M. (1988). Technologies of the self. In: P. Rabinow (Ed.), *Ethics. Essential Works of Foucault 1954–1984,* Vol. 1 (pp. 223–251). Penguin, 2000.

Foucault, M. (2004). *Naissance de la biopolitique. Cours au Collège de France (1978–79).* Gallimard.

Fraser, N. (2016). Contradictions of capital and care. *New Left Review,* 100: 99–117.

Fruggeri, L. (1997). *Famiglie. Dinamiche interpersonali e processi psico-sociali.* La Nuova Italia Scientifica.

Fruggeri, L. (2005). *Diverse normalità. Psicologia sociale delle relazioni familiari.* Carocci.

Gallino, L. (2011). *Finanzcapitalismo: la civiltà del denaro in crisi.* Giulio Einaudi Editore.

Gato, J., Leal, D., Biasutti, C., Tasker, F., & Fontaine, A.M. (2021). Building a Rainbow Family: Parenthood Aspirations of Lesbian, Gay, Bisexual, and Transgender/Gender Diverse Individuals. In: N.A.D. Morais, F. Scorsolini-Comin, & E. Cerqueira-Santos (Eds), *Parenting and Couple Relationships Among LGBTQ+ People in Diverse Contexts.* Cham. DOI:10.1007/978-3-030-84189-8_12.

Geertz, C. (1973). *The Interpretation of Cultures.* Basic Books.

Grilli, S. & Zanotelli, F. (Eds.) (2010). *Scelte di famiglia. Tendenze della parentela nella società contemporanea.* ETS.

Guilé, J.M., Boissel, L., Alaux-Cantin, S., & Garny de La Rivière, S. (2018). Borderline personality disorder in adolescents: prevalence, diagnosis, and treatment strategies. *Adolescent Health, Medicine and Therapeutics*, 9: 199–210. DOI:10.2147/AHMT.S156565.

Haidt, J. (2024). *The Anxious Generation: How the Great Rewiring of Childhood is Causing an Epidemic of Mental Illness.* Allen Lane.

Halperin, S. (2024, July 12). Neocolonialism. *Encyclopaedia Britannica.* www.britannica.com/topic/neocolonialism.

Han, Byung-Chul (2015). *The Burnout Society.* Stanford University Press (original edition 2010).

Han, Byung-Chul (2017a). *In the Swarm: Digital Prospects.* Transl. by Erik Butler. MIT Press (original edition 2013).

Han, Byung-Chul (2017b). *Psychopolitics: Neoliberalism and New Technologies of Power.* Transl. by Erik Butler. Verso (original edition 2014).

Haraway, D.J. & Goodeve, T.N. (1999). *How Like a Leaf: An Interview with Donna Haraway.* Routledge.

Harré, R. & Van Langenhove, L. (Eds) (1999). *Positioning Theory.* Basil Blackwell.

Herlihy, D. (1985). *Medieval Households.* Harvard University Press.

Hermans, H.J.M., Kempen, H.J.G., & Van Loon, R.J.P. (1992). The dialogical self: Beyond individualism and rationalism. *American Psychologist*, 47: 23–33. DOI:10.1037/0003-0066X.47.1.23.

Jaeggi, R. (2018) *Critique of Life Forms* (translated by Ciaran Cronin). Harvard University Press (original edition 2014).

Jamieson, L., Morgan, D., Allan, G., & Crow, G. (2006). Friends, Neighbours and Distant Partners: Extending or Decentring Family Relationships? *Sociological Research Online*, 11 (3). DOI:10.5153/sro.1421.

Keay, D. (1987). Aids, Education and the Year 2000! Interview with Margaret Thatcher. *Woman's Own*, 31 October 1987, pp. 8–10.

Kidd, W. (2012). Utilising Podcasts for Learning and Teaching: a Review and Ways forward for e-Learning Cultures. *Management in Education*, 26 (2), 52–57. DOI:10.1177/0892020612438031.

Knight, C. (2008). Early Human Kinship Was Matrilineal. In: N. J. Allen, H. Callan, R. Dunbar & W. James (Eds), *Early Human Kinship*. Blackwell, pp. 61–82.

Kuper, A. (2005). *The Reinvention of Primitive Society: Transformations of a Myth.* 2nd edition. Routledge.

Kyung-Sup, C., Fine, B., & Weiss, L. (Eds) (2012). *Developmental Politics in Transition.* Palgrave Macmillan. DOI:10.1057/9781137028303_9.

Le Guin, U.K. (1994). Unchosen Love. In: *Hainish Novels and Stories, Volume Two.* The Library of America, 2017, pp. 207–225.

Lee, P.M. (2006). *Chronophobia: On Time in the Art of the 1960s.* MIT Press.

Levin, I. (2004). Living Apart Together: A New Family Form. *Current Sociology*, 52 (2): 223–240. DOI:10.1177/0011392104041809.

Lijster, T. & Celikates. R. (2019). Beyond the Echo-chamber: An Interview with Hartmut Rosa on Resonance and Alienation. *Krisis: Journal for Contemporary Philosophy*, 2019 (1): 64–77. DOI:10.21827/krisis.39.1.37365.

Liu, Q., He, H., Yang, J., Feng, X., Zhao, F., & Lyu, J. (2020). Changes in the global burden of depression from 1990 to 2017: Findings from the Global Burden of Disease study. *Journal of Psychiatric Research*, 126: 134–140. DOI:10.1016/j.jpsychires.2019.08.002.

Lopez, R.B. & Polletta, I. (2021). Regulating Self-Image on Instagram: Links Between Social Anxiety, Instagram Contingent Self-Worth, and Content Control Behaviors. *Frontiers in Psychology*, 12, 25 August 2021. DOI:10.3389/fpsyg.2021.711447.

Lück, D. & Ruckdeschel, K. (2018). Clear in its Core, Blurred in the Outer Contours: Culturally Normative Conceptions of the Family in Germany. *European Societies*, 20 (5), 715–742. DOI:10.1080/14616696.2018.1473624.

Malinowski, B. (1956). *Marriage: Past and Present. A debate between Robert Briffault and Bronislaw Malinowski*. M.F. Ashley Montagu (Ed.). Porter Sargent.

Marchetti, S. (2023). Michela Murgia, l'ultima intervista: "Il tempo migliore della mia vita". *Vanity Fair Italia*, 30–31, 10 August 2023, www.vanityfair.it/article/michela -murgia-famiglia-queer.

Marcoaldi, F. (2013). Remo Bodei: "Noi, poveri post umani, schiavi delle nuove libertà." *La Repubblica*, 6 settembre 2013.

McGuigan, J. (2014). The Neoliberal Self, *Culture Unbound. Journal of Current Cultural Research*, 6: 223–240. DOI:10.3384/cu.2000.1525.146223.

Melograni, P. (Ed.) (1988). *La famiglia in Italia dall'Unità a oggi*. Laterza.

Minuchin, S. (1998). Where is the Family in Narrative Family Therapy? *Journal of Marital and Family Therapy*, 24: 397–403. DOI:10.1111/j.1752–0606.1998.tb01094.x.

Odgers, C. (2024). Great Rewiring: is Social Media really behind an Epidemic of Teenage Mental Illness? *Nature*, 628: 29–30. DOI:10.1038/d41586–41024–00902–00902.

Oldman, C. & Quilgars, D. (1999). The last resort? Revisiting ideas about older people's living arrangements. *Ageing and Society*, 19 (3): 363–384. DOI:10.1017/S0144686X99007370.

O'Donnell, I. (2014). *Prisoners, Solitude, and Time*. Clarendon Studies in Criminology (Oxford University Press; online edition, Oxford Academic, 22 Jan. 2015), DOI:10.1093/acprof:oso/9780199684489.001.0001, accessed 22 Dec. 2023.

Prensky, M. (2001). Digital natives, digital immigrants. *On the Horizon*, 9 (5), 1–6. DOI:10.4135/9781483387765.n6.

Riesman, D., Glazer, N., & Denney, R. (2001). *The Lonely Crowd: A Study of the Changing American Character, Abridged and Revised Edition*. Yale University Press (original edition: 1950).

Roazen, P. (1975). *Freud and His Followers*. Knopf.

Rosa, H. (2010). *Acceleration and Alienation: Towards a Critical Theory of Late-modern Temporality*. NSU Press.

Rossi, P. (1995). *Naufragi senza spettatore. L'idea di progresso*. Il Mulino.

Rubin, G.S. (1984). Thinking Sex: Notes for a Radical Theory of the Politics of Sexuality. In: C.S. Vance (Ed.), *Pleasure and Danger: Exploring Female Sexuality* (pp. 143–174). Routledge and Kegan Paul.

Røpke, I. (2008). The New Consumers. The Influence of Affluence on the Environment. *Journal of Industrial Ecology*, 9: 295–296. DOI:10.1162/jiec.2005.9.1–2.295.

Smoliak, O., Rice, C., Rudder, D., Tseliou, E., LaMarre, A., LeCouteur, A., Gaete, J., Davies, A., & Henshaw, S. (2024). Emotion Regulation as Affective Neoliberal Governmentality. *Family Process*, 00, 1–18. DOI:10.1111/famp.13064.

Snowden, D. (1979). Robert Fripp: The Small Mobile Intelligent Pest of Rock'n'Roll. *LA Reader*, 19 August 1979.

Snyder, D.K. & Balderrama-Durbin, C.M. (2020). Current Status and Challenges in Systemic Family Therapy with Couples. In: K.S. Wampler and A.J. Blow (Eds), *The Handbook of Systemic Family Therapy*. DOI:10.1002/9781119790945.ch1.

Spencer, L. & Pahl, R. (2006). *Rethinking Friendship: Hidden Solidarities Today.* Princeton University Press.

Steinberg, M. & Schnall, M. (2000). *The Stranger in the Mirror. Dissociation, the Hidden Epidemic.* Cliff Street Books/HarperCollins.

Suszek, H. (2018). Critique of Dialogical Self Theory. In: A.M. Columbus (Ed.), *Advances in Psychology Research* (Vol. 131). Nova Science Publisher, pp. 98–138.

Tagliapietra, A. (2003). *La virtù crudele. Filosofia e storia della sincerità.* Torino: Einaudi.

Taylor, C. (1989). *Sources of the Self: The Making of the Modern Identity.* Cambridge University Press.

Tejedor, C. (2014). *The Early Wittgenstein on Metaphysics, Natural Science, Language and Value.* Routledge. DOI:10.4324/9781315850245.

Turkle, S. (1984). *The Second Self: Computers and the Human Spirit.* MIT Press.

Turkle, S. (1995). *Life on the Screen.* Simon and Schuster.

Turkle, S. (2011). *Alone Together: Why We Expect More from Technology and Less from Each Other.* Basic Books.

Valkenburg, P., Meier, A., & Beyens, I. (2021). Social Media Use and its Impact on Adolescent Mental Health: An Umbrella Review of the Evidence. *Current Opinion in Psychology,* 44. DOI:10.1016/j.copsyc.2021.08.017.

Vuorre, M. & Przybylski, A. K. (2023). Estimating the Association Between Facebook Adoption and Well-being in 72 Countries. *Royal Society Open Science,* 10 (8), 221451. DOI:10.1098/rsos.221451.

Walsh, F. (1993). Conceptualization of Normal Family Processes. In: F. Walsh (Ed.), *Normal Family Processes.* The Guilford Press.

Walsh, F. (Ed.) (2012). *Normal Family Processes. Growing Diversity and Complexity. Fourth Edition.* The Guilford Press.

Wittgenstein, L. (1953). *Philosophical Investigations.* (Edited by G. E. M. Anscombe). Wiley-Blackwell.

Wynne, L.C. & Wynne, A.R. (1986). The Quest for Intimacy. *Journal of Marital and Family Therapy,* 12: 383–394. DOI:10.1111/j.1752-0606.1986.tb00671.x.

Chapter 2

Genders

Individual therapy is, first and foremost, an encounter between two bodies (two embodied subjects). Bodies have a gender, an age, some physical as well as relational characteristics. We will now turn our attention to this complex tangle. To us, the first variable to consider in this respect is gender: we became aware of these processes when we began focusing on gender issues, probably the pivotal novelties emerging in our practice in recent years. It was for us probably the strongest push toward change. We have been reflecting on it for a long time, but only in the last few years did we fully realise the impact it has on the lives of patients, both women and men, not to mention people with a fluid gender identity. In Chapter 1 we have observed how social and economic changes have affected people asking for therapy; the same happened in regard to gender issues. It is difficult to determine whether we see more gender-related issues in our practice because they have actually increased, or because we are more sensitive to them: the fact is that they are here. This chapter outlines the consequences of such process for individual therapy.

Some questions

It is impossible, we feel, to ask patients any question if we have not asked the same question of ourselves first. This is true also of questions about gender. In the original book, *Systemic Therapy with Individuals*, gender was named, but scantily considered. The fact that the authors were two men, of course, was not incidental in this respect: they tried to consider a female point of view, but could not grasp all its implications.[1] A female voice was necessary in order to realise what had been hitherto taken for granted: the patriarchal texture is subtle, and it is easy to be unaware of it—especially for men—because it is woven within the finest threads of our lives.

Our own path toward gender awareness started with Claudia. Soon after completing her systemic therapy training, she began collaborating with the Milan Women Collective (CDM), a militant lesbian group that needed a heterosexual woman therapist to complete their staff. She was thus exposed

DOI: 10.4324/9781003381754-3

to an array of problems and issues she had never encountered—or even conceived—previously: minority stress, relationships between homosexual and heterosexual people, sexual issues she did not know. That experience lasted for a long time.

Claudia brought such issues with her when we developed our approach. Paolo realised that, as a man, he had mostly neglected them in the past. If anybody enjoys a privilege, they are unaware of it. This is even truer of gender privileges for men. Besides bringing gender to the fore, Claudia also developed some theoretical background, mainly by reading feminist authors. (We give a very brief account of the development of feminist thinking both outside and inside therapy in Appendix B.) From our exploration of feminism manifold questions arose: Does a "public" job, such as therapy, turn us into political subjects? What are the social implications that our body takes along? Does our communication—both through body and words—imply political themes? Does it have any weight within the therapeutic process? What kind of gender implications do we bring into therapy? To what extent are we conditioned by patriarchy, as a power process that regulates roles within systems such as the couple and the family?

The body, feminism and politics

We enter therapy, all of us, therapists or patients, with this body. That means: this body, the specific body we inhabit (we are). In our systemic past, we saw the body as an idea—an abstract body. The body we now consider is our actual, concrete, living body. This also means that our patients do not see "the therapist" in general. They see one of us, the physical persons that we are. Our bodies are the first experience we have of each other, and such experience is naturally gendered. Everything else is negotiable, and it will be negotiated in the course of therapy. The evidence of the body and its presence will not.[2]

The emergence of gender themes in our thinking brought us to see the abstract, disembodied nature we had hitherto attributed to systems. We, like others before us, had been questioning the time-honoured concept of neutrality for a while. Now we could see it from another angle: the neutral therapist is necessarily a genderless, bodiless, and emotionless therapist, because anyone who has a gender, a body and some emotions cannot be neutral. When Claudia was working on gender, and Paolo was working on emotions, we realised that we were reaching the same place from two different starting points. When we wondered what could be the link between gender and emotions, putting aside commonplace ideas such as emotional women versus unemotional men, we focused on our bodies, because both emotions and gender are brought in therapy through the body.

Disembodied detachment is traditionally associated with the masculine, who thinks and does not feel, or controls what he feels, who looks from the outside and judges, who subjects the other to himself instead of participating. It is one of the subtle ways to implicitly root an ultimately patriarchal vision in our thinking—therefore all the more difficult to challenge. Considering the body gives depth to our understanding.

The body, however, is not a given, something that emerges ready-made from the biological depths of our existence, as Butler (1993) aptly noticed. Body, gender, age, are something we mould in time, under the pressure of the many contexts we are embedded in. We must be aware of this, if we want to fully understand the role our body and our gender play in our lives and our profession. As therapists, we present ourselves as a woman and a man—as we are: this is a political statement, even when we do absolutely nothing. (And our very binary nature can be challenging for patients who are outside gender binarism and identify neither with male nor female identities.) All these aspects enter forcefully in the therapy room. It is not a personal implicit, it is a political act.

When we began to question ourselves about the therapist, how they enter therapy with their body, their age, and their gender, we realised it was best to start from ourselves and our own bodies, as Italian feminists did in the 1970s. The seminal issue that "the personal is political" was posed independently by American radical feminist Carol Hanisch and Italian separatist feminist Carla Lonzi. Speaking about consciousness-raising groups in the USA, Hanisch wrote: "One of the first things we discover in these groups is that personal problems are political problems. There are no personal solutions at this time. There is only collective action for a collective solution" (1970, p. 76). This means: if my problem is shared by all of us, its roots lie in society, and society should change rather than individuals. Hanisch questioned the very definition of such groups as "therapeutic", because the idea of therapy implied some notion of pathology to be cured, rather than social issues to be faced.

Italian feminist theory of 1970s, despite some similarities, was completely different from American feminism of the same period. If the latter emphasised gender equity and equality, theorists such as Carla Lonzi (1978) developed the "thought of sexual difference", arguing that everything a man or a woman experiences passes through the body. Men and women, despite having equal rights, are different in the ways they live and interpret reality: women give birth and men cannot, male and female bodies differ. Furthermore, women struggle with social relationships, because their very being as women, with a woman's experience and desires, is shaped by male desire and male imagination.

We connected this line of thinking with Judith Butler's concept of gender as a performative dimension: gender—and in this respect sex too—is created by our performing gender roles, that are scripted for us by our culture, both in the "highbrow" sense (literature, poetry, visual arts), and in the "popular" sense (films, TV series, love songs, comics). Briefly, the whole fabric of social life creates scripts that we enact, willingly or not. Even when we want to rebel against them, we still are thinking within their conceptual boundaries (Butler, 1990; see also Appendix B). A long and complex work of deconstruction is required to go beyond them: as we have seen in the past 50 years, change happened, but it was slow and painful, and never taken for granted.[3]

Feminist distinctions are central to our very definition of systemic-dialogical therapy. If politics is a way of looking at the world and living in it, all of our personal actions become political actions. We, as therapists and trainers of future therapists, are called to make an in-depth reflection on how we practise and teach, on how we relate to patients and trainees, what position of power we assume with respect to knowledge and how it is transmitted. So gender was pivotal in our evolution toward a politically aware therapy.

Gender and therapy

Do gender (and other social) issues have implications for therapy? Being rooted in the Milan systemic approach, we looked for answers to this question in the work of the different Milan teams. We did not find any. No reflection on body and gender—not to mention intersectional themes—appeared either in their theories or practices. The team of Selvini Palazzoli, Prata, Boscolo and Cecchin was an equitable group composed by two women and two men (and led by a woman), but this obvious fact was not theorised in their work, except when sometimes they used male-female co-therapy to show some parental couples a "functional" male-female relationship (see Selvini Palazzoli et al., 1978), thus confirming several gender biases about what a functional couple or family is, and how gender roles should be played out.

As Burck and Daniel write: "What happens if we do bring talk about gender and power overtly into the domain of therapy? Attempting to do so has involved rethinking many of the most cherished tenets of family system approach to therapy" (1995, p.1). We felt more or less in the same position. And this brought us to look for further information about the history of gender issues in systemic (family) therapy.[4] Three main issues were closer to our personal experience. The first was the critique to the implicit patriarchal values of most classical family therapy theories, as portrayed by Deborah Luepnitz's seminal book, *The Family Interpreted* (1988). Luepnitz outlines the main family therapy approaches of her time, highlighting their basic, albeit mostly unspoken, patriarchal values (see Appendix B).

Specifically, our own Batesonian values were challenged: Bateson's unwillingness to theorise power had always been a problematic point for systemic therapy. But this was not the whole story. Deeper theoretical prejudices were involved. Systemic therapy, especially in its constructivist version, had glimpsed very well that no theory can be considered neutral from any point of view. When Heinz von Foerster (1982) introduces the distinction between the observing system and the observed system, or Humberto Maturana and Francisco Varela establish that "anything said is said by an observer" (1980, p. 8), they seem to indicate exactly this: every theoretical statement is made from a definite point of view, and no point of view is neutral. Yet this has had minimal consequences for systemic therapists' awareness of gender—and privilege, race, culture. They continued to have a detached view of all these issues, as if they did not concern them. In embracing the epistemology of points of view, they remained blind to many of their own points of view.

In fact, von Foerster, Maturana and Varela gave an abstract definition of their quite correct principles. The very idea of "the observer" refers to the typical (male) Western detachment, the theoretical philosopher who looks at the world from outside, rather than living and acting inside it. On some level, ancient Stoic philosopher Seneca—who recommended re-examining our actions of the day every evening (Foucault, 1990)—is closer to us than Heinz von Foerster. At this point, we realised that we needed to develop our approach in such a way as to consider both gender power and gender values.

The second issue concerned power in systemic therapy institution. In Italy, in the years after 2000, the situation was very similar to the one described by the Women's Project of the Ackerman Institute in 1978 (see Appendix B): most practitioners were women, most directors were men. We decided that our school would have two directors, a woman and a man, on a totally equal base, and that such equality would be the base not just of the school, but of our very approach, re-balancing patriarchal privileged positions every time they emerged.

The third had again been stressed by Luepnitz: the complete absence, in family therapy up to her time, of any allusion toward family violence, abuse and incest, that outside the field already were important matters of concern. Apparently, the basic prejudice that couple, marriage and "the family" were good in themselves, and should therefore be protected and enforced, made family therapists blind to an already very apparent social plague.

The change in our premises, in that period, was also favoured by the appearance of new kinds of patients. As we have seen in Chapter 1, society as a whole, and individuals within them, became liquid, with fluid and manifold identities, polyamory, new family forms. At the same time, gender-related issues came to the fore: the growing intolerance toward patriarchy, the recognition of homosexuality and different sexual orientations as legitimate forms of life, the emergence of gender identities, fluid identities, non-binary identities, identities in transition, plus all the challenges posed by social media, such as sex bombing or slut shaming, created a whole new terminology. We realised that our theories and frames of reference were rapidly becoming dusty and academic.[5] As clinicians, we had to face unprecedented themes within the social landscape of liquid modernity.

Slowly we delved into these subjects, exploring and analysing the micro-dynamics shown in the therapy room as binding premises and prejudices. For example, in a recent supervision group with six participants, we found two cases of gender fluidity, one of unaccepted homosexuality (internalised homophobia), plus a polyamory situation. The latter especially was extremely difficult to accept for the therapist involved, who tended instead to subtly pathologise it.

This is more common than one might expect: often with polyamory we adopt, without realising, a normalising position, seeing the eccentric (non-standard) behaviour as deviant or pathological, with the underlaying and unaware aim to correct it. If we adopt such a stance, we try to bring back polyamory—or any other gender-related eccentricity—to "normality", failing to wonder what "normal" means. We must be wary of our implicit assumptions about normality.

Gender identities

Chinese thinking emphasises the continuous and the gradual (Jullien, 2009), rejecting dichotomies. Western thinking, instead, entails a deeply rooted binarism: after all, at the beginning of Genesis, God separates "the light from the darkness, and the waters from the land". Then, as we well know, God creates first the man and from him the woman: in this way the man/woman dyad is born, inserted simultaneously into a series of dichotomous oppositions and into a discourse of subjugation. Dichotomous thinking finds its definitive consecration with Aristotelian logic, with its excluded middle and law of non-contradiction, which will become the basis of all subsequent logics for centuries (see Russell, 1946).[6]

Hence an endless series of dichotomies: right/wrong, good/bad, functional/dysfunctional, normal/deviant, normal/pathological, healthy/sick, sane/insane, problem/solution, fluid/blocked—and also male/female, dominant/subjugated, rational/emotional, and so on. Dichotomies that prevent us from thinking about situations that are neither on one side nor the other, or both on one side and the other, as in the now overworked metaphor of Schrödinger's cat. Besides being dichotomous, moreover, binary gender is a relational category: one is female because somebody else is male. And male and female exist through an act of distinction that is made by somebody.

As an example, let us consider the dichotomy between normal and pathological. Allen Frances, former head of the committee that shaped the fourth edition of the American *Diagnostic and Statistical Manual of Mental Disorders* (DSM-IV: American Psychiatric Association, 1994), criticised the abuse of diagnostic categories in its subsequent edition (DSM-5: American Psychiatric Association, 2013). He claimed it contained an excess of psychiatric pathologies, therefore characterising "normal" people as "pathological": for example, normal grief is subsumed by Major Depressive Disorder, normal forgetfulness in old age becomes Minor Neurocognitive Disorder, and so on (Frances, 2013). The point is: Frances does not consider that there may be conditions that are neither exactly normal nor exactly pathological (Freud understood this very well). In order to deal with them, we need to rethink the very concepts of normal and pathological.

Today, gender identities too challenge this dichotomous common sense. More and more, as therapists, we have to deal with people who recognise themselves as neither male nor female, or as both male and female. And the relationship with them leads us to question precisely the categories of masculine and feminine.

When we say that feminist thinking made us aware of gender issues, we mean that initially we were brought to consider the female gender on the same level as the male, overcoming the long-standing idea that the standard human being is implicitly and necessarily male. The goal was to empower women as women. In dealing with gender identity, in other words, we took for granted the existence of two genders, male and female. But is this the case?

If we adopt a non-essentialist position, gender identities—and the roles and functioning expectations related to them—are conditioned by the macro-contextual cultural system. Gender and what we think and practise of it is linked to the historical period we are living, with its roles, expectations, behaviours and inclinations. In contemporary Western societies, we usually expect both women and men to be heterosexual, and to have positive certainty about their belonging to one of the sides of this gender dichotomy.[7] Specifically, women are expected to be kind, thoughtful, elegant, firm but not aggressive, to know how to look after the house and children, and above all to be beautiful. We ask men to be strong, decisive, confident, successful with women and at work and not to show vulnerability.

The process of acquiring a gender identity begins before birth and continues throughout the lives of women and men. Discriminatory processes based on gender affiliation are actualised by family influences, children literature, school education, mass media messages, institutional reinforcements. All social agencies contribute to this process, thus confirming gender polarisation through the production and reproduction of stereotypes and clichés. Culture shapes minds—and genders: "it becomes impossible to separate out 'gender' from the political and cultural intersections in which it is invariably produced and maintained" (Butler, 1990, p. 6).

The process of reproduction of gender identities is not as linear as it seems, though. And it has been challenged in postmodern society, where daily life is characterised by the collapse of the elements of stability, trust and meaning on which certainties were based in pre-modern times (Chapter 1). A fracture is created in the horizon of meanings that preserves identities (roles, functions, goals), generating an individual and collective crisis.[8]

Today, the existence of more than two genders is slowly becoming part of common sense. People with identities that challenge binarism came to the fore. It is easier to see transsexual persons who do not feel they belong to the gender to which they were assigned at birth, determined on the basis of their external genitalia, or intersex persons who were born with reproductive or sexual anatomy that did not fit the boxes of "female" or "male" (United Nations OHCHR, 2015). And there are many more ways of being non-binary. (It is irrelevant to wonder whether they were already there, but silent, or whether the possibility of speaking out led to the emergence of character-istics that would have remained hidden in past societies: in any case, they are here to stay.)

Where is the difficulty then? Cisgender people find it difficult to conceive such a fluidity as a form of life and therefore to understand this kind of indeterminacy. We live in a world that still asks us to justify ourselves for traits that deviate from an ideal, reassuring and understandable norm (Godman, 2018). If our personality is built on a binary gender identity, coming into contact with non-binary people confuses us, breaks the mirror of social expectations.

The role connected to gender identity is one of the elements being reconfi-gured in present days. Ideally, one could be male, female, male and female at the same time, neither of the two, sometimes male, sometimes female, or any other possible variant of gender identity, without having have to justify one-self for this. The fourth wave of feminism, a revolution that moves through the body, incorporates differences and the strife for the existence of different people. The issue is to break down long-standing prejudices through the most powerful, most primitive and most dangerous vehicle: the body (Clarke & Peel, 2007).

The tension between tradition and (liquid) modernity redraws the bound-aries of gender identities, even for those who identify with more traditional binary categories. Women's lives become even more challenging: growing education, increased employment, reduced fertility, economic and decision-making autonomy. Men's lives, in turn, are involved in the redefinition of male identity, but its contours appear blurry and the final effects unclear. One point appears clear: patriarchal roles should be put into question.

Queerness

A possible way to challenge patriarchal prejudices can be the adoption of a queer position. What is the precise meaning of "queer", though, and how can a queer stance be useful to us in therapy? Broadly speaking, the word "queer" is used today to describe those gestures or analyses which emphasise and dramatise incoherencies in the (allegedly stable) relations between chro-mosomal sex, gender and sexual desire. According to Rosemary Hennessy, queer embraces the very categories that were used to shame presumed sexual deviants, reversing their value: "Touting queerness is a gesture of rebellion against the pressure to be invisible or apologetically abnormal. It is an in-your-face rejection of the proper response to heteronormativity, a version of acting up" (1993, p. 967).

We can consider queer both transvestite performances and academic deconstructions, insofar as they claim the problematics of any "natural" sexuality, and call into question even such apparently unproblematic terms as "man" and "woman". As Eve Kosofsky Sedgwick writes, queer questions all of the basic gender assumptions we have outlined in the preceding sections: gender and its self-perception, sexual attraction, gender self-definition, sexual fantasies, communities. "What I hear in queer is the question: What things in that list don't line up monolithically?" (1993, p. 27).

Queer theory's debunking of stable sexes, genders and sexualities developed out of a specifically lesbian and gay reworking of identity. It conceives gender identity as a constellation of multiple and unstable positions (Doty, 1993). Queer should not be considered, however, as a simple shorthand for "lesbian and gay" (see Walters, 1996). Queer's analytic framework also includes such topics as cross-dressing, hermaphroditism, gender ambiguity and gender-corrective surgery. Many theorists welcome queer as "another discursive horizon, another way of thinking the sexual" (de Lauretis, 1991, p. IV).

Our own understanding of queer is a political positioning in the broadest meaning of the term (see Haraway, 1988). In this sense, no individual could be called "queer", because queer is not an essence, nor an individual psychological characteristic (de Lauretis, 2007): instead, a practice, a relationship, a situation can be queer, a point of view and a political or even micropolitical approach can be queer, to the extent that they destabilise the binary and naturalised categories of sexes and genders. Alexander Doty in his book on queer culture puts into question "the cultural demarcation between the queer and the straight ... by pointing out the queerness of and in straights and straight cultures, as well as that of individuals and groups who have been told they inhabit the boundaries between the binaries of gender and sexuality: transsexuals, bisexuals, transvestites, and other binary outlaws" (1993, xv-xvi).

How can queer positions help therapists in their work? Amanda Middleton (2022) encourages therapists to forget their presumed knowledge about sex and gender, and seek new discourses engaging with queer people. We came in contact with queer culture as white heterosexual cisgender therapists—apparently the most distant from a queer environment. At the same time, we were aware that therapists work better when they stay on the fringe, rather than in the mainstream. In order to understand the lives—always problematic, often eccentric, sometimes deranged—of our patients, we had to step out of our default middle-class position. We were embracing a form of queerness without fully realising it, certainly without putting our own gender in doubt. We were inadvertently following queer sociologist Alessia (Leo) Acquistapace's (2022) suggestion: therapists can use the little bits of queer they have in themselves, and try to understand viewpoints that can be very distant from their own. We could well understand Michela

Murgia's queer family, and from that position criticise the normative idea of the family that is still so relevant in family therapy.

Queer ideas may infiltrate practices that are not straightforwardly queer in themselves. After all, Judith Butler herself (1993) stated that the importance of a queer position resides precisely in the fact that it is impossible to predict its future directions. What we consider essential for our therapeutic activity is not taking for granted patriarchal rules. Patriarchy, though, is much more resilient than we think.

Patriarchy

Doris is 33. Despite coming from a family of middle-class city employees, she now lives on a farm with her husband. She finds herself trapped within a traditional, patriarchal family where her 60-year-old father-in-law is still the dominant male and her 30-year-old husband is totally submissive to him, and in turn adopts his father's chauvinist vision. After marrying at a very young age, she is now stuck in this archaic system. Despite the heavy workload, her in-laws deem it impossible to hire additional labourers—a hiring that would be perfectly possible from an economic point of view. It is a family of farmers; Doris, with her city background, feels like the servant of the animals: the cows must be fed, cared for, and milked, without considering personal hardships. Mostly out of pride, she insists on staying there, despite the oppressive position her in-laws adopted from the beginning, resistant as they are to change.

Doris has been in this situation for 14 years, with a husband she hardly speaks to anymore. Sometimes she feels like she is staying in the relationship almost in spite of him. "If I leave," she says, "I lose some hard-earned advantages. I'm now recognised for what I'm worth, since I've learned to do things that I'd never imagine before; now I'm in charge of the cheeses, and everybody, within and without my family, grants me this expertise. If I leave here, I'll lose everything I worked so hard to build."

At the same time, she is unable to change the patriarchal system of that family, where male power is transmitted through the generations. She appears even ambivalent about changing it, because now her position within it has become a source of pride. She has been in therapy for many months now, and she has realised that the only change possible, if she does not want to give up her position in an apparently unchangeable system, is to change his way of staying in it. Now once a month she allows herself to go to the seaside for two days, and every now and then she takes short trips with her sister. It may seem very little from outside, but for her it is a lot: if she cannot change this system, if she still gets rewards from it, including the relationship with her animals, she has created some compensation chambers that allow her to stay there. She has found her place (Chapter 6). The price to pay is to perpetuate patriarchy.

This situation may be read from different viewpoints: family alliances and coalitions, family structure and boundaries, power relationships, the story that Doris tells about herself, the possible stories others tell about her, and so on. Once one is aware of the lens of patriarchy, however, it is almost unavoidable to see Doris's case in this light.

To what extent are we conditioned by patriarchy? And what is patriarchy, first of all? According to the Cambridge Dictionary, patriarchy is "a society in which the oldest male is the leader of the family, or a society controlled by men in which they use their power to their own advantage". Which means that patriarchy is a word with a double meaning: "There are theories of 'patriarchy' as hierarchical authority in the family and there are theories of 'patriarchy' as a ubiquitous or universal structure through which men dominate women" (Pierik, 2022, p. 71). We have to remember that patriarchy exists and thrives in connection with specific modes of production. Even gender performativity is connected to specific material conditions. Interestingly, in Doris's case both meanings are at play: her acquired family is traditionally patriarchal, with an elder patriarch in a dominating position; at the same time, it exists in a society where that kind of patriarchy is no longer the rule, but a subtler, more diffuse patriarchy is still alive and well.

Patriarchy, as a power system, is detrimental to both women and men. The difference is that women are more easily—albeit not necessarily—aware of their lack of privilege, whereas men are mostly unaware of the male privilege they are embedded in. Most (white, cisgender, heterosexual) men believe they were born free from any kind of conditioning. In fact, despite their upper hand in gender issues, granted by the fact that "man" is the standard for any social position, they are conditioned as well, although in a subtler, more invisible way than women. The education of a "real man", an alpha male, begins with the admonition: "if you try hard enough, you will get everything you want". Hence, the incitement to performance and exhortation to challenge, where work becomes a question of identity. Hence, too, the impossibility to develop an emotional body. In other words, whereas women are almost forced to be aware of and express emotions, men are compelled to be more competitive and less emotionally developed. In childhood, they are ordered not to "cry like a girl". In adolescence, they tend to live in a peer group similar to a pack (Brown et al., 1986), where every individual struggles to run faster than the others, be tougher than the others, getting more sexual relationships ("more women") than the others.[9] Growing up, competition is displaced to things—cars, houses—or, as we have seen in Chapter 1, to experiences.

As a pack, the male group tends to suppress individual differences (Wade, 1998). The pack code is activated through comparison with the other men: one can be in or out, and if he is out, he is publicly shamed and discriminated, risking being labelled as a nerd.[10] A different path of development creates a difference that may lead to suffering. At the same time, a man can feel—and be—distant from the pack's prevailing values, and yet be influenced by them at a subtler, deeper level. For example, Roberto grew up detached from the male groups he encountered in childhood and adolescence. He felt he did not share their values. He was fairly uncompetitive in sports, he never joined the usual football of basket team his peers practised; he did not even buy a car when he turned 18. He felt completely free of patriarchal values. Still he, describing himself as an intellectual, was extremely competitive on the cultural level. He was conditioned by the same kind of patriarchal and neoliberal values, only in a less obvious way. His attitude was revealed to him at work, where he found several women colleagues, who had a different way of processing their own ambitions, and made him see the extent of his competitiveness. Patriarchal modalities are contained within micro-processes and language dynamics that are very hard to see without a comparison with the other gender(s) (Bartky, 2020).

Women, in turn, are required to be sensitive, to show what Italian writer and activist Michela Murgia (2021) defined as "aphonic thought", i.e., being able to think without speaking out. Men must be rational, women must be relational. Whereas men in their leadership are meant to be assertive and authoritative, a woman who raises her voice is considered aggressive, and easily reproached for that. Women must stand back and remain quietly in the background; this is not told to men, thus creating another power micro-practice, what we could call an example of *micromachismo*, i.e., of subtle and imperceptible strategies of male domain in everyday life (Bonino, 2004).

The fact that, as an average, women are more sensitive to other people's emotion, and more able to tune in with the other has been experimentally demonstrated (Hall, 1984), so we cannot consider it untrue. But, since often women have found themselves in subordinated positions, they had to learn what subordinates must do: respectfully listen to others, getting all nuances of their emotional states (Snodgrass, 1985). Evolutionary psychologists have hypothesised that natural selection drove women to develop a more sophisticated emotional sensitivity, in order to care for children of pre-verbal age (Graham & Ickes, 1997). But it is equally easy to imagine that "such a characteristic ... has probably been amplified later by culture, so that we not only think that women tend to be better in guessing the others' emotions: we expect, and take for granted, that they do it" (Bertrando, 2015, p. 55).

Patriarchal masculinity reflects a binary position that sharply divides men from women, just assuming a sexist language and a male hegemony (Connell & Messerschmidt, 2005). It legitimates a cultural position that has been defined "rape culture", i.e., a culture that implicitly—without acknowledging it—legitimates rape (Williams, 2015). Movements like "Me Too" and its international equivalents popularised one of the most frequent misunderstandings in men/women relationships, i.e., the role of a "no" in the face of a male advance. Men tend to refuse denials, because patriarchy makes them believe that everything is possible with enough commitment—most of all, winning a woman. Denial is easily interpreted as just teasing, with a right for the man to insist. This led some women to share such interpretation, up to the idea that "he hits me because he is jealous, so he really loves me"—sometimes with the worst consequences.

We have realised that, on average, it is comparatively difficult to make men reflect on the patriarchal construction of their gender. They are mostly unaware of it. This has important implications for therapy, since a feminist position may be easily resented by male patients, even when their own masculinity causes them problems. On the social level, men need male figures, men who can talk to other men about how the patriarchal system harms everyone (Gasparrini, 2016). Dealing with such issues in therapy is more complex, although a therapist aware of the issue can—regardless of their gender—find ways to engage male clients in this kind of discourse without becoming a social engineer or an open militant.

Feminism is linked to the universal theme of human rights, but we want to preserve the term and its specificity, because it reflects the voice of women who have been excluded for centuries, and spoken about by men. Men should become feminist. This does not mean they should experience what women do—which is impossible. They should, instead, understand and use their own patriarchal privileges in order to help change them.

Women and competition

The fact that men compete in our patriarchal (and neoliberal) society does not mean that women do not. Some women adopt a patriarchal position themselves, struggling to become "like men" and seeking power. Other women compete from a more traditional, more or less aware, position: they may compete for beauty or for children; they remain inside a patriarchal view all the same.

The myth of beauty

"Art must be beautiful, artist must be beautiful," tirelessly repeated (female) artist Marina Abramovich, while furiously brushing her hair, in a famous 1975 performance. Besides being quiet and sensitive, women—artists or not—must be beautiful (Wolf, 2015). Let us go back to the (white, Western middle-class) female stereotype of the sweet, quiet, elegant woman: when seen up close, it is one with the myth of the princess, taken from fairy tales, simplified and vulgarised by American popular culture (Lieberman, 1972). It is a resistant myth: sumptuous clothes, long shiny hair, elegance, prettiness, slenderness, candour, and above all a prince who falls madly in love with her beauty and virtue, and marries her with great pomp in front of everyone, jealous stepsisters and envious stepmothers included. The princess is sleek, charming, sweet, able to endure miserable circumstances without losing humanity or sinking to the level of her oppressors.

Present-day women have mostly been introduced to the myth of the princess by Disney movies (England et al., 2011), that represent a comprehensive collection of female stereotypes: Cinderella is the humble, helpful housewife; Snow White the prototypical young, dreamy woman, who immediately shifts to a housewife position arriving in the Seven Dwarves' home; Aurora, the Sleeping Beauty, willingly accepts all her parents decide "for her own good" what she will do; Ariel, the Little Mermaid, submits herself to pain and loss for the sake of love; Belle falls in love with her own jailer, turning a violent relationship into a loving one.

(In more recent movies, princesses like Mulan or Pocahontas became more assertive, until, in *Brave*, the rebellious princess even refuses the script of a happy ending in marriage. This only highlights, however, the enormous ability of entertainment industry to turn self-affirmation into saleable products. These new princesses are still unbelievably beautiful: the myth of beauty is hard to break.)

Since we live in a competitive society, as we showed in Chapter 1, beauty becomes in turn competitive. A woman should not simply be beautiful, she should also be more beautiful than the others. After all, the princess is the most beautiful of all. Being beautiful becomes for a woman a way of affirming herself above the other women. The wildest criticisms of women often come from other women, for example sexist comments on social media regarding women with nonconforming bodies.

Celeste, 17 years old, lives in a small provincial town. Due to chronic illness—a serious form of nephritis—she underwent steroid-based treatments which made her gain a lot of weight and bulk in the critical years of her development. She sees herself as stocky and ungainly, with breasts too big for her to "wear". She finds it really hard to be so radically different from the idea of beauty proposed by social media influencers: all these agile, slim, cool female bodies she watches day after day.

Therapy with her focuses on her nonconforming body: the painful contrast between her basic disposition—she has always considered herself competitive, eager to excel—and an aesthetic diversity that makes it impossible for her to compete on that terrain. It was not just a subjective experience: at school she suffered bullying and harassment, because she initially refused to hide, and exhibited her body, drawing bloody mockery and ferocious disqualifications (fat shaming, body shaming, and so on; see Gilbert & Miles, 2002), both on social media and in face-to-face interactions.

This incurable contradiction made her withdraw so much that she began to have panic attacks when it was time to go to school. In the end, she left her prestigious school, moving to an evening school attended by older students, so to avoid the constant comparison between her body and other, "beautiful", ones. In order to avoid online shaming, she withdrew from social media altogether, and so she ended up being entirely excluded from her peer group, since social interaction at her age happens mostly through social networks. Therapy aims at helping her to accept her body again, re-developing an ability to bring it in public without the defiance she showed at the beginning, so to gain acceptance at least from some female friends.

Social media—Facebook at first, and later Instagram, TikTok and others—are shaping the ideal of beauty today, but the female body has always been subjected to social standards, hidden in details we are often unaware of. Over the decades, women have fasted, taken tonics, trained to tone their bodies, then sculpted them, put on prostheses, inflated lips, filed down bones. How women are with women is a product of patriarchy, which dictates that pleasing a man—usually the most powerful of men—is a natural woman's task. They have been subjected to the colonisation of an imagery dominated by the "male gaze" and by capitalism.

The "male gaze" is a male-gendered perspective that became the presumed natural lens to look at women, initially in film (see Mulvey, 1975). Most movie directors, especially in popular cinema, are, and have been, men. Male (white, heterosexual, cisgender, affluent) directors saw women according to their own set of patriarchal prejudices, instilling that same gaze in the presumedly objective eye of the camera. That view became, in time, so customary to be everybody's default view. Thus, a male-informed imagery passed under everybody's skin, fostering what we define as internalised patriarchy. The male gaze is just one example of a tacit patriarchal attitude that nobody questions.

Maybe we, as therapists, do not come from overly patriarchal families, but all the same we feel that everybody lives an internalised patriarchy, embedded in social, economic, cultural, and, most of all, intimate relationships—what we can define, paraphrasing Foucault (1977), as a "microphysics of patriarchal premises". Besides movies, advertising, too, usually implies and confirms patriarchal archetypes, such as traditional family or romantic love, and the same happens to popular literature or music: this combined activity produces scripts that everyone accepts and performs (Butler, 1990). The eye of the standard white, bourgeois, heterosexual, cisgender male has decided and continues to decide how the world should be seen, what is important and what is not. Such a perspective is so dominant that it is considered neutral. It makes it harder for both women and men to maintain an awareness of their positioning, a necessary step towards reflecting on—and possibly changing—gender roles.

The right body for a woman is necessary in order to find the "right man", who will solve all of her existential problems—as it happens in Cinderella's fairy tale, where the sisters compete for the best mate, the prince. This myth is endlessly replied today on social media, where young girls compete with each other to get the best boy.[11] They compete for the male gaze, subjecting their own value and self-approval to it. A war among girls emerges, where the man acts as an organising principle: the "rooster in the henhouse" phenomenon. If young women see themselves through a male gaze, they will try to get men's attention by disqualifying other women, at the same time idolising women influencers who appear to embody that perfection they are seeking.

This may foster toxic relationships between women, that easily find their way into the therapy room. Thus the myth of beauty is perpetuated, together with the whole texture of patriarchal society.

It becomes crucial for the therapist to help female patients develop a sense of where they want to be in regard to their bodily ideal. They should, in our terminology, find their place in relation to their body (Chapter 6), through a reconstruction of how they built their own gender imagery: where did it come from? Who are the people, what are the myths, that inspired them? We make them bring to therapy pictures in order to better understand this pathway. The same may apply—albeit in a different form—to men, too. Men, although clearly advantaged in this process, are nailed by the same male gaze to become Prince Charming and to show all the attributes of patriarchal masculinity. They too have to find their place in this regard.

This is a clinical gender theme that necessarily implies the therapist's awareness of their own body and gender. Only through such awareness we can help patients to shift from the search for "the right man" (or "the right woman") to the quest for "a right relationship". This also entails some sensitivity to the different forms that relationships take today, putting in parentheses the usual frame, that implies a ranking in intimate relationships: partner first, then parents, then siblings, then other relatives, then friends; and, when a new family is created, children first, then partner, and so on. Patients can be helped to legitimise the complexity of their affective needs (Chapter 1).

What else can we do, in our everyday therapeutic practice, to defuse the male gaze and detoxify gender relationships? First, we put into question the tendency to comment on other people's bodies, especially women's; we try to unveil and discuss power games, both between men and women, and among women; we help patients to centre their self-esteem on other characteristics apart from their bodies. Most of all, we help them decentring from themselves: if they realise they are not the centre of the world, it will be first a distress, but ultimately a relief.

In order to detoxify female relationships, patients should see the non-competitive aspects of them, especially on the bodily level: everybody has the right to exist, to be loved, to show or to cover their bodies, as they prefer. Adopting a therapeutic direct talk (Bertrando, 2015), we can give back patients the freedom to play openly, to reveal the games, to expose themselves.

We are very careful about how we and our patients use language. We use inclusive language when we talk. We believe language is performative: sexist language generates—and is generated by—sexist practice. We "do things with words" (Austin, 1962): if patients think about what they say, they may also think about what they inadvertently do. When any patient makes a sexist comment, we suspend the flow of the dialogue and analyse what is happening. As Wittgenstein (1922, 5.6) says: *"The limits of my language* mean the limits of my world."* To correct our language means to correct our way of thinking: a gender insult—or a sexist appreciation—in itself maintains discrimination. We ask them what could happen if they changed the kind of comments they make: a generic insult or appreciation is very different from a sexist comment. Linguistic choices are political choices.

Gilda is 15. She is in the twelfth grade, a girl who appears cheerful and bright. She has known her best female friends since grammar school. In her little group she never stood out either for beauty, precocity of romantic involvement, or seductiveness. She offered a stable and solid presence; she was the friend to rely on, the nice one.

After beginning high school, some experiences changed her a lot: a study holiday abroad and a residential tennis course made her feel more independent, prettier and more confident. She met new friends and experimented with new communication codes. She brings her novelty to her friends group. At this point her old friends join in a coalition and exclude her. She discovers her exclusion on Instagram: her friends spent a weekend out of town without her. She brings exclusion as a theme for therapy.

Therapist and patient work on dominant emotions (Chapter 5): surprise ("What happened? Why? What did I do wrong?"), pain, distress, betrayal. Together they analyse the group dynamics and co-create hypotheses (Chapter 3). The most likely one concerns Gilda's differentiation from the group: the group joins forces against the element that threatens its uniformity. Patient and therapist reflect that Gilda positioned herself as the unruly one, the one who wants to differentiate. They then work on Gilda's awareness of her positioning and responsibility (Chapter 7). Gilda must choose: "Do you want to be in the group? Do you prefer to leave it? Do you want to stay inside, but to dictate your rules?" According to her answers, different positions will emerge, triggering counterpositions by the group. Now, anyway, Gilda has the possibility to choose and become an active part of her life again.

Understanding is important for her so as not to make judgements, choosing instead where she wants to be. In this way she can avoid being passively positioned by the others (Chapter 6). Gilda in the end chooses not to give up her evolution, but at the same time not to give up her old friends. She chooses to talk to them about her exclusion, to share with them her ideas about what happened and what she felt. This is not necessarily aimed at changing the state of things: in therapy she realised that telling people where she is and how she feels is part of a circular, open and continuous dialogue. The result is uncertain, but Gilda is now well equipped to take care of it.

Competition and motherhood

Apart from beauty issues, women compete in work too. They easily face a terrible alternative, between focusing on career and job opportunities, losing the possibility to bear children, or focusing on children and letting go their career. Diletta, 32, is a social media manager. She comes from Naples, where her parents still live. After a satisfactory career start in London, she decided to come back to Italy to reconnect with her ageing parents. Instead of

Naples, she relocated to Milan, that she considers as the only metropolitan city in Italy. Things did not go as she hoped, though. She believes that her difficulties in advancing her career depend on the Italian system, hardly meritocratic and mainly based on personal and family relationships—the infamous Italian amoral familism (see Banfield, 1958).

In the middle of her struggle, she meets a man a few years younger, who works as a sailboat skipper. Due to his erratic job, he travels around the world all the time and cannot guarantee the stability she—somewhat ambivalently—desires. In this stuck situation, where both her work and her couple relationship are dragging on, she gets more and more anxious to advance her career, and at the same time to fulfil her desire for motherhood.

When she turns 30, her gynaecologist proposes her a solution: she can freeze her eggs, and wait until she will feel ready to bear a child. The proposal backfires, increasing her sense of being a woman "with an expiry date". Diletta, together with her therapist, must retrace her own whole story. She must put in place at least ten years of experience, narratives and suffering, starting from mourning her mother, who died when she was 18 years old.

Another patient, Carla, took her PhD in Brussels during the pandemic, and in turn found herself with a career to build in the complete absence of the committed relationship she wants so badly. Most of her friends married and had children; she feels forced to look outside her circle to find suitable men, but she does not know where to look. She is prey to a strong feeling of injustice. Once again, a gynaecologist proposes the biomedical solution to her existential problem: egg freezing. Beside feeling uncertain about this perspective, Carla also has to face her parents, both doctors, who consider it an aberration and severely criticised her even raising the issue of accepting it or not.

Here we have two 30-year-old white, cisgender women, coming from higher middle-class families. Both are in a dilemma between career and motherhood.[12] In both situations we find a contrast between the urgency of a real or presumed deadline, time that will pass inexorably, and work goals to be achieved at all costs. The dilemma is complexified by the nature of such work goals. They are liquid: rather than being a beautiful house or a series of objects, they concern job characteristics, experiences, social recognition and so on. However, with age they feel a stronger and stronger desire for children, and therefore for family, and therefore for solid relationships—which in turn contrasts with the life choices of the men they really like.

Both women receive the same medical advice: freeze the eggs, so that they can safely postpone motherhood to a time when their career will be more mature and therefore allow a maternity leave when necessary. The submission of Diletta and Carla to neoliberal values is thus supported by technique, which allows the changing of biology itself in order to keep the competitive system unchanged, rather than changing values and priorities when they collide with desires. Once again, neoliberal assumptions are unassailable. The very idea of having children, following a presumed "biological clock", becomes part of the competition. A really successful woman necessarily must have children, to make the most of their potential. If she is affluent enough, technology will solve her problems.

(Even in liquid modernity, everyone, younger or older, is subjected to liquid and solid elements at the same time. There is always some conflict at the interface between the values and modes of liquid modernity, that cannot be eluded, and a substrate dating back to the solid era, which is much more durable than we might think. Competition is at the heart of neoliberal novelty, having children is the base of traditional families. The situation here is made more complex by an actual biological issue, a limit imposed by nature: fertility at some point ends. Freezing eggs is a technical response to such conflict: if we cannot change the economy, we can change biology. Ironically, in turn, an issue created by neoliberalism fosters the new industry of egg freezing, that in turn will generate new profits in the best neoliberal vein (van de Wiel, 2020).)

In order to deal with such an issue in therapy, we must first deconstruct some premises. In both cases, the therapist discovers that her patients had an internalised list of goals, that they had to fulfil in a specific time, in order to live their lives in the top or in the second tier. Now she can ask questions: "Where does that binary order come from? Why do you feel you have to subscribe to it? If these premises make you feel bad, why did you accept them, and why do you still live according to them? Can you discuss the dominant social values, or do you feel this is impossible? In the end, do you think that this is the best solution at your disposal?", and so on.

The goal does not lie in their rebuttal or acceptance of the egg freezing solution: this is something that belongs to their responsibility, and the thera- pist has no say about that. What we consider essential is that they gain awareness of the implicit premises and prejudices that guide them in making their choices. When they feel they are able to choose in full—as possible— awareness, we respect their choices as they are. What a therapist can do is to expose the process, make the patient see all the facets of her dilemma, and then help her to take responsibility for her decision, whatever it may be (Chapter 7). Once again, the therapist must find her place and avoid the temptation of teaching patients how to live their lives.

Race, class and other intersections

First of all, we consider race a social construct, rather than a biological rea- lity: race is better understood as a process of racialisation, that differentiates individuals by generating a hierarchical space. In this way, the construct of race and the process of racialisation become powerful forces impacting the lives of people. We all have a race, in this sense, but some races are more visible than others: white Caucasian race is a sort of gold standard in Wes- tern countries, and therefore it is invisible: "racialised" people are the ones who do not correspond to this standard. Whiteness is another privilege white people are unaware of.

Racism is a complex issue. It is not simply an instrument of domination, it is rather a social and cultural co-construction depending on bottom-up as well as top-down pressures. According to Balibar and Wallerstein (1991), racism is a way of imagining one's own identity by naturalising and hierarchising existing differences. It marks at the same time belonging and exclusion, guaranteeing a stable differential of power. From this standpoint, there is no essential difference between a racist community and sexist one.

Race is not biological, but the visibility of race is embodied, and impact people as such. Racial prejudices easily lead to stereotypical thinking, especially when they are implicit and untold (Snyder & Miene, 2013). Such (invisible) prejudices change the point from which we see the world. We should respect, as therapists, the delicate balance between not seeing the difference, and problematise the difference as such. We must be sensitive to the others' bodies—including our own: everybody is the other of someone else. We have to explore our racial identity, first of all—including, of course, whiteness for white people. For us, both categorised as white, working on our position in terms of racial identity is uncomfortable. We try to use our own discomfort as information.

Theoretically we developed our perspective on racial issues first of all through feminism.[13] reading first Angela Davis's (1981) pioneering suggestions, then Patricia Hill Collins (Andersen & Hill Collins, 1990) and bell hooks's (1990) works. To us, racial and gender issues are inextricably linked to each other. Initially we were shy about taking race into consideration during sessions. Today we ask questions about it: levelling patients as if they belonged to the same group is not useful. We try to recover the anthropological perspective we mentioned before, to be curious about their (perceived, cultural) differences in terms of race, and class too. This in turn brought us to the concept of intersectionality.

Intersectionality became one of the key feminist concepts at the emergence of third wave feminism (Carbin & Edenheim, 2013; see also Appendix B). Intersectionality theory seeks to understand how different systems of inequality interact and intertwine in people's experience. This meant initially to go beyond the original feminist issues in order to embrace, together with gender, the dimensions of race and social class. Later, other issues, such as education, sexual orientation, disability, and so on, were considered and assimilated into the intersectional perspective. This challenges simplistic approaches that consider different aspects of identity in isolation, recognising that both identities and human experiences are inherently multifaceted. It is, from our viewpoint, a wholly systemic approach to complexity (McCall, 2005). The intersectional perspective has given voice to women of different cultures and contexts who have been historically marginalised and excluded from the dominant feminist discourse, emphasising the importance of making the diversity and complexity of experiences visible through representation and inclusion.

The term "intersectionality" was coined by Kimberlé Crenshaw (1991), a black critical feminist jurist, in her seminal article "Demarginalizing the intersection of race and sex". She argued that black women face a dual form of oppression—as women and as black persons—that cannot be fully understood if its two dimensions are analysed separately. Intersectional analyses highlight two issues: first, the multiplicity of experiences of sexism lived by different women and, second, the existence of social positions that do not suffer either marginalisation or discrimination because they embody the norm itself, such as masculinity, heteronormativity or belonging to hegemonic ethnic groups (see Viveros Vigoya, 2016).

Intersectionality challenges the universal model of "the Woman", allowing us to see the experiences of poor and racialised women as a product of the dynamic intersection of gender, class and race in historically constructed contexts. Whereas in the United States intersectionality is strongly influenced by black feminism, in Europe it is rather linked to a postmodern perspective, conceptualising identities as multiple and fluid and meeting Foucault's (1977) perspective on power (Bilge, 2010).

Crenshaw herself was not originally so much interested in identity and representation, but rather in the deep structural and systemic questions that concern discrimination and inequality. She distinguished structural intersectionality—the position, for example, of black women in society as women and persons of colour and its consequences on their lives—from representational intersectionality—the cultural construction of women of colour (Crenshaw, 1991): a black woman, to remain in her famous example, is not just a woman and a black person; she has a supplementary identity as a black woman, that combines two different kinds of discrimination and produces another discrimination altogether; this argument could be repeated for any instance of intersectionality. Such dynamics entail a set of practical consequences, facts that happen in the reality "out there", rather than simply "within" the person (Crenshaw, 1989). As such, it highlights the necessity of understanding the ways in which we belong to different groups and act accordingly.

Intersectionality, however, has often evolved an issue of identity politics, becoming part of the so-called "culture wars", often neglecting the material basis of many phenomena, including gender and race issues. As a consequence, identity claims can easily be turned into earning opportunities: capitalism always finds ways of profiting from both gender binarism and non-binarism. Changing cultural games does not mean changing economic games. The risk is to leave inequalities unchanged (Cangiano, 2024).

We feel that considering intersectionality in therapy means, for therapists and patients alike, to find their place in the multiple overlapping contexts that give shape to their experience, and understand the network of actual power practice that happen within them. It is, once again, a political positioning, and requires an understanding of concrete political, social, and economic conditions. In Chapter 6 we will present an intersectional case, where gender, race, and class are considered from an institutional perspective.

Intersectionality also brought us to acknowledge the relevance of privilege in our lives, and therefore in therapy. First of all, we became more aware of our own privileges. For example, in the USA, 76% of therapists are white, 10% of Asian descent, 6% Hispanic, and only 4% African American (Aragão et al., 2023). The average income guaranteed by the profession usually allows therapists to be firmly located in the middle class. Apart from gender, race and class anyway, therapists are inherently privileged: they hold the power of knowledge. Despite all our best effort to be fair and not exert power, the very fact that we are positioned as therapists makes us privileged (De Varis, 1994; see also Flaskas & Perlesz, 1996). What we can do is remember that we speak from a position of privilege and power, and ensure that our patients have a voice.[14]

Male privilege, that we already have encountered in the above sections, can be played out in quite obvious, but also very subtle ways. For example, a man who participates in household chores usually describes himself in terms of "I help (the woman)", and more often than not he expects to be congratulated, since he does not consider this a default duty: the burden of organising the household routine still falls on the woman's shoulders, and the man is positioned in a sort of mother/son relationship, where he has the choice of obeying or disobeying, rather than participating in an equal relationship. Another form is economic privilege. In several of the cases that we encounter, women are economically disadvantaged in comparison to men, usually because they have totally or partially renounced their own careers for taking care of the children.

In our view, all intersectional implications should be brought forth, highlighted and openly discussed in therapy, in the very same way in which previous generations of systemic therapists learned to make premises and prejudices explicit in order to work them through (see Cecchin et al., 1994). To unveil the game and bring it to open discussion, though, we must be aware of our own position—both as a person and a professional—within the patriarchal context.

Accepting the idea of intersectionality also means that our thinking cannot encompass "everything" our patient brings to us, because of the limits of our very situatedness. A woman's and a man's gender experiences are quite different. A man cannot fully understand a woman's experience, precisely because it is outside his own. Those who are comfortable and have always been living in a binary position cannot have a first-hand experience of non-binary life. This also applies to other dimensions: those who have never been discriminated against are strangers to the experience of discrimination, those who have lived a middle-class life cannot really understand true hunger, and so on.

Which does not mean that dialogue is impossible, of course. A male therapist can talk about his own male experience, and from his position—which is inevitably one of patriarchal privilege—he can criticise it. But faced with the experience of a woman, he can only listen. He will just be able to use his own standpoint, for example he could speak about his experience of living within male privilege. The same is true of all other sorts of privilege: we cannot talk for unprivileged people, as if we were able to put ourselves outside of our own situation—since, as we have seen, as therapists we remain inherently privileged. What we can do is to acknowledge it and help the unprivileged to speak. In short: to gain understanding, we should position ourselves and listen; we should ask questions rather than giving answers.

Male gender

How can we deal—from this point of view—with the overprivileged? As regards gender, the overprivileged are of course men. Working with men as men in therapy means, first of all, to consider therapy with men as a gendered process too. Most men, unfortunately, do not consider their gender as a subject of their therapeutic conversations. Things become even more complicated when we put some gender-related assumptions into question: as we have seen, it is not so easy to help men consider their own masculinity from a critical standpoint.

Dealing with the male gender also means deconstructing the very notion of masculinity. It was important for us to understand that masculinity is far from being a unitary trait. What it means to be a man varies depending on several social, economic, and historical factors (Connell & Messerschmidt, 2005). As therapists, we try first of all to understand the gender premises and prejudices of our male patients, then to specify their own masculinity: usually we can find one or more instances where the man in question did not conform to normative masculinity. In that case, we can begin to work on those instances, amplifying them and giving our patient the possibility of viewing himself differently.[15]

Such deconstruction is possible only if and when it is considered relevant by the male patient. This means that the therapist should scrutinise their own actions during the dialogue: when and how is it possible to open some conversation about such topics? How do the male gender prejudices of the patient impact on the therapist? Of course, there is a difference depending on the gender of the therapist: a male therapist will probably feel less challenged by open patriarchal views on the part of a male patient, whereas it can be harder to face that situation for a female therapist. In any case, the therapist must always be aware of their own gender prejudices, and wonder whether they are hindering their therapeutic actions.

(We should not immediately assume that the "man" we have to deal with is the typical white, heterosexual cisgender type. Of course, this is not necessarily the case: gay men, transgender men, black men, all have their own specific masculine issues, that are different from the mainstream. Once again, we must adopt an anthropologist's stance, never taking for granted the views, premises, prejudices cultural conditioning that our male patient may bring to therapy. In a dialogical stance, we have to ask as many questions as we can, in this as in other instances.)

Let us consider an extreme situation. The men who are less aware of their privilege, and that play it out in the most damaging manner, are violent men. We have learned from Alan Jenkins (1990) the idea of "invitational practice", namely a way of working with men who have used violence, coercion or threats towards partners and children. Jenkins believes that when men hurt others, they are acting in accordance with a violence that is accepted, or not sanctioned, at social, institutional and political levels. This means that the therapist, who is part—to an extent, at least—of that social and political context, should not work from a position of judgement or condemnation. They should be rather interested in the ethical intentions of safety and respect of individual men. Jenkins views this kind of interest as the antithesis of violence or coercion, that the therapist may model for their own patients.

Invitational practice focuses on men's particular stories and backgrounds, rather than universal generalisations, seeking to create change that is self-generated and personally meaningful, and therefore likely to be sustainable. The therapist should be curious and interested in those men's stories, rather than immediately confront them. They must also maintain a focus on women and children's safety and on men's accountability to others. Finally, it is a practice with a political dimension, since it considers violence as an expression of power relations. Invitational practice becomes a parallel journey of therapists and patients. The therapist should attune to the patients' effective experience in creating connection and to co-regulation. In this way, they can avoid dogmatic or confrontational approaches.

We appreciate Jenkins's political emphasis also because it gets out of the dichotomy between victim and perpetrator, of course without forgetting that in this case there is an actual perpetrator and there is an actual victim. Both victim and perpetrator, though, are in turn victims of a cultural context that favours violence. This makes easier to engage men in pursuing change.

What is true for extreme cases like these is even truer in ordinary practice. The best possibility to turn male privilege into a dialogical matter lies first of all in understanding the personal horizon of men. Although it has been proposed that the best person to deal with men and their patriarchal views is another man, we think that the gender of the therapist is relevant but not exclusive for a meaningful practice: in our experience, the patient may also profit from a discussion with a woman therapist on the same topics. It can be even more challenging, and therefore useful, for him, provided that the woman therapist has developed a genuine interest—as well as a critical perspective—toward him. Of course, it is also necessary that the male patient give her enough authority and credibility to challenge his long-term beliefs.

All in all, we have observed in our practice that there is no general rule about the respective gender of therapists and patient.

Clinical example: a perfect wife

Women who come to therapy often have internalised a patriarchal vision of gender roles. Here the crucial issue for therapists is: how can we question such implicit assumptions without unduly influencing and directing the patient? The answer, to us, lies in dialogue.

Gemma is 40 years old, married, with two children aged eight and five. She wants to find out how to deal with her husband Giorgio's infidelity. They got together when they were comparatively young, more than 20 years before. Gemma, an advertiser by trade, used to work as an event planner, but gave up her job when her first daughter was born. She completely renounced her career in order to look after the children—a second daughter was born soon afterwards—and support Giorgio, who became an affluent businessman. She maintains that the couple "got perfectly well", until "the asshole" (her word) began an affair with a young, brilliant and ambitious assistant in his business. Gemma experiences the betrayal simply as his fault. She cannot think that she too has responsibilities, not in the betrayal itself, but rather in having created a situation that made it possible. Although they displayed all the appearances of a "modern" couple, they functioned according to a strictly patriarchal organisation, in which Giorgio, a hard worker, was the only breadwinner and decision-maker, whereas Gemma took care of the household and the education of their daughters, also organising their social life: weekends, friendships, dinners, trips, and so on.

The entire financial aspect of the household was delegated to Giorgio. When Gemma begins to think about a separation, she discovers that no part of the estate is registered in her name, no house and no assets among those they own. Everything is co-owned and has always been managed by Giorgio. Who can now exercise what we can define as economic violence (Stylianou, 2018): she would have to fight hard in order to get what is actually hers, and there is no guarantee she can get it.

At this point, her (woman) therapist asks: "Is Giorgio just a dirty villain, or were you the one who allowed him to take up so much economic space?" This topic becomes one of the key themes of the therapy, and shifts the focus from Gemma's perceived victim position—the passive recipient of abuse of power (Giglioli, 2014; see also Chapter 7)—to a position of responsibility for her attitudes and actions throughout her marriage. Gradually Gemma begins to realise that their story could have been very different if she had made different choices: despite the strong influence of their family traditions and the values of their social groups, nobody actually forced her into passivity. Also, abuses of power certainly occurred, but she never challenged them.

(It is important for Gemma that such reflections are fostered by a woman therapist. She can resonate with Gemma's difficulties, and this process enables Gemma to revisit her story without feeling judged or subjected to secondary victimisation (Pemberton & Mulder, 2023). A male therapist in the same position should be much more cautious, questioning his gender both in the inner and outer dialogue, keeping in mind the repercussions his questions and statements may have on the patient. We think, anyway, that it is possible for a male therapist to address these issues too, provided that he positions himself carefully.)

Gemma reflects on the position she adopted toward her daughters. Since she had no job outside the family, she felt the duty to take full responsibility for them, dealing with all kinds of issues, from school to social activities to their emotional lives. Not caring for them full time would have been a failure in her responsibilities. The therapist reflects with her: children, as a rule, belong to both parents; by creating an exclusive relationship with them, Gemma not only adopted a sacrificial role, but also generated a distance between father and daughters. Parent-child bonds go far beyond sheer management. They are something much deeper, which cannot be completely delegated to one parent only. Gemma gradually begins to think that there is no contradiction between recovering her own personal and work projects, caring for her daughters, and maintaining meaningful relationships within the family.

Subsequently, the therapist decides to offer Gemma and Giorgio some couple sessions, without abandoning the framework of individual therapy, because she feels that the time has come to encourage a direct confrontation between the two. A new theme emerges. Giorgio reveals that the couple has had no sexual intercourse for four years now—a fact that Gemma did not even consider worth mentioning so far—and claims that he suffered a lot for this. During subsequent individual sessions, Gemma has an epiphany: for the entire duration of their sexual life, Giorgio had been the only mentor and guide in her sexual education. She never had any other erotic relationship—he had been her first and only sexual partner.

Once again, she had adopted a passive position, forging her own desire on her husband's desires and pleasures, first of all penetration. Penetration, however, never gave her any real pleasure. Lately it caused her pain, leading her to reject it, and without penetration the couple implicitly agreed that no sex was possible. Gemma now allows herself to consider that the primacy of penetration is mostly a male patriarchal prejudice. Many more forms and modes of sexuality are possible. This change of perspectives has strong repercussions on the couple: Giorgio, too, must now revise his own prejudices on good sex, entering, in turn, in crisis.

To sum up, Gemma granted Giorgio his patriarchal privilege in two of the main areas of couple life, money and sex. She entrusted him all responsibility in the family, assuming a passive position. After discovering his infidelity, she adopted a victim position. She is now aware of these dynamics. To get out of them, she must first position herself differently toward the patriarchal pre-judices inherited from her family of origin.

Gemma decides that she must regain an occupation outside the house. Giorgio—loaded with guilt and apparently ready for anything to win her back—supports her new business. Gemma realises that for years he found her rather dull, because she progressively limited her interests to the parental, family and domestic areas. In the past, he already had suggested she go back to work. Now Gemma no longer sees her husband's exhortations as inter-ferences. She understands that it is not necessary to do a high-flying job, being a full-fledged manager as she originally thought: a job should above all bring her out of the shallows of her life. It can also be a stimulus and an opportunity to meet new people.

Her new positioning also brings Gemma to stop competing with other women: "Who is the best mother, who is the best wife? Who is the best host, who has the best house?" and so on. She begins to see other women more positively, and this fosters in her a sense of relief. She transforms the compe-titive comparison with her female friends into mutual support and legitima-tion. The group of friends she establishes makes these feminist issues more present, thus encouraging change.

The therapy continues, with episodic inclusion of some couple sessions, which allow the therapist to monitor changes and possible regressions. The couple sessions always prove exhausting, because Giorgio struggles with his fear of change, and the presence of his group of male friends and colleagues, which reinforces his male chauvinist prejudices, hinders change. Most of all, he is afraid of losing the fundamental patriarchal privilege: the man has the last say about how to be together and do things ("You do as I say because I know how to do it"). Jay Haley (1963) would say that he is struggling for power, namely for being the one who dictates the rules of their relationship. For him, evolution will be slower and harder.

Ultimately, though, he reveals some ability to question his privilege, helped by an individual therapy that in the meantime he has undertaken. His new attitude, in turn, helps Gemma to get going again. Initially, her stance toward him was full of moralistic punctuations, repeatedly asking him to admit his mistakes, to repent and make amends, to tell the whole truth about his infi-delity, to unveil in detail all that happened between him and his lover. Now she feels they can start from scratch, or at least try to: like Giorgio, Gemma also had to review her own conditioning premises, which created strong and binding stereotyped role expectations. Reflecting on patriarchy was an essen-tial step toward change.

Conclusion

Focusing on the body that we bring to therapy led us to conceive and develop our sensitivity to gender issues, that today constitute a fundamental feature of our approach. This development, in turn, changed the very meaning of therapy for us, turning it from a mere technical enterprise to a (broadly) political activity. Political awareness made us also attentive toward intersectional issues, such as class and race. It had consequences not only on our general therapeutic theory, but also on our very practice. The way in which our practices have unfolded to constitute our present technical apparatus is the subject of the chapter that follows.

Notes

1 Since both authors were men, it seemed that systemic individual therapy would happen with an implicitly male therapist, despite the well-known fact that the majority of therapists—independent of their orientation—are women: for example, in the United States, where it is easier to find statistics, in 2023 it was estimated that 70% of therapists were women (Zauder, 2023).

2 According to George Lakoff and Mark Johnson (1980), we approach life through a complex series of metaphors, and the body is the foundation of them all.

3 In this case too, it is easier to find research on a North American population. Research result, anyway, confirm our ideas: Eagly et al. (2020) found a steady change in US public opinion polls on gender stereotypes from 1946 to 2018 (30,000 participants overall), toward an increased perception of women's competence and agency. Conversely, Haines et al. (2016) found a basic stability of stereotypes from 1983 to 2014, although in a much smaller sample. All in all, change appears slow.

4 We will not deal with the feminist critique and re-appraisal of psychoanalysis, begun in the 1970s with the work of therapists like Juliet Mitchell (2000), or philosopher and psychoanalyst Luce Irigaray (1985), and extensively developed in the following 50 years (see Rowley & Grosz, 2012).

5 Although many authors (e.g. Han, 2017) see relationships mediated through social media as something inherently negative, we do not share such a vision. Movements born online, like "Me Too" (see Baer, 2016), "*Ni una menos*" in Latin America (Caballero, 2019), or "*Non una di meno*" in Italy (see Chironi, 2019), had a strong reverberation on our clinical positioning, bringing us to investigate to what extent patriarchy enters in the premises people bring into therapy.

6 For psychiatrists and psychologists, actually, it remained a foundation even longer: Eilhard von Domarus (1944) saw in the denial of Aristotelian logic the characteristic of schizophrenic thinking, and Gregory Bateson followed him in his definition of the double bind (Bateson et al., 1956).

7 "For Foucault, the substantive grammar of sex imposes an artificial binary relation between the sexes, as well as an artificial internal coherence within each term of that binary. The binary regulation of sexuality suppresses the subversive multiplicity of a sexuality that disrupts heterosexual, reproductive, and medicojuridical hegemonies" (Butler, 1990, p. 25).

8 In "liquid modernity we are projected into a situation where everything is elusive and the anxieties, pains, feelings of insecurity caused by 'living in society' need a patient and constant work of questioning reality and how individuals 'position themselves' in it" (Vecchi, 2006, p. VII).

9 Sexual success is important in the pack, and it is measured by the number of women a man can seduce, in an imagery heavily conditioned by pornography. Rothman et al. (2021) found that a significant percentage of young adults see pornography as a reliable source of information about sex. According to Peter

and Valkenburg (2007), both boys and girls exposed to pornography tend to see women as sex objects: a (extreme) side effect of the male gaze (see below).

10 I.e., "an unstylish or socially awkward person", according to the Merriam-Webster Dictionary.

11 TikTok, an app of Chinese origin, censors posts showing ugly, imperfect, non-conforming bodies, as well as disabled or disadvantaged people (Zeng & Kaye, 2022). Such people's presence is only allowed in presumedly funny videos: they are accepted only if they ridicule and humiliate themselves in front of the camera. Social media are powerful activators of exclusion and envy: fortunately digital natives have stronger antibodies for them compared to previous generations (Jarman et al., 2024; Timeo et al., 2020; see also Chapter 1).

12 Their dilemma is exacerbated by the well-known lack of family and motherhood services in Italy, where most infant care is left to grandparents or other forms of do-it-yourself family welfare (see León & Migliavacca, 2013).

13 As far as our own social situation, the awareness of racial differences is a phe-nomenon that in Italy begun at the turn of the Millennium: despite its colonial past, Italians for decades considered Italy as a country of emigration rather than immigration, and racial minorities (especially people of African descent) were invisible to the public debate (see Curcio, 2024).

14 In the field of (broadly speaking) systemic therapies, the issue of power was first raised by Michael White (1993), who in turn drew from Foucault's (1977) philo-sophical analyses. The critique of power became one of the hallmarks of narrative therapy (Besley, 2002).

15 We have found quite useful, as points of reference, male feminist philosopher Maurizio Gasparrini's (2016) writings, and bell hooks's (2004) work on men.

References

Acquistapace, A. (2022). *Tenetevi il matrimonio e dateci la dote. Il lavoro riproduttivo nelle relazioni di intimità, solidarietà e cura oltre la coppia nell'Italia urbana contemporanea.* Mimesis.

American Psychiatric Association (1994). *Diagnostic and Statistical Manual for Mental Disorders. Fourth Edition (DSM-IV).* American Psychiatric Association.

American Psychiatric Association (2013). *Diagnostic and Statistical Manual for Mental Disorders. Fifth Edition (DSM-5).* American Psychiatric Association.

Andersen, M.L. & Hill Collins, P. (1990). *Race, Class, and Gender: An Anthology.* Wadsworth Publishing Company. 3rd edition, 1998).

Aragão, C., Parker, K., Greenwood, S., Baronavski, C., & Mandata, J.C. (2023). The Modern American Family. Key trends in marriage and family life. *Pew Research Center.* Retrieved from: www.pewresearch.org/social-trends/2023/09/14/the-moder n-american-family.

Austin, J.L. (1962). *How to Do Things With Words.* Oxford University Press.

Baer, H. (2016). Redoing feminism: Digital activism, body politics, and neoliberalism. *Feminist Media Studies* 16 (1): 17–34. DOI:10.1080/14680777.2015.1093070.

Balibar, E. & Wallerstein, I. (1991). *Race, Nation, Class: Ambiguous Identities.* Verso.

Banfield, E.C. (1958). *The Moral Basis of a Backward Society,* with Laura Fasano Banfield. The Free Press.

Bartky, S.L. (2020). Foucault, Femininity, and the Modernization of Patriarchal Power. In: McCann, C., Kim, S.-K., & Ergun, E. (Eds.), *Feminist Theory Reader: Local and Global Perspectives.* 5th edition. Routledge. DOI:10.4324/9781003001201.

Bateson, G., Jackson, D.D., Haley, J., & Weakland, J.H. (1956). Toward a theory of schizophrenia. *Behavioral Science*, 1: 251–264. DOI:10.1002/bs.3830010402.

Bertrando, P. (2015). *Emotions and the Therapist*. Karnac.

Besley, A.C. (2002). Foucault and the turn to narrative therapy. *British Journal of Guidance & Counselling*, 30 (2), 125–143. DOI:10.1080/03069880220128010.

Bilge, S. (2010). Recent feminist outlooks on intersectionality. *Diogenes*, 57 (1). DOI:10.1177/0392192110374245.

Bonino, L. (2004). Los micromachismos. *La Cibeles*, 2 (6).

Brown, B.B., Eicher, S.A., & Petrie, S. (1986). The importance of peer group ("crowd") affiliation in adolescence. *Journal of Adolescence*, 9 (1): 73–96. DOI:10.1016/s0140-1971(86)80029-x. PMID: 3700780.

Burck, C. & Daniel, G. (1995). *Gender and Family Therapy*. Karnac.

Butler, J.P. (1990). *Gender Trouble: Feminism and the Subversion of Identity*. Routledge.

Butler, J.P. (1993). *Bodies that Matter: On the Discursive Limits of Sex*. Taylor & Francis, 2011.

Caballero, G. (2019). Usos de las redes sociales digitales para la acción colectiva: el caso de Ni Una Menos. *Anthropologica*, 37 (42): 105–128. DOI:10.18800/anthropologica.201901.005.

Cangiano, M. (2024). *Guerre culturali e neoliberismo*. Nottetempo.

Carbin, M., & Edenheim, S. (2013). The intersectional turn in feminist theory: A dream of a common language? *European Journal of Women's Studies*, 20 (3), 233–248. DOI:10.1177/1350506813484723.

Cecchin, G., Lane G., & Ray, W.L. (1994). *The Cybernetics of Prejudices in the Practice of Psychotherapy*. Karnac.

Chironi, D. (2019). Generations in the Feminist and LGBT Movements in Italy: The Case of Non Una Di Meno. *American Behavioral Scientist*, 63 (10), 1469–1496. DOI:10.1177/0002764219831745.

Clarke, V. & Peel, E. (Eds.). (2007). *Out in Psychology: Lesbian, Gay, Bisexual, Trans and Queer Perspectives*. John Wiley & Sons Ltd. DOI:10.1002/9780470713099.

Connell, R.W., & Messerschmidt, J.W. (2005). Hegemonic Masculinity: Rethinking the Concept. *Gender & Society*, 19 (6): 829–859. DOI:10.1177/0891243205278639.

Crenshaw, K. (1989). Demarginalizing the Intersection of Race and Sex: A Black Feminist Critique of Antidiscrimination Doctrine, Feminist Theory and Antiracist Politics. *University of Chicago Legal Forum*: Vol. 1989, Article 8. DOI:10.4324/9780429499142-5.

Crenshaw, K. (1991). Mapping the Margins: Intersectionality, Identity Politics, and Violence against Women of Color. *Stanford Law Review*, 43 (6): 1241–1299. DOI:10.2307/1229039.

Curcio, A. (2024). *L'Italia è un paese razzista*. Derive Approdi.

Davis, A. (1981). *Women, Race, and Class*. Random House.

de Lauretis, T. (1991). Queer Theory: Lesbian and Gay Sexualities. *Differences: A Journal of Feminist Cultural Studies* 3 (2): iii–xviii.

de Lauretis, T. (2007). *Figures of Resistance: Essays in Feminist Theory*. Patricia White (Ed.). University of Illinois Press.

De Varis, J. (1994). The dynamics of power in psychotherapy. *Psychotherapy: Theory, Research, Practice, Training*, 31 (4), 588–593. DOI:10.1037/0033-3204.31.4.588.

Doty, A. (1993). *Making Things Perfectly Queer: Interpreting Mass Culture.* Minneapolis: University of Minnesota Press.

Eagly, A.H., Nater, C., Miller, D.I., Kaufmann, M., & Sczesny, S. (2020). Gender stereotypes have changed: A cross-temporal meta-analysis of U.S. public opinion polls from 1946 to 2018. *American Psychologist,* 75 (3), 301–315. DOI:10.1037/amp0000494.

England, D.E., Descartes, L., & Collier-Meek, M.A. (2011). Gender Role Portrayal and the Disney Princesses. *Sex Roles,* 64: 555–567. DOI:10.1007/s11199-011-9930-7.

Flaskas, C. & Perlesz, A. (1996). *The Therapeutic Relationship in Systemic Therapy.* Karnac.

Foucault, M. (1977). *Discipline and Punish: The Birth of the Prison* (translated by A. Sheridan). Allen Lane. (original edition 1975)

Foucault, M. (1990). *The History of Sexuality Volume 3: The Care of the Self.* Penguin Books (original edition 1984).

Frances, A. (2013). *Saving Normal an Insider's revolt against Out-of-Control Psychiatric Diagnosis, DSM-5, Big Pharma, and the Medicalization of Ordinary Life.* Morrow.

Gasparrini, L. (2016). *Diventare uomini. Relazioni maschili senza oppressioni.* Settenove.

Giglioli, D. (2014). *Critica della vittima.* Nottetempo.

Gilbert, P. & Miles, J. (Eds.). (2002). *Body Shame: Conceptualisation, Research and Treatment.* 1st edition. Routledge. DOI:10.4324/9781315820255.

Godman, M. (2018). Gender as a historical kind: a tale of two genders? *Biology & Philosophy,* 33 (21). DOI:10.1007/s10539-018-9619-1.

Graham, T. & Ickes, W. (1997). When women's intuition isn't greater than men's. In: W. Ickes (Ed.), *Empathic Accuracy.* New York: The Guilford Press.

Haines, E.L., Deaux, K., & Lofaro, N. (2016). The Times They Are a-Changing ... or Are They Not? A Comparison of Gender Stereotypes, 1983–2014. *Psychology of Women Quarterly,* 40 (3): 353–363. DOI:10.1177/0361684316634081.

Haley, J. (1963). *Strategies of Psychotherapy.* Grune and Stratton.

Hall, J.A. (1984). *Nonverbal Sex Differences: Communication Accuracy and Expressive Style.* Johns Hopkins University Press.

Han, Byung-Chul (2017). *In the Swarm: Digital Prospects.* Transl. by Erik Butler. MIT Press (original edition 2013).

Hanisch, C. (1970). The personal is political. In: S. Firestone & A. Koedt (Eds.), *Notes from the Second Year: Women's Liberation,* pp. 76–78. Reprint in: *Radical Feminism: A Documentary Reader,* Barbara A. Crow (Ed.). NYU Press, 2000, pp. 113–117.

Haraway, D. J. (1988). Situated Knowledges: The Science Question in Feminism and the Privilege of Partial Perspective. *Feminist Studies,* 14 (3), 575–599. DOI:10.2307/3178066.

Hennessy, R. (1993). Queer Theory: A Review of the Differences Special Issue and Wittig's The Straight Mind. *Signs: Journal of Women in Culture and Society* 18 (4): 964–979. DOI:10.1086/494854.

hooks, b. (1990). *Yearning: Race, Gender, and Cultural Politics.* South End Press.

hooks, b. (2004). *The Will to Change: Men, Masculinity and Love.* Washington Square Press.

Irigaray, L. (1985). *Speculum or the Other Woman.* (Engl. trans. by Gillian C. Gill). Cornell University Press (original edition 1974).

Jarman, H.K., McLean, S.A., Marques, M.D., Slater, A., Paxton, S.J., & Fuller-Tyszkiewicz, M. (2024). Understanding what drives adolescent social media behaviours: Informing approaches for interventions. *Body Image,* 51, 101793. DOI:10.1016/j.bodyim.2024.101793.

Jenkins, A. (1990). *Invitations to Responsibility: The Therapeutic Engagement of Men Who Are Violent and Abusive.* Dulwich Centre Publications.

Jullien, F. (2009). Les transformations silencieuses. Paris: Grasset. Engl. Transl. *The Silent Transformations*, 2011.

Lakoff, G. & Johnson, M. (1980). *Metaphors We Live by.* University of Chicago Press.

León, M. & Migliavacca, M. (2013). Italy and Spain: Still the Case of Familistic Welfare Models? *Population Review*, 52 (1): 25–42. DOI:10.1353/prv.2013.0001.

Lieberman, M. R. (1972). "Some Day My Prince Will Come": Female Acculturation through the Fairy Tale. *College English*, 34 (3): 383–395. DOI:10.2307/375142.

Lonzi, C. (1978). *Taci, anzi parla: diario di una femminista.* Scritti di Rivolta Femminile.

Luepnitz, D.A. (1988). *The Family Interpreted. Psychoanalysis, Feminism, and Family Therapy.* Basic Books.

Maturana, H., & Varela, F. (1980). *Autopoiesis and Cognition. The Realisation of the Living.* Dordrecht: Reidel Publishing Company.

McCall, L. (2005). The Complexity of Intersectionality. *Signs*, 30: 1771–1800.

Middleton, A. (2022). Adventures in time, gender and therapeutic practice. Embracing a queer systemic way of working with gender expansive families. *Murmurations: Journal of Transformative Systemic Practice*, 5 (2): 28–44. DOI:10.28963/5.2.4.

Mitchell, L. (2000). *Psychoanalysis and Feminism.* London: Allen Lane and Penguin Books. Reprinted: Penguin (with a new introduction) (original edition 1974).

Mulvey, L. (1975). Visual Pleasure and Narrative Cinema. *Screen*, 16 (3): 6–18. Reprinted in *Visual and Other Pleasures* (1989). Macmillan, pp. 44–77. DOI:10.1007/978-971-349-19798-9_3.

Murgia, M. (2021). *Stai zitta e altre nove frasi che non vogliamo sentire più.* Einaudi.

Pemberton, A. & Mulder, E. (2023). Bringing injustice back in: Secondary victimization as epistemic injustice. *Criminology & Criminal Justice*, in press. DOI:10.1177/17488958231181345.

Peter, J., & Valkenburg, P.M. (2007). Adolescents' Exposure to a Sexualized Media Environment and Their Notions of Women as Sex Objects. *Sex Roles*, 56: 381–395. DOI:10.1007/s11199-006-9176-y.

Pierik, B. (2022). Patriarchal power as a conceptual tool for gender history. *Rethinking History*, 26 (1): 71–92, DOI:10.1080/13642529.2022.2037864.

Rothman, E.F., Beckmeyer, J.J., Herbenick, D.*et al.* (2021). The Prevalence of Using Pornography for Information About How to Have Sex: Findings from a Nationally Representative Survey of U.S. Adolescents and Young Adults. *Archives of Sexual Behavior*, 50: 629–646. DOI:10.1007/s10508-020-01877-7.

Rowley, H. & Grosz, E. (2012). Psychoanalysis and feminism. In: Gunew, S. (Ed.), *Feminist Knowledge: Critique and Construct.* Routledge.

Russell, B. (1946). *A History of Western Philosophy.* Simon & Schuster, 1972.

Sedgwick, E.K. (1993). *Tendencies.* Duke University Press.

Selvini Palazzoli, M., Boscolo, L., Cecchin, G., & Prata, G. (1978). *Paradox and Counterparadox.* Jason Aronson.

Snodgrass, S.E. (1985). Women's intuition: the effect of subordinate role on interpersonal sensitivity. *Journal of Personality and Social Psychology*, 49: 146–155. DOI:10.1037/0022-3514.49.1.146.

Snyder, M. & Miene, P. (2013). On the functions of stereotypes and prejudice. In: Zanna, M.P. & Olson, J.M. (Eds.), *The psychology of prejudice* (pp. 33–54). Psychology Press.

Stylianou, A.M. (2018). Economic abuse within intimate partner violence: A review of the literature. *Violence and Victims*, 33 (1): 3–22. DOI:10.1891/0886–6708.33.1.3.

Timeo, S., Riva, P., & Paladino, M.P. (2020). Being liked or not being liked: A study on social-media exclusion in a preadolescent population. *Journal of Adolescence*, 80: 173–181. DOI:10.1016/j.adolescence.2020.02.010.

United Nations Office of the High Commissioner for Human Rights (2015). *Free & Equal Campaign Fact Sheet: Intersex*. Archived (PDF) from the original on 4 March 2016. Retrieved 12 February 2024.

van de Wiel, L. (2020). The speculative turn in IVF: egg freezing and the financialization of fertility. *New Genetics and Society*, 39 (3): 306–326. DOI:10.1080/14636778.2019.1709430.

Vecchi, B. (2006). Prefazione. In Bauman, Z., *Intervista sull'identità*, Laterza.

Viveros Vigoya, M. (2016). La interseccionalidad: una aproximación situada a la dominación. *Debate Feminista*, 52: 1–17. DOI:10.1016/j.df.2016.09.005.

Von Domarus, E. (1944). The specific laws of logica in schizophrenia. In: J.S. Kasanin (Ed.), *Language and Thought in Schizophrenia: Collected Papers*. University of California Press, 104–114.

von Foerster, H. (1982). *Observing Systems*. Intersystems Publications.

Wade, J. C. (1998). Male Reference Group Identity Dependence: A Theory of Male Identity. *The Counseling Psychologist*, 26 (3): 349–383. DOI:10.1177/0011000098263001.

Walters, S.D. (1996). From Here to Queer: Radical Feminism, Postmodernism, and the Lesbian Menace (Or, Why Can't a Woman Be More like a Fag?). *Signs: Journal of Women in Culture and Society*, 21 (4): 830–869. DOI:10.1007/978-0-230-21162-9_2.

White, M. (1993). Deconstruction and therapy. In S. G. Gilligan & R. Price (Eds.), *Therapeutic Conversations* (pp. 22–61). W. W. Norton & Co. (Reprinted from the *Dulwich Centre Newsletter*, 3, 1991, 1–21).

Williams, J.E. (2015). Rape Culture. In: G. Ritzer (Ed.), *The Blackwell Encyclopedia of Sociology*. DOI:10.1002/9781405165518.wbeosr019.pub2.

Wittgenstein, L. (1922). *Tractatus Logico-Philosophicus*. (K.G. Ogden, translator), Routledge and Kegan Paul (original edition 1921).

Wolf, N. (2015). *The beauty myth*. Vintage Classics.

Zauder, S. (2023). Therapist Statistics and Facts: How Many Are There? www.crossrivertherapy.com/therapist-statistics#sources. Archived 11 January 2023. Retrieved 13 February 2024.

Zeng, J. & Kaye, D.B.V. (2022). From content moderation to visibility moderation: A case study of platform governance on TikTok. *Policy & Internet*, 14: 79–95. DOI:10.1002/poi3.287.

Chapter 3

Practices

Having (provisionally) defined individuals, their relationship with the context, and their genders, the next step is to describe a practice of individual therapy based on the systemic-dialogical approach we have developed over the past few years.

We consider what we do as an approach rather than a theory: an approach is a structural representation—concise and approximate—of a phenomenon, whereas a theory is a consistent set of ideas providing an explanation to that phenomenon (Danielsson, 2023). In this sense, psychoanalysis is a theory, entailing an etiological explanation of any symptoms, and systemic-dialogical therapy is an approach, that refrains from considering aetiology. The approach is the basis of a therapeutic method ("the organisational patterns or practice protocol used both to set forth and bring forth aspects of the approach": Burnham, 1992, p. 5), which is then applied through a set of techniques ("specific activities practised by users of the approach that can be observed and even 'counted' by an observer of the activity": Burnham, 1992, p. 5).[1] The theoretical evolution that led us to establish our approach is outlined in Appendix A.

The systemic-dialogical approach is rooted in a systemic perspective, mostly based on Gregory Bateson's systemic epistemology. We have also been influenced by the original Milan team and their effort to transform Batesonian epistemology into a set of operational principles. Some of them are still part of our present practice, others have been deeply modified to accommodate present-day issues, still others we have abandoned altogether.

Starting from this foundation, we have developed the four pillars of our model, namely: dialogue, emotions, finding one's place and responsibility. The nature and character of each pillar will hopefully emerge over the course of this book. In this chapter we will focus on the practical aspects of systemic-dialogical individual work. The chapter deals first with the overall frame of therapy, then considers our practical techniques. Techniques are not the main focus of our approach—which is rather centred on the persons of the therapist and the patient. Some technical points are however essential: we will present the most important of them. This outline should be understood as a survey of the main points of our own clinical practice, rather than as a

DOI: 10.4324/9781003381754-4

recipe book on "how to do" therapy: systemic-dialogical principles should be put to work by any therapist according to their dialogue with the unique situations they encounter.

Basic points of systemic-dialogical therapy

The basic points of our systemic-dialogical view can be summarised as follows (for their theoretical underpinnings, see Appendix A):

- *Systems.* Human interaction is open and disordered. Human systems are provisional patterns emerging from disorder. We consider any human system as a network of relationships between individuals, constantly remodelled in a state of ceaseless flux. Relationships, therefore, are the basic focus of our therapeutic dialogue, where the voices of each person should be enabled to speak from their own perspective.
- *Rules.* In human systems, rules emerge, spontaneously created in interaction, not modifiable through sheer individual will. Interaction patterns within systems should be understood as circular and constantly evolving. The therapist should consider connections between circular patterns of behaviour and connections between beliefs and behaviour within systems.
- *Language.* Verbal and nonverbal languages are an essential part of the system, as well as the many stories intertwined within it. The therapist should understand the different modes of communication they participate in, the styles of the stories that are told, as well as their own language and its articulation with the others'.
- *Contexts.* Actions and discourses get meaning only within the context in which they happen, and recursively contribute to shaping the context itself. One of the therapist's first tasks is to evaluate the context. This is true both of more limited contexts, such as family and workplaces, and of wider contexts, such as society and culture.
- *Power.* All human relationships involve power, and therefore any context is a political context. Issues related to privilege are always present, and the therapist should be aware of them.
- *Gender.* The gender of therapist and patient is essential in shaping therapeutic interaction. Gender and other intersectional issues, such as race, class, disability and others, must always be considered by the therapist, who should be as conscious as possible of their prejudices about them.
- *Positioning.* The systems and contexts we are embedded in position us in manifold ways. In turn, we always counterposition ourselves, either accepting or refusing the positions we are given. The therapist should understand first the way in which they are positioned—by clients, contexts, culture, or prejudices—then their response and counterpositioning, before taking therapeutic action.

- *Emotions.* We consider emotions as systemic and dialogical phenomena. Any emotion one of us feels and displays, is—to an extent, at least—a consequence and a response to an emotion displayed by someone else. We see human systems (also) as networks of emotions, conveyed partly through discourse, partly through nonverbal interaction. Although, in our understanding, emotions happen in dialogues within human systems, the subjective experience of feelings pertains to the individual, within their interaction with others. The integration between awareness of one's positioning and awareness of one's emotions is what we call finding one's place.
- *Polyphony.* Any participant in a dialogue has something relevant to say about themselves and the others, and should get the opportunity to say it. No effort should be spared by the therapist for everybody to listen to each other, difficult as it may be. The aim of the therapeutic dialogue is not to reach unanimity, harmony, or a final agreement: the dialogue is never closed or concluded.
- *Pluridiscursivity.* [2] In any human dialogue, several (verbal and nonverbal) languages are present at the same time, and therapy should preserve such multiplicity, albeit allowing reciprocal understanding: there is no way of speaking or staying in the dialogue that is "right" or "wrong" in itself—except attempts to silence the others or the unwillingness to listen to them.
- *Hypothetical knowledge.* The therapist's knowledge is always provisional and uncertain, maintaining a constant state of doubt. Their attitude should be one of respectful curiosity. The therapist participates in the dialogue like the others. This implies that they respectfully bring their ideas, hypotheses, emotions and positions into the dialogue without trying to impose them over those of the patients.
- *Responsibility.* Both therapist and clients should take responsibility for their actions. To us, responsibility should be both relational, i.e., stemming from the relational and dialogical space individuals are embedded in (McNamee & Gergen, 1999), and positional—i.e., connected with the position individuals hold in systems and contexts.

Basic frame for individual therapy

The systemic-dialogical approach is designed to work in any kind of setting: individual couple, family, or group therapy. Individual systemic-dialogical therapy, though, has some specifics. In other books, such as *Systemic Therapy with Individuals* (Boscolo & Bertrando, 1996), and *The Dialogical Therapist* (Bertrando, 2007) some of these issues have been dealt with. Here we will consider them from the viewpoint of our more recent practice.

Therapist's privilege

Before entering more technical discourses, we have to spend some words about power and control in therapy. This means, first of all, talking about the privilege—and the consequent responsibility—the therapist enjoys when they are doing therapy. Many, albeit not all, therapists today are cisgender, white and reasonably affluent (Chapter 2); besides, any therapist, whatever their gender, race or status, has the privilege of cure, which also entails the power of knowledge (see Foucault, 1982, 2003). The latter privilege is inescapable.

The theme of privilege is complex, and uncomfortable too, because it is something that many therapists—including ourselves—dislike, yet cannot get out of. It must be managed with great care. Therapeutic dialogue must be a common enterprise. We know, however, that this is usually the final outcome of a long process: in dialogue, any actor brings forth their own words and meanings (their world), exerting a force in order to enter the world of the other (Bakhtin, 1981). The risk of colonising the other is always present, especially in the therapeutic relationship, which is asymmetrical by its very nature. This is why we try to develop consensuality within the therapeutic process: rather than taking for granted that a patient understands us, we continually ask questions about what we are saying: "Does what I'm saying make any sense to you?" We stress the "to you" part, in order to avoid to impose our meaning upon the other's.

The whole of this chapter should be read keeping in mind the dynamics of therapeutic privilege, even when an issue appears innocuously technical: no technique is neutral in itself. Systemic-dialogical therapists are always wary of their thoughts and actions, and keep them under scrutiny. Therapeutic privilege is ineradicable, but the awareness of it makes us attentive to the dynamics at play.

Indications for individual therapy

The indications for individual therapy, as opposed to family or couple therapy, have changed little over the years. The criteria we use today are similar to the ones used in systemic individual therapy (see Boscolo & Bertrando, 1996), although our model is altogether different.

We work individually with adolescents or adults who want to deal with a symptom, a problem or an existential discomfort. The age of possible candidates for therapy can be extremely variable, from quite young to very old age. At the time of writing this book, our caseload varies in age from 14 years old for the youngest patient to 85 years old for the oldest, with a time span that exceeds 70 years. We do not work individually with children, since we both have been focused on adults and sometimes adolescents for the whole of our professional lives. Other colleagues who have adopted our approach, though, are using it with children, with encouraging results. We have no mandatory technical prescriptions for dealing with particular age groups, except that we adapt our language and our way of presenting ourselves to the age of the person involved. The same applies to specific problems, e.g., psychiatric diagnoses: we try to find a way of having a meaningful exchange with any patient, and so we tailor our approach to the person rather than to their problems.

If, during the first interview, we find that the issues presented require family or couple therapy, or the involvement of other people in a different, non-normative intimate relationship (Chapter 1), we point this out to the person. However, we suggest our preferred modality but do not impose it: if the person, even in the face of our recommendation, continues to choose individual therapy, we agree to do it, clearly specifying its limits. The last word always belongs to the patient.

Sometimes, though, patients have other kinds of requests involving third parties. Helen, a woman of 62, asks for therapy in order to recover a relationship with her older, 33-year-old daughter, who has severed most of her interaction with her mother due to mutual incomprehension. The daughter accepts to meet once the therapist on her own, but refuses family therapy altogether. Helen accepts individual therapy, with the aim of devising strategies to induce her daughter to change her approach. The therapist accepts individual therapy with her, but discusses Helen's strategic stance. He proposes to work together with her on her share of the relationship with her daughter, on how she found herself in the situation she describes, and what she can do to feel better (to find her place: Chapter 6) in the situation. Briefly, if there is a request to influence other people who refuse to be involved in therapy, we renegotiate a different contract.

Of course we take into account the presenting problem and its importance, whatever it may be, but we consider it as connected to the patient's relational life. Generally we do not centre our therapy on symptoms or diagnoses, or even on one specific problem. The presence of a more or less serious psychiatric diagnosis, which can range from an anxiety disorder to a bipolar disorder, borderline disorder or psychosis, obviously suggests some difference in our approach: for example, medication can be prescribed by a psychiatrist colleague, and this must be taken into account. Conversely, even when facing a diagnosed or diagnosable disorder, for example panic disorder or mild depression, a patient may prefer to deal with it with the sole aid of therapy without requiring medication. In both cases, we accept our patient's choices.

Diagnosed symptoms, when present, are obviously relevant in a patient's life. We take them into account and we deal with them in the course of therapy, but we never place them exactly at its centre. Our interest lies in the person's relationship with herself and the others, and we are always focused there, even when considering specific symptoms. For example, Deborah is a 35-year-old professional, who comes after a psychotic episode that required hospitalisation plus antipsychotic drug treatment. She requests to better understand the psychiatric event, which has currently been resolved without residual symptoms. The therapist accepts trying to understand the possible connections between the events of her life and the emergence of the symptoms, but abstains from an etiological investigation. The final contract is therefore to deal with the whole of her life, in order to better understand what happened.

During the first meeting we also describe the characteristics of our way of working. We make it clear that our systemic focus will be maintained during the course of therapy. This of course will not prevent us from exploring what the patient's internal world may be like; it will be seen, anyway, against the background of their relationships, put into perspective and reframed in a systemic way.

Overall, our basic method can be summarised as: "We do not do problem solving". A way of emphasising such an attitude is to begin the first session by asking questions about the person's life, relationships, occupation, interests, and so on, arriving to the presenting problem only after this preliminary conversation. This procedure, however, is not mandatory, and depends on the urgency of the request and the person's state of distress or anxiety.

In short, people come to us with variable demands, which sometimes do not correspond to what we can offer. The patient makes requests, the therapist may agree or not. There is always a negotiation, which usually takes place during the first meeting, but sometimes a second one is advisable, to give therapist and patient the opportunity to reflect on their mutual positioning (see Bertrando, 2007, Chapter 5).

At the end of the negotiation phase, the therapist makes a proposal. If the proposal is accepted, therapist and patient will work together according to the terms of this agreement rather than the initial request. As regards the therapeutic relationship, our habit is to ask at the end of the first session how the person felt with us. We discuss the sense of ease or unease felt in the conversation, the gender and age of therapist and patient, so that most matters that may create discomfort are addressed right at the start of therapy. Generally we then consider an initial period, three or four sessions, when therapist and patient get to know each other, to see if the initial experience of their relationship is confirmed.

Time frame

The time frame of our individual therapy has become more and more flexible as years went by. First of all, let us consider the duration of therapy. When the Milan systemic approach was originally created, it adopted the timing of MRI's brief therapy (Watzlawick et al., 1974), with a maximum of ten weekly sessions, which could be increased to no more than another ten in case of necessity. Soon the Milan approach moved to an interval of one month between sessions (Selvini Palazzoli, 1980), maintaining the same maximum

number of sessions. Such practice, besides being convenient from an organisational and economical point of view, allowed the duration of therapy to be
extended without changing the number of sessions: 20 sessions, at this rate,
allowed a therapy of approximately two years. Luigi Boscolo and Gianfranco
Cecchin called this model "brief-long therapy" (Boscolo & Bertrando, 1993).

When the first model of individual systemic therapy was devised, the choice
was to maintain a fixed number of sessions, which once again could not
exceed 20. The interval between sessions varied from a fortnight to a month
(Boscolo & Bertrando, 1996, Chapter 2).

In our present practice, we have realised that neither a fixed number of
sessions nor a fixed interval between sessions are advisable. We abandoned the
maximum number of 20 sessions quite early, and today in individual therapy
we do not use the monthly interval from the beginning except in specific
cases, for example financial reasons, institutional restraints, or patient avail-
ability. Some people request weekly therapy, many others propose or accept
fortnightly therapy. We, in turn, are comfortable with both options. This type
of request is also negotiated with patients. Usually, the initial interval is either
fortnightly or weekly.

As regards duration—and therefore the overall number of sessions—we
have chosen complete variability. The therapy goes on until therapist and
patient agree that it has given all possible results in the presenting situation,
and that prolonging it would be useless. When there is no agreement
between patient and therapist on the conclusion, negotiation is once again
necessary. If the patient decides they want to end therapy and the therapist
does not agree, the therapist will discuss the reasons for their position; the same
will happen if the therapist considers a conclusion advisable, but the patient
would prefer to prolong the therapy. In both cases, the last word belongs to
the patient.

In the past, within the Milan approach, it was quite common for therapists
or therapeutic teams to terminate therapy independently from the decision of
the patients, because therapy had to be mandatorily kept as brief as possible
(Boscolo & Bertrando, 1993). In our present practice, we refrain from such
position because we have found that often, if the patient does not agree on a
one-sided termination from the therapist, they will easily end up looking for
another therapist and will have to start all over again. We realised than an
authoritative conclusion risks being counterproductive rather than useful for
the patient, because it will force them to start therapy from scratch. The only
exception is when a therapist irrevocably realises that they are no longer able
to work with that specific person.

Therapy as a result can last from a very short period, for example ten sessions or even less, up to a much longer time span which can reach a few
years. In our practice, the most frequent duration of individual therapies
varies between one or two years. Periodic monitoring is always useful. In
these moments, therapist and patient re-evaluate the progress of therapy and

the point it has reached. This helps both of them to decide whether to prolong or end therapy. In case of need, however, we may accept to extend the therapy even for rather long periods of time.

We also make extensive use of a variable interval between sessions. Each therapy has its own prevalent frequency, but we can always change it according to needs. Leaving out the many therapies that maintain the same frequency from beginning to end, generally therapy begins with briefer intervals and ends with longer ones, for example from weekly to fortnightly or from fortnightly to monthly. When therapy has already reached a substantial duration, monthly intervals are acceptable. It is also possible that specific complications lead to a momentarily increase in frequency: for example, some therapies begin as fortnightly, go through a period of weekly frequency, to return to fortnightly and end with a monthly frequency. Sometimes the final phase involves bimonthly sessions. We had patients who, at the end of therapy, requested some meetings every six months "to take stock of the situation". We do not consider such a request as a patient's attempt to maintain dependence, but rather as a progressive shift towards independence, which we are happy to accept.

Of course, when we conclude a therapy we leave the door open for subsequent meetings, should a patient feel that new difficulties or new issues to address have emerged, or even if they need a one-time consultation with their former therapist to deal with a specific event. All in all, we consider that when a course of therapy ends, the process is completed, and that specific therapy can never be resumed. What will possibly begin is a new course of therapy, with new goals and new rules. This also applies when a person interrupts therapy, often against the therapist's advice, and returns two or three months later: we still consider it a new therapy, based on new assumptions, since the patient's condition has changed so much to make them change their mind.

Shape of sessions

We originally moulded our sessions according to the standards of the Milan approach (Boscolo et al., 1987). That kind of session, originally devised for a therapeutic team doing family therapy, is divided into five parts: pre-session, where a therapeutic team discusses basic information (in a first session) or the events of previous sessions; the proper session, where one of the therapists in the team conducts a conversation with the patient, while the others observe through a one-way mirror or a TV screen; the team discussion, where the active therapist exits the therapy room and discusses with the others the course of the session and possible hypotheses; the final intervention, where the therapists re-enters the therapy room and delivers an intervention based on the team discussion; and the post-session, after the patient has left, where the therapists discuss the patient's reactions and hypotheses for conducting the next encounter.

This same format was employed in many of the cases presented in *Systemic Therapy with Individuals*, that had been treated in a training situation. After publishing the book, both Boscolo and Bertrando started conducting individual sessions on their own, with no team, and this quickly became standard clinical practice. Today we almost invariably conduct individual sessions alone with the patient, without any interruption, final intervention or post-session, and without having external observers or a therapeutic team. Sometimes it may happen that, for specific cases, we conduct individual sessions in co-therapy. The session format does not change: if the co-therapists need to discuss with each other, it happens in the course of the session, in the presence of the patient, thus resembling a brief, informal reflective team (Andersen, 1987).

Initially, this change created a difference between ordinary clinical sessions and training sessions, that were still conducted according to the Milan format. In our present-day training, we have a group of trainees observing the session, but we have dispensed with the in-session team discussion and re-entry: we think that the active therapist is responsible for the whole of their interventions in the session, and therefore any interruption may hamper the therapeutic relationship—not to mention that in actual clinical practice putting together a team for individual therapy would be completely uneconomical. Maintaining the Milan format would mean doing a training completely dissimilar from what trainees would have to do in their actual practice.

As a result, the shape of our sessions today is very similar to the one used in most therapeutic approaches: an uninterrupted dialogue between one therapist and one patient, lasting between 45 minutes and one hour, usually with a fixed duration agreed upon during the negotiation phase in the first session.

Course of therapy

In our approach the course of therapy is quite variable. We do not adopt a rigid frame, neither for the beginning, nor for the termination of therapy. At the same time, there are specifics for different phases of therapy, which we will briefly outline.

Referrals. The attention to the referring process was one of the key aspects of the original Milan approach, epitomised in the classic article "The problem of the referring person" (Selvini Palazzoli et al., 1980b). In systemic-dialogical therapy, we take into account the whole referring system, where several dialogues usually take place, resulting in the final referral. We draw a relational map of the referring process, inviting the patient—if necessary—to reflect both on their positions in relation to it, and on their resulting expectations and demands. We are also mindful of our own position within the referring and treatment contexts, which will unavoidably influence our prejudices and expectations about the therapeutic process (Chapter 8).

Early phase. We focus our curiosity on significant systems—family and beyond. We work mostly on issues pertaining to the immediate present; they may involve the presenting problem, but are not limited to it. We try to find our place within the systems and contexts that appear in the conversation, fostering a participant dialogue between ourselves and the patient (Chapter 6). We openly bring our hypotheses and micro-hypotheses—often concerning the presenting problems and processes in the here and now—into the dialogue, discussing them with the patient, and accepting the patient's points of views, emotional states, and ideas. This helps establish both a proper dialogue and a positive therapeutic relationship, and paves the way for the subsequent phase.

Active phase. In this phase, we make use of our positioning activity in order to understand in more depth the patient and their relational life, at the same time introducing slightly more unfamiliar perspectives. We are sensitive both to the dominant and tacit emotions we feel in the patient, and put them in context. In this way, they become emotional information, that are then fed back to the patient as micro-hypotheses, in order to help them develop a greater awareness of their own emotional positioning in the session—and in their life.

We also pay attention to family stories, exploring what happened at the onset of the presenting problems and extending the dialogue to encompass wider contextual issues such as present intimate relationships (couple or not), family of origin, extended family, work, friends, peer groups, and so on. We create and develop multiple hypotheses, staying open to possible changes of the original presenting problems and goals; we periodically review the patient's opinion on course and efficacy of therapy; we use sessions with different formats when necessary—e.g., couple, individual, or sibling group format. Therapy always aims at being as brief and focused as possible. We re-evaluate, from time to time, whether our interventions are meaningful to the patient, by openly questioning them.

Late phase. When it is clear that the therapy is nearing its conclusion, we begin exploring the patient's future projects. Most of our interventions are now aimed at expanding future options for the patient's life. The issue of termination of therapy is openly considered, while, at the same time, the door is kept open for the future.

Thinking and feeling

What does actually happen during a systemic-dialogical session? Our activity as therapists is double-sided: on the one hand our internal dialogue unfolds, where we reflect on our thoughts and feelings; on the other, there is an outer dialogue, where we interact with the patient, usually by asking questions and making statements.

This apparently entails a quite deliberate, sometimes strategic, activity on the part of the therapist. However, a substantial part of the emotional interaction between therapist and patient is unspoken, and for many aspects unconscious. Dialogue cannot be prescribed as a series of steps that are invariably performed one after the other. If we become too intentional in it, we are prey to what Bateson (1968) defines as an excess of conscious purpose. In our experience, this often leads to rigidity in our thinking, and to a directive stance that, besides being at odds with our principles, more often than not alienates the patient. On the other hand, this does not mean that everything goes, that we simply enter a session and do as we please. If we just keep the conversation going, without structuring the dialogue somehow, we risk losing the possibility to open perspectives for change. There are principles governing what to do, and—especially—what is preferable not to do.

Here we will try to outline our views about all sides of therapeutic dialogue: inner processes and outer processes (Rober, 2005), intentional actions and unintentional events. We will first focus on how we think and feel during the session. Of course, following what we have just said, such a process does not correspond to a fixed procedure. In systemic-dialogical therapy dialogue comes first, and dialogue is made out of the—mostly—unpredictable interactions that happen in the here and now.

We start from ourselves

We always start from ourselves, first of all: our bodies, our positions, our ways of being in the situation. What we think depends on where we are and how we feel (Chapter 6). At the beginning of a session, we now prefer not to focus too much on what happened in previous sessions. From this point of view, we mostly apply the principle that "every session is the first" (Boscolo & Bertrando, 1993). We may keep record of previous sessions, and in that case we easily consult our notes at the start, but we do not necessarily rely on them in conducting the session: the possible novelties brought by the patient should come first. In the case of a first encounter, we limit the amount of information we get in advance. The patients themselves are our main source of information. This also helps to strengthen the therapeutic relationship. After the first session, we may have a talk with the referring person, if necessary.

When we encounter the patient, an instant emotional communication happens (Bertrando, 2015). Entering the dialogue, we pay attention to our reactions, trying to be as aware as possible of our inner dialogue (Rober, 2005). During and after the session, we review more than once our position, both toward the patient and within the wider context. We wonder what prejudices are triggered in us by the encounter (Cecchin, Lane, & Ray, 1994). These processes as a whole help us finding our place (Chapter 6) and review our expectations (Chapter 8).

We believe that any course of action that we take in therapy is positioned, in the sense that our position—and our emotional reaction to our position—dictates it. Our position influences what we can see and what we cannot see in the session, and also the possible worlds we are able to create in dialogue (Goodman, 1978). This also applies to the hypotheses we are able to make: they are dictated by our position. The attention we pay to our position is a constant in our therapies.

We are aware of what we feel

We should be aware of what we feel and the position we take in response to the other's feelings. We consider emotions as systemic and dialogical phenomena. Any emotion anyone of us feels and displays is—to an extent, at least—a consequence and a response to an emotion displayed by someone else. Other people are usually affected by the emotions we display, and in turn develop their own emotions toward us, and so on. We can see human systems as networks of emotions, conveyed partly through discourse, partly through nonverbal interaction. Emotions are important in mutual understanding because they are not mere discharges, they have a rationality of their own, which is necessary for the activity of everyday life. Although, in our view, emotions emerge in the space between people, the subjective experience of feeling pertains to the individual, elicited by the individual's interaction with others (Bertrando, 2015).

In sessions, we pay attention both to the more apparent (dominant) emotions, and to emotions that seem to be hidden in interaction (tacit emotions). We focus on the emotions displayed by the patient when they interact with us, as well as the emotions that appear in the stories the patient tells, and, at the same time, we are attuned to our own feelings in the course of the session. We may highlight some emotions that we see or feel, but that the patient appears not to be aware of. Emotions are also central to the process of micro-hypothesising in session.

In Chapter 5, we will deal extensively with one specific emotion—shame—in order to detail our approach to emotions in therapy.

We make hypotheses

Once we have understood the emotions at play within the session, we further the therapeutic process by creating therapeutic hypotheses. We have described in detail hypothesising both in the traditional Milan approach and in its evolution in other works, that the reader can consult for a more comprehensive view (see Boscolo & Bertrando, 1996; Bertrando & Toffanetti, 2003; Bertrando & Arcelloni, 2006; Bertrando, 2007, 2014). Here we will focus on the systemic-dialogical way of dealing with hypotheses, trying to give a summary of its basic characteristics.

There are multiple ways of hypothesising, that lead to different kinds of hypotheses. We consider our hypotheses to be tentative, processual, perspectival, embodied, dialogical, and emotional. Let us make some distinctions.

Our hypotheses are tentative, and they remain such throughout the course of therapy. We draw a distinction between naive realistic hypotheses and provisional hypotheses. The former aim at reaching certainty about what we are describing. To paraphrase Korzybski's statement, made famous by Bateson (1970), they are maps that can lead to a full knowledge of the territory. These are the kind of hypotheses even Freud made. The idea is that progressively the therapist will narrow their hypothesising, until they achieve certainty about the "real" state of things regarding their patient.

The original Milan team introduced in the field the notion of provisional hypotheses. In the article "Hypothesising-circularity-neutrality" (Selvini Palazzoli et al., 1980a), they proposed that therapeutic hypotheses should be considered as "neither true nor false" (p. 4), thus challenging the positivistic view of therapy as discovery of a hidden truth, and introducing an endless quest, where a hypothesis can be substituted for another, and so on *ad infinitum*. We have remembered elsewhere (Bertrando, 2007) how that idea changed our way of conceiving therapy. It was a kind of epiphany. One us wrote that:

> for me, the hypothesis is not a technique, it is a world view: as a systemic therapist, I see the world hypothetically rather than "realistically" (at least to a certain extent). I do not presume that I can reach the "real", "authentic" core of a family anymore. All I can do is to have a hypothesis about it. The consequences of such a shift in my convictions are enormous.
>
> (Bertrando, 2007, p. 55)

Such interpretation, though, obscured the strategic implication still embedded within those hypotheses: according to the original Milan team, they introduced "the powerful impact of the unexpected and the improbable" to the attention of patients, and, by so doing, they acted as strong reorganisers, influencing and redirecting the patients' views.[3] A good part of classical Milan hypotheses (see several examples in Boscolo et al., 1987) were explicative—or, medically speaking, etiological—hypotheses: they explained "why" a problem or a symptom had arisen, and so offered the therapist, and the patients, an alternative explanation of what was going on.

From the very beginning, however, we tended to hypothesise in a different way. We considered our hypotheses neither as progressive approximations to one presumed final truth, nor as ways of leading patients to pre-determined conclusions, nor as explanations of the present state of things. They took the form of proposals for a redescription.

Our hypotheses centre on process rather than (as well as) content. This introduces a second meaningful distinction, between explicative hypotheses and process hypotheses. Explicative hypotheses focus on the content of the patient's narrative, whereas process hypotheses focus mostly on the here and now, on what is happening in the session between the patient and the therapist, or what is happening in the life of the patient, in their interactions with others, and are reported in therapy. Once again, our hypotheses thus become mostly ways of offering different descriptions of these processes.

Our hypotheses stem from our own position and perspective. As our practice grew, we gave more and more importance to the understanding of the therapist's position within the therapeutic system (Lini & Bertrando, 2020). We realised that our hypotheses, too, were influenced, if not dictated, by such a position. Rather than being an all-seeing disembodied entity, that creates infinite possible worlds (Goodman, 1978), the therapist is an embodied person, who can only create what their position allows. This refers to another distinction, between all-encompassing hypotheses and positional, perspectival hypotheses.

When we propose a hypothesis in a dialogue, we create a world; if we change our position, we change the world we are creating. That is very resonant with what we think today about therapy: the core of the therapeutic enterprise lies in our positioning and in the other's counterpositioning. First we find our mutual places in therapy, then everything descends from that. So we can hold multiple possibilities depending on how we change our position and every time we can generate another "universe bubble" (see Larner, 2024).

Of course, such unlimited openings must also take into account the actual, embodied possibilities we have. We do not like to create unlikely, extravagant hypotheses anymore, since we aim at helping patients to develop alternative but plausible views of their lives, rather than challenging them through eccentric propositions.

Our hypotheses are embodied rather than abstract. Discussing the pitfalls of some straightforward postmodernist approaches to therapy, communication theorist John Lannamann wrote: "Social constructionist inquiry that highlights the indeterminacy of meaning without a corresponding emphasis on the responsive embodied practices of family members glosses over the material conditions shaping the politics of interaction" (2004, p. 393). Here Lannamann draws attention to the illusions of postmodernism (Appendix A), that fostered a sense of omnipotence in therapists, who believed that any hypothesis could create a better world for the patient, and all obstacles could be removed by simply changing language, description, or stories. Such a position may still influence us too, when we overemphasise opening possibilities over the limitations we all have.

To overcome this objection, hypotheses should take into account the embodied experiences of both patients and therapists. Since our hypotheses always involve our selves, they also involve our bodies. We are aware of our embodied condition, that always is on the background—sometimes to the fore—of any hypothetical scenario. Such embodied perspectivism unveils the limitations and the pitfalls of any point of view, including the therapist's, and shows how external realities limit the possibilities both of therapists and patients (Bertrando, 2014).

Our hypotheses are dialogical, and involve patients in the very act of their creation. Our hypothesising was of course influenced by the dialogical view we were developing. More and more we considered our hypotheses as the result of a collaborative enterprise, jointly developed by therapist and patient (Bertrando & Arcelloni, 2006). The distinction, here, is between monological and dialogical hypotheses. Traditional systemic hypothesising was monological, despite the fact that most hypotheses were developed by a team, because the conversations where the hypotheses took shape happened only within the therapeutic team. Discussing hypotheses with patients creates a true dialogue, where the patient has their say about the hypothesis in the very moment when the therapist is trying to give it shape. It is also a way of creating consensuality. This is even truer in individual therapy, where one therapist is facing one patient, and the only possible hypothesising dialogue is between the two of them.

Our hypotheses are emotional. Finally, we became more and more aware of our emotional world, and the way in which emotions shape both our interactions and our worldview (Bertrando, 2015). We realised how much our hypotheses were affected by our feelings, and began to see them as emerging at the intersection between our emotions and our position. In short, we became aware of the distinction between cognitive and emotional hypotheses. This was useful in going beyond the cognitive emphasis of our previous, Milan-style hypothesising.

Thus, we can say today that we see our hypotheses as multiple ways of connecting and framing the different statements, perspectives and emotions that the patient—as well as the therapist—bring into the therapeutic dialogue. Hypotheses that foster doubt and uncertainty, rather than trying to resolve it. We also see them as incomplete: they show a face of reality, a facet of life, some connections, but we all know (therapist and patient alike) that reality is larger and more complex than any hypothesis of ours can imagine.

Clinical example: Zelda

Any therapeutic situation may give rise to any kind of hypothesis. We try to avoid explicative, causal, rationalistic ones, although this is not always as easy as it seems: the risk of falling into old-fashioned Milan hypotheses is always present. Let us try to illustrate this process with an example.

Zelda has always been considered the problem solver in a difficult family, with an alcoholic father, a mother dominated by anxiety, a brother who turned out to be an alcoholic himself and a sister who takes her as a point of reference for her life. Lately, after a period in which she had been able to safely distance herself from her family, it turns out that her brother relapsed and went back to drinking. Her sister calls her, alarmed, asking her to take action, possibly unbeknownst to their parents, who she feels could not tolerate the umpteenth problem brought by their son. Zelda is reluctant, tired, she does not want to return to a way of being with the family that belongs to the past.

In this same period she is seriously considering whether—having reached the age of 35—she should think about having a child: she has a partner she trusts, enough financial resources, so why not? Yet she hesitates, she finds herself worried, more anxious than she should be, tense. Talking about it in therapy, she cannot understand why.

In this case, it would be very easy for the therapist to imagine a typical systemic hypothesis along the lines of Boscolo et al. (1987). It would be something like: Zelda has a strong role within the family, towards which she still feels an active loyalty; her duty would be to take immediate action in the interest of her parents and siblings. At the same time, she would like to free herself from it. Left to herself, she would maybe go on with her project of a new family. But if the family once again positions her as the saviour, she must unconsciously respond by preventing herself from moving into the future—as she might do if she had a child—but stopping before going back into the past—as she would do if she rushed to the rescue of her brother. The result is her current paralysis.

This hypothesis is apparently convincing. But it has the flaw of neglecting both Zelda's own positioning and her emotions. The question from which the systemic-dialogical hypothesis arises is rather: "How do you feel in this situation?" "Angry!" she replies vehemently. She is very angry with her family. At the moment, she feels it as an unbearable burden. The therapist must consider this anger in trying to properly understand Zelda's position. In the end, she agrees that perhaps the anger towards her family makes her experience the possibility of pregnancy—of creating a new family, of getting new responsibilities—as an additional burden. She feels pervaded by thoughts about the changes in her body, the pain of childbirth, the breastfeeding she refuses. Maybe her family experience has something to do with it, but in the sense that it may make her feel the burden more than the joy of motherhood—and the uncertainty of shifting from a laboriously built couple to a family still to be imagined.

This exchange between Zelda and the therapist led to a very different, jointly constructed hypothesis compared to the therapist's original idea. The therapist understands that the interplay of loyalties that was so central in his hypothesis was entirely internal to his own logic, nourished by his intergenerational readings (for example, Boszormenyi-Nagy & Spark, 1973) and by a perspective that he recognised as mostly centred on a traditional family structure. Through the dialogue with Zelda, a new hypothesis was born, where the pivotal role was held by her anger and her (physical) feelings. Zelda experienced this hypothesis as meaningful, and it helped the therapeutic dialogue to unfold.

Clinical example: Isadora

Isadora is 38, with a five-year-old daughter, Maia, whose birth was very controversial: at first unwanted, then dutifully accepted—with a little help from her therapist. Isadora then became a quintessentially anxious mother, attentive to any possible issue regarding Maia, whom she cared for with almost excessive intensity. Isadora entertains a very difficult relationship with her mother-in-law. She does not tolerate this woman's intrusiveness: like many Italian grandmothers, she tends to know everything about how children of other women should be raised, and constantly tries to impose herself. When she arrives at Isadora's house, she always inexorably puts himself in the position of Maia's mother. Isadora recounts that she and her own mother had a very special story: they lived alone together for a long time, because her father had Isadora while he was in another marriage, and never lived with them.

One day her mother points out her intolerance towards her mother-in-law. Isadora stands up and says to her: "Look, you made me live for years in this unbearable situation where I was thrown between your house, grandma's house, dad's house with his new partner, and also the house of dad's first wife!" Isadora is very resentful towards her mother, and at the same time she has a hard time getting away from her.

Here an easy "classical" hypothesis would be that Isadora has maintained her loyalty to her biological mother, to whom she feels indissolubly linked, and therefore struggles to adopt a mother position, as Maia's mother. At the same time, it is impossible for her to accept surrogacy on the part of the mother-in-law, which ends up being unbearable. But this is not the only possible hypothesis: another one would concern the fear and the stress of a possible repetition of that mother-daughter relationship with another woman: her mother-in-law would be the duplicate of her mother, sharing with her the same intrusiveness, that Isadora cannot of course stand. An emotion-centred hypothesis would involve Isadora's anger, implicit toward her mother and open toward her mother-in-law, and so on.

We can also complexify the hypothesis by including Nico, Isadora's partner. Being the only son of his mother, he tends to be peculiarly attached to her, and to his whole family of origin. In this case, Isadora's anger would be displaced from him to his mother.

In actuality, the therapist let her hypothesising fluctuate from one hypothesis to the other, without embracing any of them, allowing instead different angles of the situation to emerge. She interacts with Isadora, giving her ideas from time to time and maintaining an open position: it will be Isadora's task to find the hypothesis that fits her best, guided by her own emotions.

The devil is in the detail

Probably, the basic characteristic of explicative hypotheses—those aimed at "explaining" the patient's life to the patient herself—is that they are broad, all-encompassing ones. These are also the kind of hypotheses criticised by postmodern authors like Andersen (1987), or Seikkula and Olson (2003): strong explanations, with the value of a truth, created by a therapist or a team using the patients' statements just as raw data.

The hypotheses we mostly use in practice are what we define as "micro-hypotheses" (Bertrando, 2015), i.e., small and simple hypotheses based on emotional events happening during the therapeutic dialogue. The micro-hypothesis is closely linked to the here and now, and it is offered to patients in a partial, unfinished way. Founded upon a detail, it is centred on one specific—albeit, to us, important—aspect of the patient's life.

Micro-hypotheses are also open. They can generate links with other elements appearing in the therapeutic dialogue, allowing new hypotheses, ideas, or emotions to emerge. Their very openness and incompleteness foster the evolution of the therapy over time. The interweaving and superimposing of micro-hypotheses, rather than the search for one big systemic hypothesis, may stimulate the patient to create their own connections between what they feel and the world of their relationships, developing a relational sense of their own emotions and actions. In the course of a session, we may offer several different micro-hypotheses, encouraging the patient to elaborate and propose their own. In this way, hypothesising becomes a way of generating multiple options for seeing and feeling a given situation. At the same time, it is also a way to foster consensuality.

This does not mean that we have completely cancelled the other kind of hypotheses, that we may call "macro-hypotheses". A macro-hypothesis, provided that it is a systemic hypothesis, i.e., a hypothesis based on relationships, is useful if we can maintain it as a background for micro-hypothesising. We build the macro-hypothesis on the events of the session and the memories of previous sessions. It is helpful to maintain a focus on the network of relationships both the patient's life and the events in the session are embedded in. Sometimes it can be useful to let the patient know the wider frame of our hypothesising; in these cases, we may offer them macro-hypotheses too. In doing that, it is essential that we remain mindful of their provisional nature, and make this clear to the patient, too.

We are aware of the context

We never forget the context where things happen. Pluridiscursivity implies a complex tangle, in which different languages intermingle in dialogue, influencing and conditioning each other. The same happens with contexts and frames: contexts are themselves liquid and mutable, generating a complex imbrication already described by Bateson (1955). Freely emerging from interactions, contexts are manifold and subjected both to change and to different framings: different people experience different contexts even in the very same situation, depending on their own positions within them. Hypothesising about contexts means an ability to see—imagine—many different contexts at the same time.

According to Donald Schön (1983), a professional—in our case, a therapist—is in dialogue with the whole situation they are embedded in, not only with their patients. While we promote dialogue with our patient, and between this person and their significant others, we also dialogue with the therapeutic situation as a whole, and also with ourselves within the situation. Dialogue with the context is, of course, a metaphor: it means to be able to monitor our own words and actions in regard to the larger significant system, and evaluating the various actors' different responses, again both in word and action. As therapists, we are inside the relationship; at the same time we should see it from the outside, and from that position question it—and ourselves. We talk and act within the therapeutic context, and in so doing we change and reshape it: we become part of the context. Meanwhile, we are aware that the context exists independent of us, and as such resists our attempts to change it. This metaphorical dialogue, in our opinion, is as important as the actual conversations with patients going on in sessions.

Talking and acting

In systemic-dialogical therapy, most of the therapist's actions in the session happen in the form of talking. We consider the words that we put into the therapeutic dialogue as performative, as ways "to do things with words" (Austin, 1962). Words are accompanied by innumerable nonverbal interactions, that convey mostly emotional meanings (Bertrando, 2015). When we use the word "language", we are always implying this interplay between the verbal and the nonverbal.

We use a plain language

We use the simplest way of talking, avoiding psychological or technical jargon. We accept and encourage the patient to speak in their own unique voice (pluridiscursivity). Through simplicity, we keep as close to the patient as possible. At the same time, we try to allow other voices to enter the therapeutic dialogue: the voices of significant others (polyphony). Rather than translating the patient's statements in the language of therapy, we allow their language and style and our own to mix up freely. What is really relevant will emerge by leaving people free to express themselves and interact with us. Or, better, there is nothing "relevant" in itself: what is relevant will be jointly decided in the course of dialogue.

In therapy we position ourselves, at first, as listeners. Asking questions is more important than getting answers. Promoting a free language dance is more relevant than looking for conclusions. Not all patients, though, find it is enough to have their voice in the dialogue: sometimes the therapist has to intervene with their own voice and respectfully doubt and challenge the patient's.

Strategic and Erickson-informed systemic therapy favour ambiguity in the therapist's talk (see Haley, 1973). They aim at changing the patient through confusion. In *Systemic Therapy with Individuals*, Boscolo and Bertrando favoured an extensively metaphorical language, that promoted change through ambiguity. In the past, we have contrasted such an approach with the idea of direct talk, of speaking the truth of what we think and feel to our patients, rather than choosing words in order to obtain a rhetorical effect.[4] Today we are going a step further.

We have observed that, in the present cultural condition, the patient prefers to know the rationale for the therapist's actions. We choose today to risk unveiling our professional "tricks" and to accurately describe our position in the session: this usually strengthens the therapeutic alliance. Ways of obtaining this effect are, for example, sharing the process of creating hypotheses, as we have shown in the previous section; or discuss what we expect from the therapeutic process in a specific phase of a therapy.

We also try to avoid, through our linguistic choices, problem-centred and problem-saturated dialogue. We prefer to widen the perspective, asking as soon as possible questions that move away from the presenting problem, trying to generate a comprehensive view of the patient's relational life. This means that we find it acceptable to talk about something else, apparently unconnected to presented problems or symptoms. This allows novelty to emerge and helps the patient in developing their own perspective and positioning. It is also eased by the use of plain, everyday language.

We ask questions

We ask a lot of questions during therapy. We do not see the therapeutic process as a continuous exchange of questions and answers, but we consider questions the best way to open dialogues. We use questions to explore the patient's worlds together with them, to widen their—and our—perspectives, and to help them discover options they were not originally aware of, trying to create a context where the patient may surprise the therapist—and themselves.

We keep our question open and nonstrategic: we never ask a question if we think we know the answer; we make a statement instead. We do not ask leading questions either, i.e., questions that, by their very structure, lead the patient in a specific direction. In this case, we may make a (very doubtful) statement, and see how the patient reacts to it.

Questions may be circular, future, or hypothetical in the Milan tradition. We may use questions theorised by other approaches, such as narrative questions. We have dealt with our questioning in detail in previous writings (see for example, Bertrando, 2007, Chapter 8). Here we summarise some of the types of questioning we use. This list, of course, is not exhaustive—it only gives some indications that readers can expand according to their own style, background and sensitivity.

Simple (linear) questioning

First of all, it is important to ask questions as such. So even the most linear, apparently trivial questions bear some relevance: at the very least, they are useful to accumulate details, that sometimes seem unimportant, but may reveal their value later.

Simple questions help creating a relationship in which the therapist makes it clear that they have, rather than answers to give, curiosities to satisfy (Cecchin, 1987). The therapist's curiosity also encourages the patient to become curious in turn. As such, linear questions are the first, minimal building block of a therapeutic dialogue.

Circular questioning

This type of questioning was established initially in 1980 by the original Milan group (Selvini Palazzoli et al., 1980a), and subsequently developed by many authors in different contexts: Peggy Penn (1982), Karl Tomm (1988), Boscolo et al. (1987); its specific use in individual therapy was first proposed by Boscolo and Bertrando (1996). Circular questions are the kind of questions that are able to bring forth differences (in the Batesonian sense of "a difference that makes a difference", and therefore a relationship). There are several kinds of them, from triadic questions—the "investigation of a dyadic relationship as it is seen by a third person" (Selvini Palazzoli, 1980a, p. 8)—to ranking questions, to difference questions and so on.

We will not deal extensively with circular questions here, since we have developed this subject elsewhere. Suffice to say that they help creating in the patient an awareness of their relational life without statements or declarations on the part of the therapist. As such, they remain important instruments for systemic-dialogical therapists. Once again, we use them in order to propose a relational perspective, and only when we find that they can be introduced into the dialogue without an effort.

A typical example of a circular question would be a triadic question, such as: "What do your children do (or say, or feel) when your wife comes back home and the two of you begin a quarrel?" Here the question enlightens the fact that a couple fight has an effect on people other than the couple, and fosters in the patient some awareness of it.

Future and hypothetical questioning

The same applies to future and hypothetical questions (see Penn, 1985; Boscolo & Bertrando, 1993). Both kinds of questions introduce specific perspectives in the questioning process: the former open possibilities in the future, the latter propose specific hypotheses within the question itself. Future questions "allow clients to construct possible future worlds by exploring the temporal horizon of the family and any discrepancies there may be between the times of individual members" (Boscolo & Bertrando, 1993, p. 172). With hypothetical questions, "the therapist includes one or more possible futures in hypothetical questions and presents clients with a stimulating hypothesis. This enables him or her to challenge their premises quite openly" (Boscolo & Bertrando, 1993, p. 172).

The inherent risk is to use such questions in order to "plant" a specific idea or perspective in the patient's mind, without openly stating it. We avoid such a strategic stance when asking those questions too. For example, when asking: "What do you think would happen if you really left your job for trying something different in the near future?", we would add: "I'm asking this because you fantasised about this possibility some time ago, but I don't mean that you should do it if you don't feel like it."

Narrative questioning

Narrative questions were originally devised by Michael White to inquire about unique outcomes (i.e., unpredictable experiences or events that contrast the patient's problem-saturated narrative), externalise problems and stabilise change (Carr, 1999). The therapist may ask patients about particular instances in which their problem was prevented from having a major negative influence on their lives. Unique outcomes may then be incorporated into a story and the plot enriched by mapping them with "landscape of action" and "landscape of consciousness" questions. Landscape of action questions aim to plot the sequence of events as they were seen by the patient and others. Landscape of consciousness questions aim to develop the meaning of the story described in the landscape of action, mapping motives, purposes, intentions, hopes, beliefs and values. White (1993) developed an extensive list of questions for the different moments of narrative therapy: these questions aim at "thickening" the experience of the unique outcome in order for the patient to "re-author" her life.

Narrative questions have a centripetal effect, in that they usually centre individuals on themselves. In this sense, they are reciprocal to circular questions, that tend to de-centre them and focus on their relational network instead. The potential risk of narrative questions is to foster egocentrism together with self-reflection.

Reflexive questioning

The notion of reflexive questions can be attributed to Karl Tomm (1987b). It referred to a kind of

> questions asked with the intent to facilitate self-healing in an individual or family by activating the reflexivity among meanings within pre-existing belief systems that enable family members to generate or generalise constructive patterns of cognition and behaviour on their own.
>
> (Tomm, 1987a, p. 172)

In other words, these questions foster a circular process within the patients' communication patterns and beliefs, acting as "probes, stimuli, or perturbations" (Tomm, 1987a, p. 171) for change.

For example: "How do you think your husband would respond if you didn't cook meals anymore as you have always done in the past?" "How do you feel about this idea?" "What would you say or do if he didn't accept it? And if he accepts it...?" and so on.

Despite their heavy reliance on cognitive processes, these questions may be useful for challenging the patient's ideologies and open a different landscape of understanding and of actions to them.

Positional questioning

We consider two distinct kinds of questions as positional. In the first, the therapist is aware of their own position when asking the question (such position can be openly articulated in the question or not). In the second, the question openly addresses the position(s) that the patient takes. They both aim at clarifying positioning, and at increasing the patient's awareness in this regard.

They may be considered specific examples of reflective questions, and perhaps they are, but they deal with a specific point in our theory and practice, namely our work on position and positioning.

For example, if a patient feels excluded by her group, like Gilda in Chapter 2, a good set of positional questions would be: "How do you feel you are considered by the group? How do they position you? Is it possible for you to make a choice? And if so, what would you choose?"

Another girl befriends a group that two cousins of hers are part of. In her extended family, the relationships of her nuclear family with that part of the family are getting more and more strained. She discovers that they had a holiday without inviting her. She is asked: "What position did you take toward them?" "I didn't realise it, but in practice I had begun to stand up to them. I created a distance..."

Emotional questioning

Since the other pivotal characteristic of our approach is the emphasis on emotions, we frequently ask questions about them. Emotional questions are all the questions that have a definite emotion, feeling or mood as their subject. They can be linear (when we ask questions about the patient's feelings), circular (when the patient is asked questions about other people's emotions), reflexive and so on (see Bertrando, 2015). For example:

"How did you feel, then and there?" "Can you give me an idea of the atmosphere, the emotional tone of the situation you are talking about?" "What did you feel was the disposition of the other(s)?" "Are you able to get back to what you were feeling in that moment and describe it?"

Or (in the present): "How do you feel now?" "How do you imagine are others feeling now?" "The others, how do they imagine you are feeling now?", and so on.

When therapists ask an emotional question, they should, at the same time, ask questions to themselves about that same emotion, to avoid taking for granted that the emotion that they see is the patient's reality, rather than an effect of the therapist's own emotional sensitivity. We will give more detailed examples of emotional questioning in Chapter 5.

We presentify others

Systemic therapy is characterised by its emphasis on relationships. In individual therapy, relationships are not present in the here and now of the session. The only relationship that is active in the session is between therapist and patient—and that relationship has been theorised by therapists of all orientations, most of all by psychoanalysts with transference analysis. There is a relevant difference, however: transference-based psychoanalysis tends to bring all the events and relationships happening in the life of the patient within the therapy room, referring them to the relation with the analyst (Gill, 1982). In the book *Systemic Therapy with Individuals*, Boscolo and Bertrando developed a specific therapeutic technique defined as "presentification of the third party", i.e., making the significant others in the patient's life present in the session as if they were in the room. The presentification of the third party can be considered as the reciprocal of transference analysis: the therapist metaphorically takes the patient outside the therapy room, to "visit" the most significant people in their relational life.

Such attention to significant others has multiple meanings. First, it is a need of the therapist's: we want to understand these other people, since they influence and determine our patient's feelings, thoughts and actions. We cannot content ourselves with knowing the effects that the others have on a patient. Second, presentifying others move the patient outside their own frame of reference, recovering one of the most important aspects of systemic family therapy: the comparison of viewpoints and experiences. Milan systemic family therapists foster connections among family members, all of them present in the therapy room. After all, one of their main tools are circular questions, i.e., questions that require one family member to comment on the relationships between other members of the family. This has an effect on the others: it puts them in the position of observers of what the member being questioned is thinking and feeling about them. In individual therapy, necessarily such connections must be built by therapist and patient in *absentia*, rather than in *praesentia* of the others. To keep the relational focus, we try to consider what the others (would) feel, think or do in any situation we are considering together with a patient.

For example, Milena, 60, has been recently divorced—against her will—by her husband Carlo, father of their 18-year-old son Silvano. She is furious with Carlo: immediately before their separation, he had been quite seriously ill, and she had to take care of him. Despite their already strained relationship, she had resolved to purchase a new, bigger apartment, with the aim of living together in a sort of cohabitation in separateness. Now she feels betrayed, and cannot understand why her son is angry toward both parents. The therapist tries to help her understand Carlo's position, hypothesising that he had reluctantly accepted her proposal as a form of unwelcome charity, and that his clumsy moves toward independence were the result of this ambivalence; at the same time, the therapist points out that Silvano may feel recruited by both father and mother as an ally, and this split loyalty makes him suffer—hence, his anger. Accepting this reading is extremely hard for Milena, and the therapist is very careful to propose his hypotheses as mere suggestions. In the course of dialogue, through a reflection about Carlo's and Silvano's positions, the therapist enables Milena to see what is hidden by her anger: her fear of a desolating, all-encompassing loneliness.

Third parties can be presentified by asking (mostly circular) questions about them, or by hypothesising and imagining their thoughts, actions and feelings, as we have seen in Milena's case. Our questions and hypotheses regard the others as such, rather than their effects on the patient. For example, a question like: "How did your mother feel when you told her you wanted to leave?" is usually preferred to a question like: "How did you feel when your mother told you she didn't want you to leave?" In other words, the presentification emphasises the other rather than the patient. This allows the introduction of voices, presence, points of view—briefly—of the worlds of the third parties that are relevant to the life of a patient within the dual relationships with the therapist. The therapist should then reconnect the presentified others to the here and now of the patient.

A virtual community is thus created, which participates in the development of novel points of view. This modality has, among others, the effect of bringing the patient to reflect or make assumptions about the thoughts or emotions of the others regarding himself, as opposed to just his own.

Circular questions as such have a similar effect; the presentification of the third party enforces the process by focusing on one person at a time, making their (virtual) presence stronger.

Our practice bears some similarity to Karl Tomm's (1998) interview with internalised others, that consists of a process of questioning directly aimed at an internalised third party. The goals of the two procedures are the same, and both focus on making the patient more aware of their relational world and their reactions to it. Usually, though, we do not use Tomm's way of questioning, preferring a more informal style, where the patient is directly questioned about the others.

In later years, we went one step further: the context that defines both the therapeutic relationship and the patient's existence is a third party too (Bertrando, 2002). The individual, their conversations and their relationships make sense only within a contextual matrix, which is made up of the significant third parties who intervene in their lives. Of course, contexts can be much wider, and involve ideas, ideologies, cultures, and even dimensions like gender, race, or economical factors.

> Thus a third party may represent a person (or several people), an idea, an aspiration, and a "something". For the therapist, this means the need immediately for an awareness of her own position, not only vis-à-vis the client, but also vis-à-vis the various systems in which therapeutic relationships are steeped, for example, family and extended families; referral and referring person; health structures and the likely public services attached to them; work; school; other social systems; politics and culture in general.
>
> (Bertrando, 2002, p. 354)

The introduction of the third party into therapy is no mere technique, or a way to formulate questions, but rather a basic stance of the therapist. The presentification of the third party is a constitutive element which characterises our approach as compared to other forms of therapy.

Working in institutions

Many of the examples we present are connected with our everyday work. Being private practitioners, we mostly see individuals coming from a middle-class environment. In the past, however, we both worked with disadvantaged people in institutions, and many of our trainees still work in similar situations. We want to present here some of our ideas about systemic-dialogical individual therapy in an institutional setting.

First of all, the systemic-dialogical therapist must determine who is their patient and who is their client. The distinction is between the person who actually participates in the sessions, as the therapist's interlocutor, and the person(s) or entities who determine the possibility and the course of therapy—or, briefly, who pay for the therapy.

In many instances, the clients themselves pay for their own sessions. When working with adult individuals in a private settings, client and patient are the same person. When working individually with children or adolescents, the patient is the young one, the clients are their parents, which may create challenging situations. For example, in one of our therapies the patient was 17-year-old Sofia, a young woman with dissociative and depressive symptoms. In two years of therapy, the proper symptoms waned and almost disappeared. Therapist and patient, anyway, wanted to keep the therapy going because Sofia had to face a new situation: after completing high school, she had to begin university and at the same time to find a part-time job to pay for at least part of her studies. Her parents, instead, wanted the therapy to end with the end of high school, because after that moment they felt that Sofia should stay on her own feet. What the therapist could do was to negotiate with them an additional three months, that she and Sofia employed to review the point she had reached, her new abilities, and the challenges she would have to meet in her new life. The final meeting was all in all positive, albeit with some regrets. Therapist and patient had to adapt to the restraint posed by Sofia's parents, and find the best way out possible in that situation: they both found their place (Chapter 6).

When institutions are involved, things are more complex. Actually, the therapist's client in those cases is the institution itself, that may determine not only the duration, but also the conditions of therapy, such as the interval between sessions, of even the choice between individual and family, couple, or group therapy. The therapist here is in a sense a mediator between institution and patient, especially in cases when the patient comes from a disadvantaged situation, and has little leverage in dealing with the institution and its more authoritative representatives.

Let us take a more complex case, involving several professionals and institutions. Abigail is a 35-year-old Caucasian Australian, who had several children from two previous partners, both Aboriginal. Brenda, her seven-year-old daughter, is the actual patient in this case. Abigail now lives with a new partner, in what she describes as her first non-abusive relationship—"now I understand that what I found normal in the past was not normal at all..." she says—although both are drug users. Most of her children are now in foster care. Brenda and one of her older sisters now live with Cheryl, a single mother with a ten-year-old biological daughter.

The colleague who asks for supervision is Brenda's individual therapist. She works on behalf of Evolve, a tertiary mental health service providing mental health assessment and intervention for children in care, under the supervision of the Department of Child Safety (DOCS); Brenda's sister has another individual therapist. Brenda is considered the troublemaker, and Cheryl often complains that Brenda's therapist is not good enough: she is not giving Brenda a therapy as effective as her colleague is giving to Brenda's sister, Cheryl says. The therapist feels that Cheryl is undermining her therapeutic efforts.

The central event, actually, happened when Brenda disclosed to Cheryl's biological daughter that her 13-year-old brother had physically abused her and her sister. The daughter told her mother, who in turn forced both sisters to tell DOCS. According to the therapist, this was a wrong procedure by Cheryl, who should have discussed this with her first. A legal process was set in motion, and as a consequence Abigail cut all her relationships with her son.

The therapist's dilemma is: "How can I go on with my therapy without entering in a competition with Cheryl, and without Cheryl damaging my reputation in front of DOCS? I am very angry at her…"

The supervisor tries first of all to draw a map of the situation, and of the many systems involved: a family, a foster family, DOCS, Evolve, schools, mental health services (for both Abigail and her partner). Our therapist had originally been a friend of the other girl's therapist, but now they are drifting apart due to professional differences. Finally, the therapist is also worried about what DOCS management could think about her.

The supervisor begins to discuss possible hypotheses with the therapist. Who is her client? To her, it is Evolve (but, at times, DOCS); Cheryl, though, believes she is the actual client. Who is the patient, then? Obviously Brenda, but sometimes the therapist sees Cheryl as a patient.

They discuss how the therapist wants to be accepted by Cheryl as a good professional; at the same time, she seems to enter a competition with Cheryl as "the best mother". The therapist sees Cheryl as aggressive, and she feels threatened by her; but, if we consider the situation from Cheryl's viewpoint, possibly she feels disqualified by the therapist—who actually thinks Cheryl is not a good carer, and that she behaved improperly. So we could reframe Cheryl's aggression as self-defence.

The wider network is relevant too. For example, neither DOCS nor Evolve considered the possibility for Abigail to take care, in her new situation, of her children: Abigail has no voice in this story. The race element is also neglected: Cheryl and her daughter are white, Brenda and her sister partly Aboriginal. Is this why she is necessarily the troublemaker? Also, the politics of giving separate therapy to the two girls is consistent to the tendency of the overall system of creating divisions and to separate the persons from each other. Finally, nobody is taking into account the time element: how long is the situation going to stay the same?

As usual the supervision leaves many questions unanswered, since the important element is to enable the therapist to ask herself—and later ask others—new questions. As a consequence of the supervision, the therapist begins to feel that possibly she can talk openly about what goes on, (first) to her therapist colleague, (second) to her managers at Evolve, and maybe (third) to Cheryl herself. In the latter case, she should probably be slightly more educational in explaining the rationale for therapy: she cannot take for granted that it is properly understood by Cheryl, independently from her presumed agenda of getting rid of her. In this way, the therapist can go beyond the prevailing parallel process of splitting that is happening in the system, and also against the tendency of defending oneself by putting blame on the other. In this way she can promote a proper dialogue with all the other main actors in the system.

Conclusion

To sum up, our approach to individual therapy involves the use of many practices. Some of them, such as the hypothesising process, define the approach itself, and are in a way mandatory, if we want to do therapy according to the systemic-dialogical approach. Other ones, such as circular questioning, definitely pertain to our approach, but are not necessary for us to follow if we want to consider ourselves as belonging to the approach. All in all, those practices make sense only if they are framed in the context of the four systemic-dialogical pillars. We will extensively describe our pillars in the following four chapters.

Notes

1 In short, we adopt John Burnham's categorisation, which distinguishes approach, method and techniques. In the past one of us used a similar three-part distinction between theory, principles and techniques (Bertrando, 2007). We feel that Burnham's designation is best suited to our present thinking.
2 Polyphony and pluridiscursivity are both terms related to Mikhail Bakhtin's (1981, 1968/1984) dialogical theory. After a long reflection on terminology, we maintained the term "polyphony" to denote the presence of many voices in the session, but we decided that, in order to denote the acceptance of many languages at the same time, we prefer the term "pluridiscursivity" to the one officially adopted by most English-speaking dialogical theorists, namely "heteroglossia", a term created by Bakhtin's scholar Michael Holquist (2002) to translate the Russian word *raznorecie*, literally, "varied-speechedness".
3 The strategic value of the original Milan team's hypotheses was brought to our attention by Raphael Cadenhead and Richard McKenny in a still unpublished article that was shared with us by the authors, whom we thank.
4 For a more extensive discussion of this position, see Bertrando (2007), Chapter 7.

References

Andersen, T. (1987). The reflecting team: Dialogue and meta-dialogue in clinical work. *Family Process*, 26 (4): 415–428. DOI:10.1111/j.1545–5300.1987.00415.x.
Austin, J.L. (1962). *How to Do Things With Words*. Oxford University Press.
Bakhtin, M.M. (1981). Discourse in the novel. In: M. Holquist (Ed.), *The Dialogic Imagination* (pp. 259–422). Texas University Press (original edition 1935).

Bakhtin, M.M. (1984). C. Emerson (Ed.). *Problems of Dostojevski's Poetics*. University of Minnesota Press (original edition 1968).

Bateson, G. (1955). A theory of play and fantasy. In: *Steps to an Ecology of Mind* (pp. 177–193). Chandler Publishing Company, 1972.

Bateson, G. (1968). Conscious purpose vs. nature. In: *Steps to an Ecology of Mind* (pp. 426–439). Chandler Publishing Company, 1972.

Bateson, G. (1970). Form, substance, and difference. In: *Steps to an Ecology of Mind* (pp. 448–465). Chandler Publishing Company, 1972.

Bertrando, P. (2002). The presence of the third party. Systemic therapy and transference analysis. *Journal of Family Therapy*, 24 (3): 351–368. DOI:10.1111/1467–6427.00224.

Bertrando, P. (2007). *The Dialogical Therapist*. Karnac.

Bertrando, P. (2014). Il postmoderno è un lusso? La visione postmoderna di fronte alla crisi. *Rivista di Psicoterapia Relazionale*, 39: 5–23. DOI:10.3280/PR2014-039001.

Bertrando, P. (2015). *Emotions and the Therapist*. Karnac.

Bertrando, P. & Arcelloni, T. (2006). Hypotheses are dialogues: sharing hypotheses with clients. *Journal of Family Therapy*, 28: 370–387. DOI:10.1111/j.1467–6427.2006.00358.x.

Bertrando, P. & Toffanetti, D. (2003). Persons and hypotheses: The use of the therapist in the therapeutic process. *Australian and New Zealand Journal of Family Therapy*, 24 (1): 7–13.

Boscolo, L. & Bertrando, P. (1993). *The Times of Time: A Perspective on Time in Systemic Therapy and Consultation*. 2nd edition. Routledge, 2020.

Boscolo, L. & Bertrando, P. (1996). *Systemic Therapy with Individuals*. Karnac.

Boscolo, L., Cecchin, G., Hoffman, L., & Penn, P. (1987). *Milan Systemic Family Therapy: Conversations in Theory and Practice*. Basic Books.

Boszormenyi-Nagy, I. & Spark, G. (1973). *Invisible Loyalties*. Harper & Row.

Burnham, J. (1992). Approach, Method, Technique: Making Distinctions and Creating Connections. *Human Systems*, 3 (1): 3–26.

Carr, A. (1999). Narrative Therapy: One Perspective on the Work of Michael White. *Feedback*, 8 (3): 15–24.

Cecchin, G. (1987). Hypothesizing-circularity-neutrality revisited: An invitation to curiosity, *Family Process*, 26: 405–413. DOI:10.1111/j.1545–5300.1987.00405.x.

Cecchin, G., Lane, G., & Ray, W.L. (1994). *The Cybernetics of Prejudices in the Practice of Psychotherapy*. Karnac.

Danielsson, U. (2023). *The World Itself: Consciousness and the Everything of Physics*. Bellevue Literary Press.

Foucault, M. (1982). The subject and power. In: H.L. Dreyfus & F. Rabinow, *Michel Foucault: Beyond Structuralism and Hermeneutics*. University of Chicago Press.

Foucault, M. (2003). *Le pouvoir psychiatrique. Course au Collège de France 1973–1974*, ed. J. Lagrange. Gallimard.

Gill, M.M. (1982). *Analysis of Transference*. International Universities Press.

Goodman, N. (1978). *Ways of Worldmaking*. Harvester Press.

Haley, J. (1973). *Uncommon Therapy. The Psychiatric Techniques of Milton Erickson, M.D.* Norton.

Holquist, M. (2002). *Dialogism: Bakhtin and His World*. 2nd edition. Routledge.

Lannamann, J. (1998). Social constructionism and materiality: The limits of indeterminacy in therapeutic settings. *Family Process*, 37: 393–414.

Larner, G. (2024). Family therapy and the ecology of parallel universes. *Journal of Family Therapy*, 46: 264–280. DOI:10.1111/1467-6427.12464.

Lini, C. & Bertrando, P. (2020). Finding one's place: emotions and positioning in systemic-dialogical therapy. *Journal of Family Therapy*, 42, 204–221. DOI:10.1111/1467–6427.12267.

McNamee, S. & Gergen, K.J. (Eds.) (1999). *Relational Responsibility. Resources for Sustainable Dialogue*. Sage.

Penn, P. (1982). Circular Questioning. *Family Process*, 21: 267–280. DOI:10.1111/j.1545–5300.1982.00267.x.

Penn, P. (1985). Feed-forward. Future questions, future maps. *Family Process*, 24: 299–310. DOI:10.1111/j.1545–5300.1985.00299.x.

Rober, P. (2005). The therapist's self in dialogical family therapy: some ideas about not-knowing and the therapist's inner conversation. *Family Process*, 44: 477–495. DOI:10.1111/j.1545–5300.2005.00073.x.

Schön, D.A. (1983). *The Reflective Practitioner: How Professionals Think in Action*. Basic Books.

Seikkula, J. & Olson, M.E. (2003). The open dialogue approach to acute psychosis: its poetics and micropolitics. *Family Process*, 42: 403–418. DOI:10.1111/j.1545–5300.2003.00403.x.

Selvini Palazzoli, M. (1980). Why a long interval between sessions? The therapeutic control of the family-therapist suprasystem. In M. Andolfi & I. Zwerling (Eds.), *Dimensions of Family Therapy*. The Guildford Press, pp. 161–169.

Selvini Palazzoli, M., Boscolo, L., Cecchin, G., & Prata, G. (1980a). Hypothesizing-circularity-neutrality. Three guidelines for the conductor of the session. *Family Process*, 19: 3–12. DOI:10.1111/j.1545–5300.1980.00003.x.

Selvini Palazzoli, M., Boscolo, L., Cecchin, G., & Prata, G. (1980b). The problem of the referring person. *Journal of Marital and Family Therapy*, 6: 3–9.

Tomm, K. (1987a). Interventive Interviewing: I. Strategizing as a Fourth Guideline for the Therapist. *Family Process*, 26: 3–13. DOI:10.1111/j.1545–5300.1987.00003.x.

Tomm, K. (1987b). Interventive Interviewing: II. Reflexive questioning as a Means to Enable Self-healing, *Family Process*, 26: 167–183. DOI:10.1111/j.1545–5300.1987.00167.x.

Tomm, K. (1988). Interventive Interviewing: III. Intending to Ask Circular, Strategic or Reflexive Questions?, *Family Process*, 27: 1–15. DOI:10.1111/j.1545–5300.1988.00001.x.

Tomm, K. (1998). Honorating Our Internalized Others and Ethics of Caring. In: M.F. Hoyt, *The Handbook of Constructive Therapies*. Jossey-Bass.

Watzlawick, P., Weakland, J. H., & Fisch, R. (1974). *Change: The Principles of Problem Formation and Problem Resolution*. W. W. Norton.

White, M. (1993). Deconstruction and therapy. In S. G. Gilligan & R. Price (Eds.), *Therapeutic Conversations* (pp. 22–61). W. W. Norton & Co. (Reprinted from the *Dulwich Centre Newsletter*, 3, 1991, 1–21).

Chapter 4

(Systemic) Dialogues

This chapter and the next three deal with the four pillars of our models. The first pillar is dialogue. Once again, our version of dialogue is rooted in a systemic view: dialogue makes sense to us only in a dialectical relationship with systems. Every time we speak of dialogue we see it on a background made of multiple systems and contexts interwoven with each other. A dialogical approach to therapy, however, changes the conduction of therapy in many ways compared to a straightforward system approach.

Dialogues within systems

We do not consider our systemic-dialogical model to be an integration of pre-existing models, such as the Milan approach we originally practised, with other ones, such as Jaakko Seikkula's open dialogue—or Tom Andersen's reflecting team, or Peter Rober's inner conversation.[1] What we propose here emerged independently as an evolution of our own systemic practice, through our reflections on it.

Some etymology may help clarifying issues: "dialogue" derives from Latin *dialogus*, in turn derived from ancient Greek *dialogos*, from *dia* "through" + *logos* "word". We see it as an exchange where we let ourselves be affected by the other (the other's words), while asking their permission to be affected by us (our words). Dialogue is actually the basis of Western philosophy: Socrates is considered in many respects its true founder, and his philosophy mainly consisted in engaging his fellow citizens in dialogue. His thinking—never put in writing—reached us through Plato's written dialogues. And their very dialogical nature has challenged interpreters for 25 centuries: Plato's dialogues are open-ended, leaving the reader to find their "true" interpretation, or to distinguish between Plato's own thoughts and Socrates's (see Press, 1993).

The theoretical evolution of our thinking and practising, together with their main references, are outlined in Appendix A. Here we mainly want to describe its practical implications. Why dialogue, first of all? Because we realised that the affirmative, strategic stance of the original Milan systemic therapy was no longer fit to the times. The process was fostered by our patients, that in

DOI: 10.4324/9781003381754-5

most cases wanted to share the therapeutic process, rather than being sub-mitted to it. We found more and more difficult to adopt the heroic, messianic position of the traditional systemic therapist (Bertrando, 2007). At the same time, we did not want to be just witnesses to our patients' evolution; we felt that our activity, questions, hypotheses, and involvement was necessary to further the therapeutic process.

As Michael Guilfoyle (2003) has observed, adopting a dialogical stance in therapy means to be aware of its power dimension: power can be considered as a common factor of all therapies, and it is impossible for us, as therapists, to escape it. The only thing we can do is to be aware of it and question our own position all the time. Guilfoyle also noticed that dialogical therapists, in contrast with therapists of the previous generations, make wider use of "uncertainty markers", which "remove the authority of [their] voice, replacing it with a voice that is … uncertain rather than certain, personalised rather than objective, and relative rather than universal" (p. 338). He refers to minimal utterances, such as, "maybe", "possibly", "in my opinion", "I don't know", and so on. They enable patients to see that the therapists is uncertain and fallible as they are, thus fostering a proper dialogical exchange.

A dialogical position allowed us to pay closer attention to our patients and their discourses, and to ask questions without necessarily looking for definite answers. It made us more sensitive to the processes happening in the here and now of the session, as opposed to the content—the stories, facts, opinions brought into the session by therapists and patients.

What do patients perceive of the therapist in the therapeutic dialogue? Our body, its form and its "staging", our gender, our age, our sexual orientation, our religious and political beliefs, our privileges. Our words, our manners, our looks, the questions we ask and the ones we do not ask, talk about us, about our linguistic, aesthetic and political choices. Briefly, the same that we look for and perceive in them: dialogue is a perfectly reciprocal process. The awareness of this process is essential to the conduction of therapy.

The system, a concept that has been too often conceived as an (essential) abstraction in systemic therapy, becomes an embodied system, where all interac-tions are free-flowing. Bodies interact through (in) emotions; exchanges exceed verbal language. The very questioning process becomes something very different from a gathering of information. We still use all of the technical questions we have outlined in Chapter 3, but with a different emphasis: a question is a way of raising an issue; it may remain unanswered, and still be useful for creating a possible new frame. The question stays with the patient—and the therapists themselves. It may thus trigger a process that goes well beyond the specific moment, or even the specific session, when it was asked.

Positioning becomes more than a simple awareness of where we are, intertwined with all the emotional processes happening in the session and around it. All in all, therapy becomes less cognitive, more of an overall experience for both participants in the session. And the shift toward dialogue also provides a very different way of conceiving systems.

Order and disorder

In embracing dialogue, we overcame a methodological stalemate. Our passage through postmodernism already had freed us from the idea of finding underlying systemic mechanisms in the lives of our clients. At the same time, we found the reliance on patients as the experts of themselves (Anderson & Goolishian, 1992) too simplistic, especially in an age where nobody feels that they are an expert on anything anymore. We needed a theory that could safely deal with disorder. In a dialogical perspective, therapy could be an unordered, albeit fruitful, process.

Gregory Bateson (1972) saw the world as inherently organised according to systemic principles, and believed that the human tendency to deny them was the root of an ecological crisis (Harries-Jones, 1995). With a strange symmetry, Mikhail Bakhtin believed the world to be inherently anarchical, and maintained that to give free rein to different languages was in itself liberating (Holquist, 2002). A systemic perspective emphasises rules, a dialogical one emphasises freedom. Systemic therapists' insistence on order and rules (Guttman, 1991) obscures the fact that in most cases well-balanced systems emerge from self-organisation rather than from planning.[2] At the same time, no human aggregate can exist without rules, and language exchanges themselves—not to mention "proper" dialogue—depend on them: in any dialogue we can find patterns organised according to dialogical rules. Such patterns are not pre-established by any authority, they are rather emerging phenomena (see Johnson, 2001).

Dialogue, as such, cannot be planned, and therefore it is disordered; at the same time, it can be disordered only within some order, provided by dialogical rules. A completely unruled dialogue can easily become abusive, and should be corrected according to the rules of proper dialogue. We may speak of a dialectic between order and disorder (see Bateson, 1948). The Babel of polyphony and pluridiscursivity may be a cure for an excess of restriction; systemic rules appear when polyphony becomes cacophony and can be lived as disconnected garble.

In our practice, order takes the form of hypotheses. When the original Milan team first proposed the idea of systemic hypothesising, their arguments were actually ambiguous. On the one hand, their systemic hypotheses were considered "neither true nor false" (Selvini Palazzoli et al., 1980a, p. 4), and therefore undetermined and undecidable. On the other hand, they aimed at "introducing the power" (Selvini Palazzoli et al., 1980a, p. 4) of some modification dictated by the therapist. A hypothesis of this kind was a strong statement on the therapist's part, aiming at finding causal—albeit provisional—explanations of the patients' lives. Hypotheses were created by the therapeutic team as an all-encompassing description of the state of the patient's significant system, and gained power from being presented as a team effort, with few possibilities on the part of patients to rebut, restricting, when not cancelling, dialogical openness.

We see the hypothesising process from a different standpoint: if a hypothesis is a way of getting one's bearings in the often chaotic interactions between therapist and patients, we wonder whether it is in fact possible not to make any—maybe minimal, very tentative—hypothesis when doing therapy. Perhaps the best we can do as therapists is being aware of our own hypothesising. If we propose multiple hypotheses rather than one, encouraging our patient to propose and elaborate their own, hypothesising becomes a way of generating manifold options to see and feel a situation; a conception that would fulfil and amplify the notion of a "neither true nor false" hypothesis imagined by the Milan team (Chapter 3).

Such provisional and manifold hypotheses maintain, rather than reduce, uncertainty: Gianfranco Cecchin in his later years used to define them as "fantasies", to eradicate the reference to scientific methodology implicit in the concept (see Bertrando, 2004). They are proposals, continuously corrected and revised through dialogue (Bertrando & Arcelloni, 2006). We neither try to explain to the patient what they are doing, nor are we looking for causes or hidden motivations; we try to show the patient new points of view, that can dialogue with theirs. Of course we, like any other therapist, try to develop our own discourse with some consistency. We never try, though, to prevail over the discourse of the patient.

We embrace the precariousness, the uncertainty of Bauman's liquid modernity, not (only) as an undesirable consequence of late neoliberalism, but as an existential condition of humankind. In this way, we can reclaim uncertainty and turn it into a strength. Dialogue has enriched our systemic perspective through the practice of uncertainty, with radical consequences. We moved from considering systems as actual entities, inherently stable, to seeing them as sets of complex, disordered interactions that are stabilised only transiently and provisionally. Systemic rules, in this perspective, emerge from disorder and are always unstable. Hence our emphasis on uncertainty. Remaining in uncertainty, we work on internalised systemic patterns appearing in the patient's inner dialogue—since in individual therapy, by definition, significant others are usually absent from the therapy room.

At the same time, we moved from a disembodied notion of systems to one that brings to the fore the therapist's and patient's positions in their significant systems: we can reclaim uncertainty only if it is positioned, only if we find our place in systems and contexts (Chapter 6). Such positions are embodied and concrete, influenced by the material determinants of the context.

The nature of therapeutic dialogue

Operationally, the dialogue we are discussing pertains to the domain Karl Jaspers defines as "understanding": a way of comprehending from inside the lived experience of patients through our own.[3] To Bakhtin (1981), understanding is an active process, where the speaker's words must be assimilated by the listener in another conceptual frame. We cannot be in dialogue if we do not act—or react—toward the others, and we can act only if we enter the conversation with all of our ideas, opinions, emotions. We have no guarantee either that our intention can be perceived as such by our patients, or that we are immediately able to understand theirs. Mutual understanding is the result of a long, probably endless, process of negotiation.

If we see therapeutic dialogue as a form of (reciprocal) action, this means that it cannot consist of just words. Extra- and paraverbal activity is equally important, especially in emotional communication—possibly the key element of therapeutic dialogue (see also Seikkula et al., 2015). A purely logocentric idea of dialogue reminds us what Pollard says of Bakhtin, that he "expects too much of language; it cannot account for all aspects of human consciousness, social life and experience" (2008, p. 80). As therapists, we have to better understand our own and the others' emotions, and the ways in which they are expressed within and around discourse, in the form of actions, as we will see in Chapter 5. We should be able to modulate such discursive actions according to dialogical principles.

Applying Bakhtin's thinking to our practice produced a new scenery for our clinical work. Living interaction took the place of the therapist's—or therapeutic team's—personal scrutiny. We had to accept patients in their emerging humanity, without submitting them to categories. Or, better, they could belong to one or more categories, but they could not be fully contained in any of them. The last word did not belong neither to us nor to our patients: the dialogue never ends, and its interruptions are but arbitrary. The technical equipment employed by former systemic therapists was severely reduced: directivity, strategies, reframings, prescriptions, rituals, even some rules of setting, faded out, replace by a less formal, everyday speech, where only specific kinds of questioning survived, occasionally accompanied by some techniques, used for specific purposes, as we have seen in Chapter 3.

One of Bakhtin's key concepts is incompleteness. We see our patient as incomplete, in the sense that any description we can have of them is necessarily limited, that they could always surprise us, preventing us from closing them within any systemic determinism. Our hypotheses must then become even more tentative and minimal. Rather than aiming at an overall view of a situation, they describe a cloud of possibilities, focusing from time to time on different details, without any final point. Subjecting patients to a multiplicity of views, sometimes contradictory, may in turn help them to see the others, the third parties, as incomplete. This process fosters a basic respect for the uniqueness of the others, which, to us, is the very core of the dialogical experience.

Dialogue and context

Sometimes dialogical approaches risk underestimating contextual issues. We never wanted, instead, to renounce to the notion of context, that we consider the first step of systemic understanding (Bertrando, 2000). Actually, contexts became more and more relevant in our therapies. From a systemic perspective, the context contains the dialogue. We cannot choose in total freedom the meaning of what we say and do, because meanings are shaped by the context we are embedded in (Bateson, 1955). In a sense, pluridiscursivity is context reframed in dialogical terms: our words do not belong just to us, they emerge from interaction with other words, from the very history of the language we speak, which, in turn, intersects many other languages or speech genres (Bakhtin, 1981). I develop my way of speaking by assimilating and comparing other discourses. Therapy is a continuing process of re-negotiation of meaning, where an awareness of the context in which it happens is needed. Any negotiation, in turn, opens new contexts, that generate new meanings, and so on.

The Bakhtinian idea of polyphony allows us to challenge notions that often constrained systemic therapy on a Procrustean bed, such as the possibility of fostering "systemic harmony" in patients' lives. On the other hand, it apparently presupposes that any group—and even any individual—is a set of dissonant voices, and any human interaction is completely disorganised, forgetting that "the orchestra has a conductor, the music a composer, and the book an author" (Pollard, 2008, p. 77). Therapy cannot be an encounter of naked, decontextualised people, as if they did not emerge from the complex crossing of contexts where we all live, that in turn we contribute, for our part, to shape, and that give meaning to our actions and words. Lack of context would risk depriving the therapist of their ability to position themselves and their patients in the world.

We dialogue not only with individuals, couples, or families; we also dialogue with the situations and contexts we, as therapists, have to deal with (Schön, 1983). At the same time, we are aware that the context is always a political context, as Michel Foucault (2003, 2004) has shown us. As we stated in Chapter 2, our therapeutic activity is never neutral, and we have to take positions that may be challenging or difficult to hold, because we cannot take refuge in scientific explanations of what happens. We are always constrained by the microphysics of power (Foucault, 1977).

We must, then, perfect our ability to read relational contexts—family, work, school, the therapeutic relationship, up to the wider social and cultural ones. If we can dialogue with the situation, we can find our own place in it, regarding our premises, feelings, expectations, and also understand its evolution in time. If we find our place in the system, we can foresee its possible evolution, and imagine, within its limits, our possible answers—giving people the tools to help them find their place (Chapter 6).

The activity of finding one's place gives depth to the dialogical perspective. On the other hand, we are aware that we see contexts through our premises and prejudices. Contexts do not simply exist "out there", although they influence and restrain us. The context that we see in a situation is necessarily interpreted, modified and possibly distorted by our perspective. What we propose to our patient in dialogue is our interpretation. We should always wonder: is this context that I am seeing the real thing or not? We cannot reach any final certainty about it. This state of doubt about what is real is an inherent characteristic of the systemic-dialogical model. In order to deal with these issues, we can rely on our internal dialogue, what Peter Rober (2005) calls inner conversation. Using the theory of the dialogical self (Chapter 1), we can become aware of the various I-positions we and our patient take in the course of a session, and challenge both.

For example: a patient tells the therapist about a fight with her father; she feels he is blaming her because, after a long course of studies she is earning little money without contributing to the family welfare. The therapist may tend to react from a daughter or son I-position, thus siding more or less openly with the patient. This will enhance the therapeutic alliance but, at the same time, validate the patient's version of her experience without doubting it. If the therapist is able to shift to a parent I-position, they may allow the patient to see the father's view too, and help her to realise the one-sidedness of her own position, possibly opening herself to an alternative perspective.

Consensuality

As we have repeatedly hinted in the previous chapters, the therapeutic process that we envision needs a consensus between therapist and patient. This does not mean that they have to agree about the content of dialogue: as Bakhtin (1984) suggested, therapeutic dialogue—like any form of true dialogue—is not a way of reaching a final agreement. Therapist and patient may dissent about content, and this is not detrimental to the therapeutic process: on the contrary, it is from disagreement with the therapist that the patient may get the new perspectives that they need. Consensus is something different. It regards the therapeutic process.

Since we do not try to impose our views on the patient, we must get their permission to intrude with our views in their world, in every step of therapy. To get consensus means that the patient is informed of what we are saying, of the meanings we attach to it, and of our goals and perspective in doing it. The most important question in this regard is: "Am I making sense? Does what I say make sense to you?" Asking this simple question indicates that we do not take for granted that the patient is passively accepting all that we are saying, and means that the patient can challenge us, ask us what we want to do. It gives back agency to the patient within the dialogue.

Consensuality is a linguistic practice that refers to the performative properties of language (Austin, 1962), to language as politics. If we ask the patient whether what we are saying makes sense, this means that we do not try to impose our meaning over theirs, that we do not believe that our proposal are truer than theirs because we are the experts. It is a linguistic decolonising practice, a way of minimising the impact of our power/knowledge (Foucault, 1982).

Since we are not (only) focused on symptom resolution, or on well-delimited problems that allow for instant solutions, the effects of our intervention are necessarily limited. When the issues that a patient presents are not strictly individual, but entail social, economical, or cultural dimensions, we cannot expect to solve them on the individual level. We can help that patient to understand the context, their position in it, and their possibility for taking action. Taking proper action—and taking responsibility for their actions—will be a consequence of their finding their place, as we will see in Chapter 6.

Dialogue in individual therapy

We developed our systemic-dialogical approach in an interesting period of our professional lives. Although we had both been trained—Paolo especially—within a family therapy perspective, at the turn of the century it was increasingly evident that family therapy could not become the choice treatment for most psychiatric and psychological issues, as many early pioneers had wished (see Bertrando & Toffanetti, 2000). Family therapy remained relevant in particular settings, such as child and adolescent problems or psychotic conditions. Most of our referrals, however, were for individual therapy, due both to economical reasons and to a general tendency to individualism. That process had already begun at the time of the book *Systemic Therapy with Individuals*—actually it had been the main impulse for writing it in the first place.

As a consequence, our approach is probably the first Milan-informed therapy that was born mainly as individual therapy. This is why we do not feel the necessity to detail specific guidelines for individual therapy: the approach itself is oriented toward an individual setting.

At the same time, the form of dialogue is dictated by the setting: it is different to participate in a dialogue with a family, a couple, or an individual patient. In the latter case, our main preoccupation is to introduce the context in the dialogue. We always strive to amplify and complexify contextual references in the dialogue, since no other representative of the context is in the room with us and our individual patient. We foster polyphony in individuals by using internalised others (and related techniques, as we have seen in Chapter 3), internalised communities, and the concept of dialogical self. We pay attention to pluridiscursivity too. We respect the different linguistic codes or ways of speaking our patient displays, without reducing them to our own speech, and from time to time we meta-communicate about speech genres.

We take care to respect the individual. In the individual setting, inevitably closer and more intimate compared to family or couple therapy, we are aware of the possibility to influence the patient beyond our intentions. We are even wary of our own openness and informality, that may become a way to influence them without them noticing. As we have shown in Chapter 3, it is essential for us to check periodically with the patient if they feel understood and accepted, or if they feel we try to force their consent.

Clinical example: an uncertain relationship

Flavia is 21 when her therapy begins. She is studying architecture at the university of Milan. She is living together with other students, and she is very conscious that her studies have a price for her parents, both low-wage labourers. She has a sister and a brother; both are much older than she (33 and 31 respectively) and live in distant cities: her experience, all in all, is close to an only child's.

She comes to therapy full of uncertainty and doubts: she does not know what she wants, she does not want a romantic relationship—and least of all a sexual one. She wonders whether she is in fact asexual. She has had a boyfriend years ago, but she never enjoyed sex with him, and she feels attracted neither toward men nor women. The dominant emotions she brings to therapy are sadness, bewilderment, and anxiety (Chapter 5).

Therapy begins, as usual, with an exploration of her present state, and of the different relationships she is embedded in. When, later, the discourse opens toward the past, the therapist discovers that Flavia's family life has always been somewhat disconnected: her parents are affectionate and kind, but she does not feel their love; the same applies to her siblings, to whom she feels she has no real connection since they left home when she was a small child. She has a group of good friends, but all in all she exudes an aura of loneliness. She loves her university course and is highly engaged in it.

The therapist follows her in her reappraisal of her own life, proposing ideas and hypotheses from time to time, and engaging with her in an ongoing dialogue. There is no "wow moment" in this therapy, but slowly she begins to feel more motivated in what she does, sometimes even enthusiastic, for example when she finally gets her BA. Apparently, she stops feeling good when she is at home: her cohabitation with her parents is claustrophobic, but she lacks financial resources to live on her own. In this situation, the positive event is Daniel, a 27-year-old she meets in this period, with whom she begins a quite rewarding romantic as well as sexual relationship. The therapist is surprised, because that theme has been absent from the therapeutic dialogue for quite a while. Flavia cannot link her ease in beginning the relationship with any specific event, and she states that "it simply happened".

(This is quite common in our therapies. Sometimes a specific session may produce a dramatic, discontinuous change, similar to what was commonplace wisdom in systemic therapy (Boscolo & Bertrando, 1993). Such events, however, are exceptions rather than the norm: usually, our therapeutic dialogues remain open-ended, without the emphatic, sometimes theatrical reframings of Milan systemic therapy. Changes happen through small movements that are fostered by processing in dialogue an array of micro-events. From this process new micro-practices emerge, in a silent, unpredictable way. What changes is not the ideology of our patients, it is their tacit knowledge (Polanyi, 1966): the implicit knowledge that underpins most actions of ours, without us being aware of it. As such, change in tacit knowledge happens outside the consciousness of patients. Change seems continuous rather than discontinuous because it is made of a myriad of tacit micro-changes, and it becomes visible only by hindsight.)

The situation seems rather improved, and therapist and patient begin to discuss the conclusion of therapy. Suddenly, the picture changes: Daniel gets a job offer from the USA, that will be a giant step for his career. The problem is, he has to accept or decline the offer within a few weeks, and he would have to commit to stay in the States for the next couple of years. Which would be very good for him, much less for Flavia: she is literally panicked by the very idea of regressing to be alone in her little village, at her parents' house, with the perspective to wait for two more years. All her apparent wellbeing, all her confidence in herself and in the couple has been stripped away.

Their relationship is badly strained, with a consequent discontent on her part. The therapy has to go on, because she does not feel well with herself, despite her finding a good enough job, that allows her to save with the perspective of leaving her parents' home in a while. Flavia was unhappy without a romantic relationship, and now she is unhappy within a romantic relationship. The situation drags on for some time.

The session we will consider happens some time later.[4]

> "I'm kind of worried," Flavia says, "because things are not going well with Daniel. Last week we hardly communicated with each other, except a few monosyllables on the phone, good morning and good night and that was it. We haven't met, and I don't know what to think, because I'm confused, although I know I shouldn't, because everything tells me to let him go…"
>
> "Are you thinking of leaving him?"
>
> "Yes!"

Now the therapist must understand the evolution of their situation. Flavia points out the path to follow: she is confused, she does not know where she is—and therefore she needs to clarify.

"On the other hand," she says, "there is that part of me that thinks that everything can be fixed by being patient, but I'm fed up of being patient, and I'm also extremely tired at the moment…"

"Then let's try to understand what's going on: how do you explain his attitude?"

The therapist presentifies Daniel in the session through a circular question, then listens. Flavia has a lot to say: Daniel shows the behaviour he displayed at the very beginning of their relationship; he is almost mute, unable to express his emotions unless solicited. His aloofness makes her feel lonely and lost. Flavia thinks this is due to his fear of leaving, but this is just her assumption.

"This means that he feels bad, but doesn't understand how he feels bad?"

The therapist asks a question that is positional and circular at the same time. The question brings her to reflect on her own position: she is frustrated mainly because she cannot share with her man the burdens he bears.

(In this long sequence—a third of the whole session—the therapist is quite laconic, just asking very few questions; such questions, though, help Flavia in creating her own hypotheses about Daniel and their relationship, beyond the therapist's proposals. It is not necessary, in a therapeutic dialogue, to evenly distribute speaking times.)

Together, patient and therapist elaborate on Daniel's emotional closure. Flavia feels betrayed by his retreating. She narrates some episodes where she provoked him on the possibility that he would leave her. She is anguished by his coldness, in sharp contrast to her past claims of physical distance from everybody. The therapist proposes that maybe he tends to leave everything vague, and this prompts her to seek a definition and some reassurance at any cost. In Flavia the therapist feels anxiety, sadness, bitterness, and again a sense of solitude. The two appear to him distant, estranged. After the umpteenth description of "passive aggression" on Daniel's part, the therapist intervenes:

"I feel that he's angry with you, but I don't understand the reason!"

"I wouldn't say angry. Sometimes I provoked him, and he got angry, but that's it."

"I had the feeling he was angry before that, or at least he was flaunting indifference."

"Yes, he flaunted indifference, that's true. Not angry, removed rather than angry, yes. Passive aggressive once, but because I got pushy, and he doesn't like it!"

(When the therapist introduces an emotion, Daniel's supposed anger, Flavia acknowledges some responsibility in provoking him. They discuss the origins of his anger. In the end, she disproves the therapist's initial hypothesis, and proposes a different view of Daniel's affects, namely distance and indifference.)

Flavia seems to live a "return of the old", as if the situation had gone back in time, and the changes in their relationship had not happened at all. The therapist disagrees:

> "What you say is: 'no change was true, and now we are back to the starting point'. It seems to me, instead, that now there is a big further change that needs adaptation, the fact of having to go away. I wonder: maybe it's not something old, but something new that appears old."
>
> "It's possible. I was thinking the same too. I don't feel like excusing him, anyway, because I didn't live it as if nothing had changed. I saw that at the beginning he was trying. Now he stopped." She begins to cry. "This is why, egotistically, I was saying that I feel betrayed. He stopped trying and once again he's taking me for granted. I say 'egotistically' because I understand that the situation is new, but his way to deal with it shouldn't be the old one. All in all, he should at least attempt to let me know what's going on, he should allow me in his head, communicate the bare essential! All this should happen and instead it doesn't."

During the exchange Flavia becomes increasingly pained: she cries, she gets angry, she appears physically uneasy. She tells of her evenings spent agonisingly waiting for him to give a sign. "For better or worse, now in my everyday life I'm happy. The only thing that doesn't work for me is my relationship." Perhaps it is not worth staying in a relationship that makes her feel bad.

(The therapist listens and tries to weigh up possibilities: what could make her feel better? And how can he help her understand? At the same time, as a man, the therapist feels Flavia is slightly edgy toward him, as if he was a representative of the reviled male sex. Now he realises that he is implicitly trying to save the relationship, and to absolve Daniel. He decides to put his position into the open.)

> "I don't know why, when I was speaking I felt in the position of Daniel's counsel for the defence. And I don't even know him!" Flavia laughs. "And so I wondered: why am I doing it? Probably because I know that, with all the suffering that it causes to you, this is a relationship you care about, because, even in the middle of all your difficulties, rather than doing what you—I dare say—had done in the past, that would be to break off—not now, a lot of time ago—you decided instead to take a leap of courage and remain with him, with a great struggle. So when you say: 'Enough is enough, now I can't take it anymore,' it occurs to me: 'What a pity, though!', because it was a big investment."

"This is what makes me angry. This is why I haven't broken up with him, but now I doubt this conviction. And I'm also lucky to have this session today…"

(We are now at two thirds of the session.) She tells of how in the last few days they played fast and loose about the possibility of meeting on the evening after the session. She is ambivalent about going, on the one side attracted, on the other worried of taking charge of him. The therapist tries to put himself in Daniel's shoes, and proposes the simplest emotional hypothesis: that he is scared, much more than she is, and does not know what to do. At the same time, while empathising with Daniel, the therapist emphasises the "as if" quality of his position, asking Flavia for consensuality. She, on her part, accepts many of the therapist's proposals, but continually reminds him of her weariness and disillusion. In the dialogue, they consider the situation from multiple viewpoints: fatigue, abandonment, loneliness, fear of the future, anguish at not being able to rely on each other. Rather than offering solution, the therapist tries to open discourses.

"Sometimes I feel I should love myself a little more," she says, "and that this situation is not fit for me."
"That you should love yourself more is something about which we all agree," the therapist comments, "the issue is: what would show you that you're loving yourself enough?"
"I don't know: being patient or run away from the source of my distress?"

What she finds most frustrating is that Daniel is relapsing, that they are repeating the same pattern they followed in the past, and that his distancing is always at the core of their struggles. The therapist has a proposal:

"Maybe the problem is that this is your tender spot too, distance. In your life, you have always been the first to take a step back—at least this is what you told me in the past. It is as if he were doing the same that you did, but even more decidedly, and without the awareness you have developed."
"Right! I know what he is going through, and I know how difficult it is to let other people in. I know it. On the one hand, I know what it means, and I should be patient, on the other I tell myself: you've been patient enough, he's making fun of you! I don't know what to do, and tonight I must see him, and I don't know what to do!"

The therapist takes a position:

"It's not for me to tell you what to do. But if it were, I would tell you not to anticipate anything, then when you see him, speak out all you feel and say all you have to say."

"It would be natural for me to do it, but it's not exactly right, because it's not exactly right to throw things in his face when he doesn't expect it. But I would do it!"

"Right now, as I see it, you need to communicate these things to him. If you don't, the risk is that somehow things get worse. This is the feeling I have."

The therapist tries to balance the urge to say something he feels is true for him[5] and the need to remain open to Flavia's feelings and ideas. He introduces in his speech several uncertainty markers, so that his proposal becomes less assertive and categorical. She intellectually agrees, developing many hypotheses of her own, but emotionally she remains reluctant. Her stronger fear is to get no answer. The therapist intervenes again:

"I have a proposal: don't expect answers! One thing I always tell my trainees is that in this job it's important to ask questions rather than getting answers. As you maybe noticed, in therapy one asks questions that have no answers. But just asking the question paves the way for different possible thoughts that can be developed afterwards."

The therapist tries to work on Flavia's expectations (Chapter 8): she expects answers and she is disappointed if she does not get them. Flavia acknowledges it, and in this way she becomes critical toward her own hurry. She has not overcome all of her doubts, but admits the possibility to initiate a dialogue with Daniel with different expectations. The session ends with Flavia still caught in her doubts, but with less fear. The therapist closes the session ascertaining not to have been perceived as too prescriptive.

In the end, the encounter between Flavia and Daniel will have no spectacular effects, as the therapist will learn in the following session. Their relationship, however, will go on, and in a few months Flavia will recover the trust and the positive view of the latter period. The therapy will end some time later, with the agreement of maintaining some sessions with a three-month interval, to check the irreversibility of change.

Supervision example: a musical genius

Systemic-dialogical therapy is a multi-layered activity. The possibility of holding multiple perspectives helps us when we are working in supervision too. Our supervision model, inspired to the one devised by Boscolo and Cecchin (1981) in the 1980s, is also comparable to Tom Andersen's (1987) reflecting team. We will deal with both similarities and differences between our method and the reflecting team at the end of this example.

In this case, one of us was supervising a group of four colleagues, all working as private therapists. One of them brings the case of an individual patient he has been working with for a few months, with mixed success. We will call him Norman. He is 22, and lives with his parents and a 15-year-old sister. He lives a secluded life, and spends most of his time in his room, composing electronic music—he is passionate about it—on his computer. He says he is a good composer, having authored dozens of pieces that have never been publicly aired. As per the therapist's knowledge, he could be either a musical genius, or an unrealistic dreamer.

He has been attending a musical college for two years. Each year, he grew more and more tired and disillusioned, to the point of abandoning the course. The second time he did it, the college threatened to permanently exclude him from the courses, unless he recovered enough interest to attend them. Encouraged to look for treatment, his parents found the present therapist, who, after an initial family session, began to work with Norman individually. As happened with the university, he initially accepted, then appeared less and less interested, until he abandoned therapy. Alarmed, the father convinced him to resume the sessions.

In order to help Norman get interested in his studies, the therapist first proposed a motivational method, with no results, then tried to negotiate with him attendance to another musical college, specialised in electronic music. After Norman accepted, his father got deeply involved in his attending: he woke him up in the morning, he brought him to the train station, and so on. The pattern, however, was repeated again: after a promising beginning, Norman once more lost interest in the lessons, until he withdrew, maintaining that the course was too basic for him. After that, he interrupted therapy too.

The parents came back, desperate, for the third time. Norman had grown (verbally) abusive, especially toward the mother; once, after being reproached, he reacted strongly, even spitting in her face, to her dismay. Norman was feeling scatterbrained, confused, uninterested, apathetic. After another violent quarrel, he went out of the house barefoot, scratching his arms and screaming: "I'm useless, I'm useless!" This brought the parents to involve several renowned psychiatrists, to look for solutions nobody was able to find.

Confused, the therapist resumed treatment again, facing a complete stalemate. The week before supervision he saw the parents, and advised them to try "benevolent sabotage", a strategic method where the parents should appear more inept than their son—e.g., forgetting to respect schedules, or to prepare dinner—so to give him back responsibility and competence in managing his own life. The therapist, though, has little hope for it.

He feels that Norman is a strange patient, "stone-faced", cold and unemotional, apparently uninterested in the dialogue with him, impenetrable. He always answers questions through platitudes. The only time Norman appeared genuinely involved in a session was when they once talked about his music, but the therapist had not followed through. As for the family, the parents appear activated and anguished, whereas his sister never participated.

At the beginning, the supervisor looks for parallel processes: Norman and the family, Norman and the university, Norman and the therapist (activating in his dialogical self a "first order" therapist position): Norman is always able to stalemate his interlocutors, through silence and passivity, triggering in anybody a feeling of uselessness. He then asks the therapist about his feelings and thoughts. The strongest feelings regard Norman's alienation, that in turn generates in the therapist thoughts he would not subscribe: "process schizophrenia", chronicity, a future career as psychiatrist patient. The supervisor notices that the same thoughts were beginning to exist in his mind too (psychiatrist position). He also observes that the therapist is positioning himself as a parents' ally, trying to find the right method to induce Norman to study, and, generally, to get him interested in things (strategic position, well exemplified by the benevolent sabotage idea).

One of the participants notices that nobody, apparently, is trying to understand Norman on his own terms (empathic position). The supervisor then tries to put himself in Norman's shoes (phenomenological position): how does he experience all those people who want him to do things, and have their own ideas about his outcomes? What does he actually want? What does the therapist want? Do we want Norman to become a good neoliberal young man? A dialogue is promoted. The supervisor asks: "Could we try to change our criteria for success? What is actually a success? What could Norman feel as a success? Is he feeling useless, or are we—all the others—feeling him as useless, because he is supposed to do useful things according to our own criteria?"

Another participant proposes that somebody, maybe the therapist himself, could actually get interested in his music, listening to it, discussing it with him, without implicitly—strategically—suggesting that it could become a successful profession. Another group member suggests a different view: what about the parents, and their hopelessness (parents' position)? It could be important to involve them, too. Together, the supervision group widens its perspective. The therapist begins to find his place in regard to both Norman and his parents (Chapter 6). One possibility could be to resume family sessions, also including the sister, thus going beyond the polarisation between Norman and his parents that recently has shaped both family life and therapy. To join with the whole family, shifting the setting from individual to family therapy, the therapist could acknowledge the suffering of them all: everybody is feeling bad, although in different ways. It could be useful also to consider the other professionals involved, but only after strengthening the therapeutic alliance with the whole family

As the therapist listens, he seems more and more relieved from a burden. The supervision process does not get to a conclusion, nor to the definition of any specific intervention; it just proposes and juxtaposes multiple readings, considering different levels in the system. At the end, the therapist says he feels freed from the feeling of senselessness that was pervading his work.

After a few months, a follow-up will reveal that few of the group proposals were actually put to work, but the feeling of lightness and variety activated in the supervision allowed the therapist to reconstruct a good enough alliance with both Norman and the rest of the family.

Our use of dialogue in supervision, as stated before, is close to Tom Andersen's reflecting team, that—besides its well-known use in clinical practice—has been widely employed in this context too (Friedman, 1995). We are indebted to Andersen and the other colleagues who, in different times and places, developed the reflecting team approach, for the openness of the dialogue between participants, both when therapy and supervision are concerned, and for the absence of a unified, concluding perspective. At the same time, there are differences. Compared to the reflecting team approach, we try to be more aware of the different I-positions that supervisor, supervisee and patient adopt in different moments of the dialogue. And we do not refrain from creating and discussing systemic hypotheses in the process, whereas such state is discouraged for orthodox reflecting teams from the very beginning (see Andersen, 1987). Also, reflecting teams usually fosters deeply emotional dialogues, but emotions are seldom the subject of the dialogues themselves. We have learned in time, instead, that focusing on emotions can enhance both reciprocal understanding and change. We will try to show how we do it in the next chapter.

Notes

1 In conceiving the systemic-dialogical approach we were not directly influenced by open dialogue, that we came to know later. If we must cite an influence in that field, it could rather be reflecting team. Practising it created a quite different experience compared to the use of therapeutic team we had experienced in our Milan-style training and early practice.

2 A good example can be the sharp critique of city planning and the praise of self-organisation of cities posed by architectural writer Jane Jacobs as early as 1961: she observed that citizens tended to self-organise, and to use public spaces in a way always different to the one imagined by city planners. The actual organisation of any city—successful or unsuccessful—is the result of the tension between imposed rules and unplanned initiative (Jacobs, 2011).

3 Jaspers (1997) distinguishes Explanation (*Erklären*) from Understanding (*Verstehen*). Explanation, used in natural sciences, means that we can causally explain a phenomenon by individuating the elements that make it up, interweaving those elements in temporal series, and making one the cause of the others. Understanding, used in human sciences, means that the examiner understands other humans from within, having direct access to that phenomenon that we are.

4 We will not use a full transcript here, because we just want to give the overall flavour of the session. All the sentences in quotation marks, however, are later transcriptions from the session recording.

5 A "moment of truth", as described in Bertrando (2015), Chapter 8.

References

Andersen, T. (1987). The reflecting team: Dialogue and meta-dialogue in clinical work. *Family Process*, 26 (4): 415–428. DOI:10.1111/j.1545–5300.1987.00415.x.

Anderson, H. & Goolishian, H. (1992). The client is the expert: A not-knowing approach to therapy. In: S. McNamee & K.J. Gergen (Eds.), *Therapy as Social Construction* (pp. 25–39). Sage.

Austin, J.L. (1962). *How to Do Things With Words*. Oxford University Press.

Bakhtin, M.M. (1981). Discourse in the novel. In: M. Holquist (Ed.), *The Dialogic Imagination* (pp. 259–422). Texas University Press (original edition 1935).

Bakhtin, M.M. (1984). C. Emerson (Ed.). *Problems of Dostojevski's Poetics*, University of Minnesota Press (original edition 1968).

Bateson, G. (1948). Metalogue: Why do things get in a muddle? In: *Steps to an Ecology of Mind* (pp. 3–8). Chandler Publishing Company, 1972.

Bateson, G. (1955). A theory of play and fantasy. In: *Steps to an Ecology of Mind* (pp. 177–193). Chandler Publishing Company, 1972.

Bateson, G. (1972). *Steps to an Ecology of Mind*. Chandler Publishing Company.

Bertrando, P. (2000). Text and context. Narrative, postmodernism, and cybernetics. *Journal of Family Therapy*, 22 (1): 83–103. DOI:10.1111/1467–6427.00139.

Bertrando, P. (2004). Systems in evolution. Luigi Boscolo and Gianfranco Cecchin in conversation with Paolo Bertrando and Marco Bianciardi. *Journal of Family Therapy*, 26: 213–223. DOI:10.1111/j.1467–6427.2004.00279.x.

Bertrando, P. (2007). *The Dialogical Therapist*. Karnac.

Bertrando, P. & Arcelloni, T. (2006). Hypotheses are dialogues: sharing hypotheses with clients. *Journal of Family Therapy*, 28: 370–387. DOI:10.1111/j.1467–6427.2006.00358.x.

Bertrando, P. & Toffanetti, D. (2000). *Storia della terapia familiare. Le persone, le idee*. Raffaello Cortina Editore.

Boscolo, L. & Bertrando, P. (1993). *The Times of Time: A Perspective on Time in Systemic Therapy and Consultation*. 2nd edition. Routledge, 2020.

Boscolo, L. & Cecchin, G. (1981). Training in systemic therapy at the Milan Centre. In: R. Whiffen & J. Byng-Hall (Eds.), *Family Therapy Supervision: Recent Developments in Practice*. Academic Press, pp. 153–166.

Foucault, M. (1977). *Discipline and Punish: The Birth of the Prison* (translated by A. Sheridan). Allen Lane (original edition 1975).

Foucault, M. (1982). The subject and power. In: H.L. Dreyfus & F. Rabinow, *Michel Foucault: Beyond Structuralism and Hermeneutics*. Chicago: University of Chicago Press.

Foucault, M. (2003). *Le pouvoir psychiatrique. Course au Collège de France 1973–1974*. ed. J. Lagrange. Gallimard.

Foucault, M. (2004). *Naissance de la biopolitique. Cours au Collège de France 1978–79*. Gallimard.

Friedman, S. (Ed.) (1995). *The reflecting team in action: Collaborative practice in family therapy*. The Guilford Press.

Guilfoyle, M. (2003). Dialogue and power: A critical analysis of power in dialogical therapy. *Family Process*, 42: 331–344. DOI:10.1111/j.1545–5300.2003.00331.x.

Guttman, H. (1991). Systems theory, cybernetics, and epistemology. In: A.S. Gurman & D.P. Kniskern (Eds.), *Handbook of Family Therapy*, Vol. II. Brunner/Mazel.

Harries-Jones, P. (1995). *A Recursive Vision: Ecological Understanding and Gregory Bateson*. University of Toronto Press.

Holquist, M. (2002). *Dialogism: Bakhtin and His World*. 2nd edition. Routledge.

Jacobs, J. (2011). *The Death and Life of Great American Cities*. 50th Anniversary Edition. Modern Library (original edition published 1961).

Jaspers, K. (1997). *General Psychopathology* (J. Hoenig & M.V. Hamilton, transl.). Johns Hopkins University Press (original edition 1913).

Johnson, S. (2001). *Emergence: The Connected Lives of Ants, Brains, Cities, and Software*. Scribner.

Polanyi, M. (1966). *The Tacit Dimension*. Peter Smith, 1983.

Pollard, R. (2008). *Dialogue and Desire. Michail Bakhtin and the Linguistic Turn in Psychotherapy*. Karnac.

Press, G.A. (Ed.) (1993). *Plato's Dialogues. New Studies and Interpretations*. Rowman & Littlefield.

Rober, P. (2005). The therapist's self in dialogical family therapy: some ideas about not-knowing and the therapist's inner conversation. *Family Process*, 44: 477–495. DOI:10.1111/j.1545–5300.2005.00073.x.

Schön, D.A. (1983). *The Reflective Practitioner: How Professionals Think in Action*. Basic Books.

Seikkula, J., Karvonen, A., Kykyri, V., Kaartinen, J. & Penttonen, M. (2015). The Embodied Attunement of Therapists and a Couple within Dialogical Psychotherapy: An Introduction to the Relational Mind Research Project. *Family Process*, 54: 703–715. DOI:10.1111/famp.12152.

Selvini Palazzoli, M., Boscolo, L., Cecchin, G., & Prata, G. (1980a). Hypothesizing-circularity-neutrality. Three guidelines for the conductor of the session. *Family Process*, 19: 3–12. DOI:10.1111/j.1545–5300.1980.00003.x.

Chapter 5

Emotions

The second pillar of the systemic-dialogical approach is emotions. We regard emotions as a primary factor both in human life and in therapy: we need the rationality of emotions (de Sousa, 1987) to carry on the activities of everyday life. At the same time, we consider them as systemic and dialogical phenomena. Any emotion one of us feels and displays, is—to an extent, at least—a consequence and a response to an emotion displayed by someone else. Other people are usually affected by the emotions we display, in turn develop their own emotions toward us, and so on. We see human systems (also) as networks of emotions interacting with each other. In our understanding, emotions mostly happen in interaction within human systems; the subjective experience of feeling, however, pertains to the individual (Bertrando, 2015).

In order to illustrate our way of working with emotions—already described in detail in the book *Emotions and the Therapist* (Bertrando, 2015)—we will use as an example one of the emotions that we found more intriguing and relevant to deal with: shame.

Emotions in systems and dialogues

Some of the pioneers of family therapy paid great attention to emotional experience: Murray Bowen, Ivan Boszormenyi-Nagy, Virginia Satir and Carl Whitaker among others (see Becvar & Becvar, 2013). We cannot say the same of the systemic approaches born out of Bateson's thinking, such as the MRI's brief therapy (Watzlawick, Jackson, & Beavin, 1967) or Jay Haley's (1973) strategic therapy. Early systemic therapists aimed first of all at establishing a distance from psychoanalysis and its supposedly individualistic emphasis on emotions. In their view, emotions distracted the therapist from systemic phenomena. Through the original Milan team, this attitude was transmitted to most postmodern approaches (Krause, 1993). More recently, systemic theories were revised, giving more consideration to emotional experience and their therapeutic consequences: this is apparent in David Pocock's (2010) proposals, centred on the relationship between emotions and attachment patterns, in Inga-Britt Krause's (1993) work on the anthropological

DOI: 10.4324/9781003381754-6

underpinnings of systemic therapy, and especially in Glenda Fredman's (2007) work, where emotions are connected both to discourses and bodily postures.

Similarly to Fredman, we see emotions as messages exchanged within a human system, rather than inner properties of individuals (Planalp, 1999); such messages act both as reciprocal information, and motivation to action (Krause, 1993), turning individual bodies into "social bodies" (Dumouchel, 1995). To see emotions as embedded in relationships, of course, is an episte-mological choice. We do not mean to diminish the other facets of emotion—biological, evolutionary, developmental, intrapsychic, etc (see Lewis & Havi-land-Jones, 2000). We simply choose to deal with emotions in a way that can be useful for our therapies.

As noted above, in this chapter we will use one emotion as a paradigmatic example of our emotion-based practice. We chose shame because we have discovered it is relevant in many of our therapies, although patients often are unaware it. Of course, the way we work on shame can be used with any other emotion we encounter in our clinical practice.

Shame is not a thing

What is shame, first of all? What is an emotion? We believe that emotions are processes rather than objects. Any time we name shame, it does not mean that we are considering a "thing" called shame. We are rather using a shortcut to indicate a process where someone is ashamed, someone is maybe shaming them, someone else sees and reacts to that exchange of shaming and being ashamed, and so on. When we deal with shame—or any other emotion—we must keep in mind that we are dealing with processes.

We are interested in the characteristic of the emotional process called shame: how shame appears in interaction, how it is embedded in relation-ships, how it may define (emotionally) a specific human system. This is how Sylvan Tomkins, in his major work on emotion, describes shame:

> Shame is the affect of indignity, of defeat, of transgression and of alie-nation. Though terror speaks to life and death, and distress makes of the world a vale of tears, yet shame streaks deepest into the heart of man. While terror and distress hurt, they are wounds inflicted from outside which penetrate the smooth surface of the ego, but shame is felt as an inner torment, a sickness of the soul. It does not matter whether the humiliated one has been shamed by derisive laughter or whether he mock himself. In either event he feels himself naked, defeated, alienated, lack-ing in dignity or worth. ... Shame is the most reflexive of affects, in that the phenomenological distinction between the subject and object of shame is lost.
>
> (Tomkins, 1963, pp. 351 and 359)

Tomkins emphasises the interior, private quality of shame. The very word "shame" comes from ancient German *skam*, "infamy", which in turn contains ancient Indo-European *kam*, "to cover, to veil, to hide" (Belpoliti, 2010). Shame is self-conscious, since it requires subjects to be aware of what they feel: they become even too conscious of their face and the expression of their emotions, to the point that their very shame reactions, like blushing, increase their own shame (Lewis, 2000). At the same time, shame is a social emotion too, namely an emotion produced necessarily by the presence of others. We can be happy, angry or sad without the necessity of someone else in the proximity, but we need somebody else, actual or imagined, in order to get ashamed. To feel ashamed means to acknowledge the existence and the importance of the other: our very feeling of exposure means that we have internalised the look of the other, which can make us feel ashamed even when we are alone—there is always some other, real or imagined, beside (inside) us (Sartre, 2001).

Other self-conscious, social emotions, like pride of contempt, induce us to increase our relationship with the others. If we are proud, we want everybody to see us and know it, whereas, if we are ashamed, we diminish our contact with others and we withdraw into ourselves, reducing or blocking our communication. We avoid the others' gaze, avert our eyes, lower our head, and often blush.[1] There is some ambivalence too. We avert our gaze, but at the same time surveil the others in order to understand their reactions: "In shame I wish to continue to look and to be looked at, but also I do not wish to do so ... Self-consciousness is heightened by virtue of the unwillingness of the self to renounce the object" (Tomkins, 1963, p. 361).

In most of his memorial work about his experience of the extermination camp in Auschwitz, writer Primo Levi deals with shame: the Nazi guards' contempt generated shame in the deportees. Despite the fact of being victims of unbearable violence, they became ashamed and such shame extended to their whole lives. When the Red Army freed the lager, the soldiers were, in turn, ashamed of the very scene they were witnessing: shame was contagious. In the end, survivors were ashamed of the very fact of having survived (Levi, 1986).

We can be ashamed "of" something we have done, or "for" somebody else who has done something, provided that we have some affective ties with them. We can be ashamed for the action of some member of our family, or even for the whole community we are part of. In all these cases, shame is easily accompanied by guilt, as we will see later on. Different is the case where we get ashamed for the blunder of somebody we do not even know, out of sheer empathy.

Maria comes from a family where she witnessed scenes of violence between her parents, and where both parents continually shamed her in front of others. Now she is ashamed of them, but at the same time she brings shame on herself: she gets ashamed when they create embarrassing situations. She also found a partner that exposes her to the same kind of embarrassment, due to his public outbursts. In therapy she remembers that in her family of origin her feelings, impressions, considerations, were always disconfirmed, bringing her to be doubtful of herself. Shame became pervasive, involving also the perception of her own body: shame "of being discovered", of intimacy, of sex. Therapy with her must take her shame into account, working on the relationships where she is not shamed, and trying to construct new bridges toward others. In this process, it is essential to work on the therapeutic relationship, where the therapist is very careful to create a completely shame-free environment.

Communicating shame

We do not arrive to an encounter with others coming out of an (emotional) void. Our past and recent history plays an essential part in what we feel. But the virtual emotions we may feel are actualised only in the encounter: even when we experience feelings with ourselves alone, we are engaged in some inner dialogue (Rober, 2005), that becomes an encounter of sorts.

As Kenneth Gergen (1991) has observed, the metaphor of the "deep interior" as the source for the stability of the self was created in the romantic period, and entailed a primacy of emotions, which were considered as direct expression of the "unseen power" that resides within each human being. Yet such a romantic view—or any contemporary counterpart of it—is historically and culturally conditioned, and it is not the only possible way of conceiving emotions. We prefer to locate the virtual space for emotion not underneath (or above) individual consciousness, but rather *in between* the people that constitute the interpersonal system. We think that every time we are together with another person, a relational system is created, which has—among others—emotional characteristics.

In our view, we would not feel anything unless we were part of a meaningful emotional interchange: a dialogue. Our emotions, too, are part of such interchange. As such, they are not our private property. Any emotion any of us feels or shows, we maintain, commences in some interaction, and is aimed at somebody. We like to say: every emotion comes from somewhere and goes somewhere, to emphasise the interactional, superindividual nature of emotion. Such interplay creates a network of emotions, conveyed partly through discourse, partly through nonverbal communication (see Hatfield et al., 1994; Planalp, 1999). Emotional processes also involve all other elements of human systems. Gergen (1991, p. 166) maintains that any emotion one feels at a given moment is but part of a more elaborate interaction he defines as an "emotional scenario": the emotion I feel as being "my own" is simply the part I play within the scenario. This, of course, also applies to shame: it emerges in communication, and is reciprocally influenced by other emotions, as we will see shortly.

Finally, shame—like any other emotion—has a rationality of its own (de Sousa, 1987; Damasio, 1994). Emotional processes should not be considered in opposition to rational processes, as it happened in most of the history of Western thought (Averill, 1974). As Erving Goffman (1959) has shown, the different degrees of shame, beginning with embarrassment, and ending with humiliation, are powerful social regulators. Through getting ashamed—and shaming—several kinds of social activities are performed, evaluated, and responded to.

Dominant shame, tacit shame

Carol Magai and Jeannette Haviland-Jones (2002) consider all human systems—individuals as well as families and larger units—as self-organising dynamic systems, namely unstable, fluctuating systems that are organised by some variables:

> Certain preferences for thoughts, feelings, and activity will develop over time; in dynamic systems terms, these are called attractors. Similarly, the system will also develop certain aversions for particular thoughts, feelings, and activities; in dynamic systems terms, these are called repellers.
>
> (p. 44)

According to these authors, emotions are among the most relevant and effective attractors and repellers. Drawing on their work, we think that some emotions dominate the scene of a therapeutic situation, whereas others are apparently absent, yet seem to exert some influence on the people involved. We define the former as "dominant emotions", since they dominate the feelings of everybody involved, and the latter as "tacit emotions", emotions that are there but do not speak (Bertrando, 2015, Chapter 3).

In our relational view, dominant and tacit emotions are not the product of a person's inner circumstances. They are moulded, and made either dominant or tacit, by the relational emotional network in which each person is embedded. A person living in a family where shame is a dominant emotion may become in time more prone to shame, until their shame becomes one of their dominant emotions; but they could instead deny their shame, with pride becoming a dominant and shame a tacit emotion. We found no deterministic pathway in our clinical practice: the ways in which emotions become dominant and tacit are different for each family and each individual.

Dominant emotions are not necessarily prominent in a person's whole life. The same person may feel easily ashamed with strangers, and show no trace of shame in their family or couple interaction. An emotion may be dominant just in a specific episode, e.g., a therapeutic session. In all cases, dominant emotions are the ones that occupy the centre stage.

The processes concerning tacit emotions are similar: an emotion may be avoided in public, thus becoming tacit, and be dominant in private life. Or it can become untenable in a specific moment, and at that point become tacit, which does not prevent it from becoming dominant again in a different moment. Such different possibilities show that dominant and tacit emotions are manifold: they can be solid and stable, and maintain their characteristics for the whole life of a person or even of a family, or they can be unstable and mutable, changing from time to time.

Dominant emotions are usually easy to single out for the therapist, because they tend to be loud and clear. Identifying them is a hypothesising process, since we can never be absolutely certain about what we see or feel in the other, but hypothesising about dominant emotions is comparatively easy. Tacit emotions, instead, remain hidden and are hardly detectable, although they still exert an influence on all involved. They can be key elements for therapy, because they indicate processes that are usually invisible to the patient. At the same time, they are difficult to identify: how can we know that a given emotion is tacit, rather than simply absent? How can we avoid planting an emotion in the patient? In individual therapy the situation is especially tricky, because there is no other person in the room who could bring that emotion to the fore. We must be cautious, sensitive, and most of all mindful that all we can do is proposing hypotheses rather than giving truths.

For some patients, shame is a strong dominant emotion. They propose themselves as shy, secluded, avoidant. They easily blush. Some psychiatric conditions, such as social phobia or avoidant personality disorder, are usually associated with anxiety, but appear more closely related to shame: some patients have been publicly shamed, like Maria in the previous example, other have suffered from overtly humiliating experiences. Other people feel ashamed only in very specific conditions; their shame is related to some specific system rather than their overall personality.

For example, Noemi tells a story of having been constantly shamed by her father and, at the same time, having been ashamed of her mother, a woman described as chronically depressed and passive. She has developed, in time, severe obsessive-compulsive symptoms. Now she looks for substitute mothers everywhere, first at school and the university, now in her workplace; her present substitute mother is the head of her service. Noemi is constantly haunted by mixed feelings of guilt, shame, and anxiety: nothing she does is right, but what she mostly fears is her "mother's" disapproval. This makes her feel ashamed of nearly whatever she does. The therapist tries to help her distance herself from her past experience, locating her shame in the place where it started, and fostering a dialogue between her present and her past self. Noemi is bringing her past—her mother-centred shame—into the present, the therapist tries to help her to reposition her shame in the past, freeing her from repeating the same pattern over and over again (see Boscolo & Bertrando, 1993, Chapter 6).

Some people are ashamed without realising it, or they cannot name their own shame. In those cases, shame is a tacit emotion. When we feel this may be the case, we try to understand whether shame is indeed a tacit emotion, or whether it is just not there. Here a delicate process of questioning is needed, in order not to induce the patient to say what the therapist would like to hear, or even to feel what the therapist think they should feel. We will deal with that process in the second section of this chapter.

Shame and its relatives

Shame exists within a complex tangle of emotions, that constitute the affective landscape of our experience. A shame reaction may come from an encounter with anger or contempt. Guilt and again anger can be companions to shame. We can also turn shame into opposite emotions, such as pride or indignation. We will now draw a tentative map of such interactions, in order to get our bearings in our clinical work.

The shame continuum

We can see shame as part of an emotional continuum, where the same basic affect appears with varying degrees of intensity: shyness, embarrassment, shame, humiliation.[2] Embarrassment can be considered as a weaker form of shame, and shyness as a tendency to become easily embarrassed. As we have seen, Erving Goffman maintains that embarrassment and anticipation of embarrassment are essential to social life: the subtle interplay of reciprocal embarrassment produces a distance between people that allows safe interaction.[3] The relationship between shame and humiliation is more complex: the difference is qualitative rather than quantitative, as we shall see shortly.

Guilt

Many patients of ours struggle to distinguish shame from guilt. They tend to use the word "guilt" to express any regretful feeling due to something they have done or failed to do. We think instead that the distinction between guilt and shame is relevant. We can regard shame as a violation of collective values, whereas guilt would be a violation of inner ones. Guilt is a process that may or may not involve the other; sometimes we feel guilty without anybody accusing us. Shame, on the other hand, is always public: without the gaze of somebody else—real or imagined—there is no shame. Shame, therefore, implies an exposure to others, whereas guilt involves a contradiction between our actions and our own judgement of them.[4] Briefly, shame tends to be immersive, outward-looking, and concerns the relationship between the person and the eye of the other; guilt is more punctual, inward-directed, and concerns individual actions and the relationship of the person with herself. Sometimes one can even "use" guilt to contrast shame. Guilt implies some possible atonement or forgiving on the part of the other, which is impossible with shame: there is no absolution from shame.

Contempt

Contempt is complementary to shame. Shame is inner-directed and produces a de-evaluation of oneself; contempt is outer-directed and produces a de-evaluation of others. If we despise someone, we want them to be ashamed of themselves; if we are ashamed, we feel—or fear being—despised. Contempt does not necessarily generate shame, though. According to Tomkins (1963), contempt more easily evokes anger. For the other's contempt to evoke shame instead of anger or indifference, the other must be an actual or potential source of positive affect, only partially diminished by her contemptuous stance. If contempt is associated with shame, without any of the two prevailing, the relationship will probably oscillate, thus creating an unstable emotional system, open to change. Such a change will be, in turn, unstable: the therapist must work hard to drag their patient out of such a dynamic.

Anger

Open shame is not related, usually, to anger. The very dynamics of shame—withdrawing into oneself, disconnecting from others, feeling deeply distressed about oneself—contrast with the development of anger. Shame may alternate with anger in an unstable emotional system, or it may be hidden by anger (a strong dominant emotion), thus becoming tacit. In both cases, the result can be an escalation of violence: denied shame leads to an increase of anger and destructiveness, especially in men.[5] Patriarchal prejudices may easily prevent men from accepting or even from feeling shame, believing it to be emasculating and replacing it instead with anger (Chapter 2). In studying a therapist/patient interaction, Thomas Scheff (1998) observed an early misunderstanding due to the patient's shame, that became angry withdrawal.[6] When we find in a patient this kind of angry indifference, it is useful to go beyond the mere observation of the dominant emotion (in this case, anger), and to look for tacit emotions. Usually, a careful questioning process is necessary if shame is a tacit emotion, because patients are ashamed to be ashamed. A couple, a family, a community where shame circulates without being fully acknowledged are easily subjected, as we have seen, to escalations of anger and destructiveness.

Humiliation

We can consider humiliation as the passive equivalent of shame: other people submit us to humiliation; we can be ashamed without anybody shaming us, but we are humiliated only when somebody else shames or despises us (Rigotti, 1998). Shame is connected to responsibility too: we get properly ashamed when we feel somewhat responsible for what is happening us, otherwise we are humiliated (by others).[7] Humiliation and shame have been widely used by power institutions to control minorities, as we will see in the following section. Historically, the poor have been humiliated because they were considered responsible for their own poverty; racial and gender minorities in turn have been humiliated for being "inferior", "deviant", or "perverted". Humiliation may then be subjectivated as shame, leading in turn to phenomena such as internalised racism or internalised homophobia, where minorities internalise and identify with their oppressors, despising themselves for their own very condition, and living in shame.[8]

We may wonder, too, whether a situation of disguised humiliation, where, for example, we are made responsible for events that we cannot control, may lead us to feel ashamed (see Lini & Bertrando, 2020). Humiliation may be annihilating, or, on the contrary, be the origin of indignation and furious anger.

Pride

If contempt is the complement of shame, pride is its opposite (Tracy & Robins, 2007). Pride is a twofold emotion. It can be a sense of satisfaction with ourselves, with a feeling of almost physical pleasantness; it makes us willing to show ourselves and our accomplishments to others, wishing to be seen. But it can also turn into what the ancient Greeks called hubris, the wish to go beyond our boundaries and overwhelm others, without recognising our limitations (Watt Smith, 2016a).

Any social interaction produces either pride or shame (Cooley, 1922). These emotions signal the state of the relationship: true pride signals a secure bond (connectedness), shame a threatened one (disconnect). Historically, social minorities found a way of subverting the shaming they received from the majority by turning shame into pride: black pride (Fredrickson, 1996), gay pride and queer culture (Turner, 2000) took the most stigmatised and shamed characteristic of each group, and made them into reasons for pride: the Afro hairstyle, outrageous poses, the "faggot" stigma, became symbols of pride. All this is relevant for therapy, as we will see.

Indignation

Another emotion is on the opposite side of shame, this time with a less optimistic frame: indignation. Embedded in indignation there is anger and often contempt, that seek a response from the other, together with some excitement. Contrary to shame, indignation induces the person to act.[9] If shame undergoes a positive (empowering) transformation, it becomes pride; if the transformation is negative (aggressive), shame becomes indignation. When we become proud, we address toward ourselves a positive feeling; when we become indignant, we address toward the others who we feel are outraging us a negative feeling; we get angry, aggressive, blaming (Stratton,

2003). In shame one wishes to hide and possibly disappear, whereas in both pride and indignation there is a wish to become visible. In both cases, the person leaves the victim position, and finds a different stance toward the others, getting at the centre of their attention.

Indignation is a composite emotion, containing a good measure of anger. Compared to pure anger, though, it can be considered more emotionally rational: the indignant person is aware of the consequences of their actions, the angry or quick-tempered person often is not. Indignation brings the person to act deliberately, in order to achieve specific consequences. Sometimes indignation becomes resentment, i.e., the transformation of negative self-focused emotions, particularly shame, into anger or hatred directed at presumed out-groups, such as political and cultural elites, refugees, immigrants, strangers of any kind. Briefly, the movement from shame (humiliation) to indignation to resentment easily leads to political populism (Salmela, 2019).

Shame, society and culture

Emotions are not mere biological reactions. They exist within a wider network of cognitions and institutions that constitute the texture of our social and intimate life. As such, they are standardised by culture. We attach a value to what we feel—or to how we express what we feel—depending on our cultural heritage, and this may have a deep effect on emotional exchange (Lutz, 1988).[10] Gregory Bateson spoke of the "ethos" of a culture, "which we may define as the expression of a *culturally standardised system of organisation of the instincts and emotions of the individuals*" (Bateson, 1936, p. 118, italics in the original). This means that in different cultures, and in different periods within the same culture, emotions take a different meaning, and have a different social usage.

In this respect, shame is a very interesting emotion to investigate. It is quite difficult to single out a culture where shame is irrelevant.[11] Shame is an index of the degree of social cohesion within a society: the more the society is cohesive and ordered, the more its members will tend to feel ashamed in the proper situations (Turnaturi, 2016). Since the times of the ancient Greeks, shame has been the mirror image of honour and pride. Some of Franz Kafka's narratives offer examples of a deep, pervasive shame within a patriarchal and hierarchical society. In the final scene of *The Process*, before being killed "as a dog", its hero Josef K. feels "as if his shame would live on after him" (Kafka, 2009, p. 165).

The definition of shame—i.e., what one should be ashamed of—depends in many ways on power: who has power also has the authority to decide the boundaries of shame. Traditionally, institutions like the Church or the State had exclusive access to that power, with the possibility of using it to get rid of a social minority. It happened when the Nazis used shame to undermine the

Hebrew population in Germany, and it is still happening today, as Martha Nussbaum (2004) notices in her analysis of American law. Similarly, shaming is a component of the stigma traditionally applied both to psychiatric patients and to people with disability (Goffman, 1963).

Today, social media seem to have gained a fair share of that power—for example, to decide whether a body with a presumed excess weight is shameful (Chapter 2). This kind of public shame coming "from below" can be as destructive and humiliating as shaming coming from positions of power (Ronson, 2015).[12] The opposite may also be true, however: sometimes social organisations shame the powers that be, transforming shame from a conservative force into and agent of change (Jacquet, 2015). Which brings us to the evolution of shame in a postmodern world: despite being a social emotion—possibly the most social of all emotions—shame today is becoming more individualistic.

Neoliberal shame

Shame has always been deeply rooted in social standards. In the past, people got ashamed when they did not conform to strict standards and rules in a static society. This was not necessarily desirable: unveiling non-heterosexual desires, or adultery, as in the case of the heroine in Nathaniel Hawthorne's (2003) *Scarlet Letter*, was considered shameful and condemned as such. Conversely, our present time is often described as shameless. This apparent eclipse of shame is usually attributed to the exhibitionism characterising liquid modernity (Chapter 1; see also Belpoliti, 2010). In a society where everybody must appear and perform on a metaphorical stage, there is apparently little room left for shame, which requires a community with solid shared values and a corresponding moral disposition on the part of the ashamed individual.

The fact is, shame did not disappear, it simply changed. Today, it concerns a perceived failure in maintaining the required performance, in terms of beauty, success, or money (Chapters 1 and 2). Showing one's private recesses is not shameful; we get ashamed when we cannot show what we "should". Italian psychoanalyst Anna Maria Pandolfi (2002) calls it "amoral shame", as opposed to traditional "moral shame". Philosopher Agnes Heller (1976) likewise distinguishes a more superficial "shame on the skin" from "deep shame". She thinks that moral, "deep" shame entails some sense of guilt, which is totally absent from amoral shame "on the skin", which can be instead characterised as a shame of being ashamed, of not being authentic, of lacking possessions, experiences, success, and so on.

We may call it neoliberal shame: advanced capitalism utilises discourses of shame to reinforce the sense of the citizen subject as consumer and thus shame those who cannot participate. In this process, there is no difference between an individual unwilling to conform, and an individual who simply cannot afford to conform. They are both shamed—sometimes humiliated—

as if they decided to stay out of the race, and therefore cast as losers: the definition of "loser" became one of the most humiliating of all insults.

This is how shame, in liquid modernity, becomes individualistic: the failed achievements we get ashamed of pertain individually to each one of us. The eye of the other does not look for adherence to rules, it looks for (individual) performances: shame becomes another facet of the relentless competition the postmodern individual is constantly engaged in. Neoliberal shame is performance shame: it concerns some insufficiency, a lack of something, rather than the excess, the "doing what we are not supposed to do" that characterises moral shame.

We are ashamed in the face of people we know, as has always been the case, but the people we are ashamed of can also be faceless—the invisible presence of social media. The possibility of being instantly shamed for something we have done—or neglected to do—is well-known (Frye, 2022).[13] Also, social media are present-oriented: people post images or document actions which are not shameful at all in the present, but that may become so in the future. And, once we have put anything on the Internet, it becomes almost impossible to cancel it. People are persecuted by old, shameful images of themselves they cannot get rid of. Shame always depends on communities. Social media allow the quick emergence of a weakly engaged, provisional community, not long-lasting but still powerful (Chapter 1; see also Ge, 2020).

What all kinds of shame, from the more traditional to the newest, have in common, is the presence of strong social, or family, or intimate demands, which the individual is—or feels—unable to respond properly. In a sense, in the past it was easier to avoid shame. Passive conformism was enough, whereas today active adaptation to performance standards is required. There are, however, new ways of escaping it, exploiting the flexibility of liquid society: if we are ashamed in a context, we can shift to another where we are not ashamed anymore. Shame thus becomes partial: rather than undermining the person's identity as a whole, it only affects that part of the identity that is involved and exposed in a specific situation. It becomes a situational emotion (Turnaturi, 2016, p. 63).

Such partial shame is occasional, revisable and therefore short-lived. We should not generalise, though: to some of our patients, who have shame as their dominant emotion, the risk of feeling annihilated by shame is as strong as ever. But these considerations may help us to understand how some other patients can be deeply ashamed in some moments or aspects of their lives, and be completely shame-proof in others. Both their shame and shamelessness are situational.

Emotions in individual therapy practice

Our approach considers emotions as neither "internal" nor "private": we consider them embedded in the wider system, where emotional interchanges happen, and emotions circulate. At the same time, emotions are inherently twofold: what we feel is ours. The subjective experience of feeling pertains to the individual, rather than to the individual's interaction with others. In clinical work, we are aware of this duplicity: we feel our emotions as our own, and the patient's emotions as theirs, but we go beyond these immediate feelings. Without forgetting the force of individual feelings, we try to make patients aware of the relational interplay their feelings are part of. This holds true for shame as well as for any other emotion we consider.

Regarding our (therapists') own emotions, we consider them at the same time as our personal experiences, and as news about the state of the system we are embedded in. An emotion is an important clue about what is going on within a human interaction, but this does not mean emotions "unveil" the ultimate reality of that encounter: what we feel when we come face-to-face with a patient tells a lot about our relationship with them but it is not necessarily the revelation of what is actually happening to them. All in all, in therapy we are very attentive to our own emotions, and at the same time wary of them.

In a systemic-dialogical perspective, what we can see or understand in any situation depends on our position in the systems we are embedded in, including the therapeutic one. We feel this is true of emotions, too: they change according to changes in the therapeutic system. Within a therapeutic setting, the emotional tone colours every behavioural interaction: any display of feelings sends a message to the others, and this emotional sequence can be singled out from the complex interweaving of relationships in the system. When needed, we may focus on emotions, forgetting all other aspects of the system; in other cases, it is better to connect emotions to other events and relationships.

Our view differs from other systemic theorists' positions. We do not share Kleckner and colleagues' (1993) idea that a change of behavioural patterns may be sufficient to change emotions correspondingly, since we have observed that there is no necessary relationship between a sequence of actions and the emotions attached to it: the same actions may be imbued of many different feelings. We do not consider, as Miller and de Shazer (2000) do, emotions as mere language games: descriptions of emotions are certainly language games, but emotions in themselves are largely pre-linguistic, and therefore impossible to consider only through the lens of language.

Emotional work in the session

In the session, our activity tends toward a basic goal: to give emotions some relational sense, and to share it with our patient. We pay attention both to dominant and tacit emotions, although the latter are more difficult to single out. We focus on the emotions displayed by the patient who is in the room with us, as well as the emotions that appear in the stories they tell. At the same time, we are attuned to our own feelings in the course of the session. We may highlight some emotions that we see or feel, but that the patient appears not to be aware of. Emotions also play a pivotal role in the process of micro-hypothesising in session.

Often the raw emotional material we find in the session is some form of emotional discharge. Byung-Chul Han (2017) draws a distinction between emotion and feeling (*Erlebnis*): in his view, emotion is momentary, overwhelming, and uncontrollable, whereas feeling is long-lasting, stable, and moderate. The former is something we are subjected to, like the ancient Greeks' passions (*pathos, passio*: something we suffer, by which we are invested); the latter, instead, can be lived with awareness and mastered. We define the former as "emotionality", reserving the term "emotion" to states that Han qualifies as feeling.

We try to help our patients to distance themselves from their own emotions, in order to decipher them and transform emotionality into emotions, and emotions into emotional information: the final result should be a better emotional awareness and an ability by each patient to master their own emotions (we prefer to think about "mastering" or "governing" emotions, rather than "controlling" them: control always implies some repression of emotions). In doing this, we keep some guidelines in mind, although our therapeutic work does not follow a rigid schedule: its steps are neither fixed nor so distinct from each other.

From time to time, we focus on one emotion or another, depending on the moment of therapy, on the emotions shown by the patient, or our feelings in relation to it. This is what happens when we decide to focus on shame:

- We identify a specific moment of shame during the dialogue;
- We investigate shame in the individual through questioning;
- In the meantime, we evaluate our (the therapist's) relationship to shame and its effects on the present episode;
- We try to understand the person's relational network and its influence on that moment of shame, through further questioning;
- We look for emotional patterns—e.g., the interaction between shame, guilt, contempt, anger and so on—through another set of questions;
- We create hypotheses about shame;
- (If possible), we try to arrive at some transformation of shame

Identifying a moment of shame in the session

The basic tone that we feel any time we meet a patient depends on a complex alchemy of the emotions, dominant and tacit, that each person presents, and their relationship to the therapist's. During each session we try to be very attentive to the affective presentation of the patient. At the same time, we also pay attention to what we feel during the dialogue. Although emotions are not necessarily the central point of the whole session, they permeate the interpersonal space, and influence all the actions of both therapist and patient. In each session, we always spare at least some moments to focus on emotions.

When we do this, it is comparatively easy to single out the dominant emotion(s). As we have said already, this happens through a hypothetical job, where we are guided by the impressions and feelings the patient and their discourse evoke in us. When shame is dominant, it is easy to see and feel it. A moment of shame is characterised by very definite traits: the closure of the person on herself, the averting gaze, the obvious suffering. When shame is present in the patient's account of an episode, rather than in the here and now of the dialogue, we often need to ask more questions in order to distinguish shame from sadness or guilt: as we have seen, many patients tend to interpret as guilt what we see as shame.

In a sense, we are even more interested in tacit emotions, although it may be harder to pinpoint them. Here inferences are even more indirect, since a tacit emotion is, by definition, absent from the system's horizon—or, better, it induces the system to get away from it. The result, anyway, is that we can hardly perceive it directly. Instead, we wonder what emotions we would, in that same situation, feel or show, and we work by difference. If looking for dominant emotions is circumstantial, looking for tacit emotions is much more inferential. Since we only can imagine tacit emotions (they do not directly appear in the dialogue), we must accept the possibility of being wrong, of attributing to the patient emotions that we—rather than them—would feel. Here systemic reasoning, through hypotheses that we can always falsify, is extremely helpful.

For example, Zaira, 26, came to therapy because of a difficulty in deciding the career and the life she wants: apparently she is unable to define her own wishes. She also brings some symptoms, including a binge eating disorder, that makes her feel uncomfortable in her own body. She begins the present session by saying:

"Today I'd prefer not to be here."
"Why?"
"I'd prefer not to say why…"

"… which makes quite difficult to go on with this conversation," the therapist replies mildly.

In the meantime he looks at her: she is averting her gaze, closing on herself, with an expression of resigned sadness. He feels her shame.

"Are you ashamed of speaking?"
"Yes!"
"What makes you so ashamed even before beginning to talk?"
"I think you will disapprove of me."
"Why should I?"

"Because I should be at a more advanced stage of therapy, rather than still mired in old thoughts."

"You are where you are, and that's alright for us. What thoughts?"

She goes back to a story about a past boyfriend, Boris, who was revealed in time to be manipulative and abusing. It is not a new story, but this time she adds more details: he had also been physically violent, a fact she never revealed before. The therapist begins to investigate the different levels of shame she is bringing: the present one, because she has not solved her old issues with him yet; and also the past one, because she never disclosed the secret of his violence to anybody, including her family and her closest friends. She is obviously in a state of secondary victimisation, and the therapist begins to help her getting out of it. The whole session will deal with her shame.

Investigating shame in the individual

When in a session we find evidence of shame, it is important to determine the intensity of the feeling, whether it is embarrassment or proper shame, and most of all if there are traces of humiliation; in this case, we can also verify whether that shame is connected to specific events or to the patient's very personality. This leads us to a specific set of questions, that we first ask ourselves, then transform into questions aimed at the patient:

- Is the person actually ashamed—or sad, or guilty, or maybe fearful? (Here it is important to look at the patient's face, attitude, interaction with the therapist and so on.)
- Is she simply embarrassed?
- Is she rather humiliated?
- What is she ashamed of?
- Who is she ashamed of?
- Who is she ashamed for? (If she is…)
- Who is she shamed by? (If she is…)

(In Zaira's case, she is deeply ashamed of herself, and this all-encompassing shame is the result of a history of humiliation due to Boris's violence and contempt of her. This history in turn is rooted in her distant past, as we will see.)

Evaluating the therapist's relationship to shame

Like any therapist, we build our interventions on the (emotional) material at our disposal. Elsewhere, one of us postulated that therapists, probably, interpret their preferred therapeutic model—and afterwards integrate it with other ones—according to their own emotional sensitivity, therefore their own story, enriched in time by the encounters that contributed to the moulding of their emotional personality: the therapists' emotions play an essential part in defining their models (Bertrando, 2015).[14]

As a consequence, any therapist should try to understand their own dominant and tacit emotions. Which is not an easy task, but it is not impossible either, especially in regard to dominant emotions: to get a first idea of them, we can simply wonder what characteristics of our patients we feel easier or more difficult to work with, then review the emotions that we more frequently feel in each case. As for the tacit ones, the task is harder, even forbidding, given that a tacit emotion is an emotion that disappears from our field of consciousness, which therefore we cannot fully be aware of. Here it is vital to have teamwork or supervision available.

In any case, we must focus on the emotions that we feel in the dialogue during that specific session. If shame appears, besides all the questions we ask the patient, there are several questions we must ask ourselves:

- Am I ashamed of anything?
- Do I get easily ashamed?
- Am I sensitive to others' shame?
- Can I accept my shame?
- What is the effect of this person's shame on me?
- Can I share with this person my own experience of shame?

Through this process, we aim at better understanding our response to the patient: if a therapist is particularly sensitive to shame, the shame experience of the patient can be clarified and brought to awareness; on the other hand, the therapist might also unduly amplify a sense of shame that is insignificant to the patient. If shame, instead, is a tacit emotion for the therapist, they may let shame build up outside the consciousness of both patient and therapist. The risk is for shame to become an unacknowledged factor in the session. The therapist must always question their response to any emotions shown by the patient.

(In this case, the therapist is quite familiar with all the nuances of shame. He rapidly checks his own response to Zaira, and concludes that, rather than overdoing it, he is working on a dimension meaningful for her too: she accepted his definition without hesitation, and is willing to elaborate on her own experience of shame. Therapist and patient readily agree about going on with their investigation of shame.)

Understanding the person's relational network

In order to work on a patient's emotions, it is necessary to know the world that that person inhabits: the values they adopt and share with others, the prejudices they have absorbed, their unconscious premises. This is especially true for shame. The shame that a person may feel will depend on their relationship with the whole array of those assumptions and affects, of which they are only partially aware. Usually, the first questions we ask regard the context, then we try to understand the role of shame in it:

- Is the person living in an environment prone to shame or shaming?
- Does she come from a cultural climate that gives shame some prominence?
- What is the role of shame in the person's family—and family of origin?
- Is there evidence of shaming processes in the person's past?
- Is there evidence of shaming processes in the person's present?

(Zaira comes from a family where her parents, despite being attentive and affectionate toward both of their children, decided that their first-born son was the one both to protect and elevate, whereas their daughter, considered more solid and self-sufficient, had to remain in the background, without emphasising her achievements. She was constantly led to keep her head down—or so she felt. Therapist and patient reflect that, if this is true, her family climate and relationships brought her to feel a shame connected to a sense of her own worthlessness: a template for future relationships. Zaira remembers: "My brother, five years older, was the one who taught me to read, to write, to do maths. It was obvious, since he was the older brother. But what I felt from him was a sense of condescendence and contempt.")

Looking for emotional patterns

This part of the work regards all the different emotions the patient may feel and their interaction with shame. Of course, it is impossible to go through the whole spectrum of possible emotions: we have to focus on the emotions that are more commonly linked to shame. First of all we try to distinguish feelings of shame from feelings of guilt, although we must bear in mind that the distinction is usually difficult, and that in no situation are we likely to find expressions of "pure" shame—or any other "pure" emotion—and therefore it is not unlikely to find shame and guilt in the same person and the same episode. Then we extend to other connected emotions, like anger, contempt, pride, and so on. At the same time, we have to understand what happens, in relation to shame and related emotions, to other people belonging to the patient's significant system:

- Is somebody despising the patient (Do they feel despised by anybody)?
- Is somebody angry at them (Do they feel somebody is angry at them)?
- Is somebody showing them their pride?
- Is somebody ashamed together with them?
- How is shame circulating in the system?
- Is shame present in more than one person?
- Is shame pervasive in the system?
- Does anybody feel humiliated?
- Is anybody showing contempt?

- In that case, what is the reaction of others? (Contempt/shame, contempt/contempt, contempt/anger?)
- Can I detect any self-contempt?
- Is anybody showing pride?
- Is their pride justified?
- Is anybody showing hubris (arrogance)?

(In this case, it is clear that Boris's position, with all his arrogance and contempt, fostered Zaira's shame both in the past and the present. On the other hand, she is ashamed also at people that treat her in a very different way, including good friends, which means that her shame is more deeply rooted. The therapist begins to try to formulate some emotional hypothesis.)

Hypotheses about shame

Hypotheses have a peculiar relationship with emotions. On the one hand, we can make hypotheses centred on emotions: our emotions, the patient's ones, the relationship between them, the emotional networks encompassing the patient's—and our own—life, within and without the therapy room. On the other hand, the nexus is more subtle. Our very hypothesising is conditioned, maybe dictated, by our emotions: we hypothesise because we are feeling something, and our hypotheses exist within that emotional space. Without emotions we could not even make any hypotheses.

Every time an emotion suggests a hypothesis, or vice versa, we try to frame the emotion we are perceiving within what we know and remember about the patient. Which implies a definite attention to the emotional context, to the wider (emotional) system, beyond the here and now of the session. It is always useful to take into account dimensions that go beyond immediacy. Hypothesising with emotions does not only mean exerting a (healthy) wariness toward immediate intuition. It also means including emotions within the process of constructing more complex hypotheses, which implies coupling the emotional facts we see and feel in the here and now of the session with what we can fantasise about the then and there of our patients' lives.

In many instances, however, this is not possible. Sometimes our emotional hypotheses remain minimal ones, micro-hypotheses (Chapter 4), because our attention to emotions leads us to concentrate on details. The micro-hypothesis, for its very nature, tends to be limited to the here and now. The more it widens to the rest of the patient's life, the more it becomes a complex and (basically) all-inclusive hypothesis. Being open and incomplete, the emotional micro-hypothesis allows the therapy to evolve in time. The interweaving and superimposing of micro-hypotheses in time, rather than the search for the one, big systemic hypothesis, may stimulate the patient to create their own connections between what they feel and their relational world, acquiring a systemic sense of their own emotions. Even when it grows and widens, the emotional hypothesis tends to remain partial. Founded upon a detail, it is centred on one aspect—although we can consider it constitutive—of the patient's life, without stretching connections too much.

We also try, as far as possible, to insert ourselves and our own emotions into the hypothesis. Everything that happens in the session may be read as related to the relationship between therapist and patient, therefore a hypothesis that does not include the therapist is incomplete (Bertrando & Toffanetti, 2003).

In the case of shame, the micro-hypotheses that we can construct connect our immediate observation of the patient with the event we are talking about, while we also consider our relationship with them. There are some more questions the therapist should wonder about:

- Did I do anything that could cause shame or embarrassment to this person?
- Could I be seen as despising? How?
- Did I create an atmosphere reminding the person some past or present relevant relationship?
- Was this a consequence of the story they were telling, or rather of my questions or considerations about it?
- Did I feel ashamed in any moment?
- Was I embarrassed?
- Was I reminded of any past shameful experience?

At the end of this process we can begin to weave the different bits of information together and build a preliminary micro-hypothesis. The course of the dialogue then helps us to correct, modify, amplify or abandon our hypothesis, following the patient's cues and openly discussing our work with them.

(In the therapist's original micro-hypothesis about Zaira, Boris was just a trigger for a deeper kind of shame: her first feeling of shame in the session, after all, involved the therapist. This leads him to enlarge the hypothesis to accommodate both Zaira's family past and her present network of relationships, apparently affected by the same kind of shame. She seems to have learned to be ashamed of herself as a way of coping with her family's requests—or the requests she felt from it. Then she has lived the same shame every time she reached, or failed to reach, a milestone in her life, accepting persons like Boris because they confirmed her status of submission. Boris added violence to the picture, a much more extreme kind of contempt, making her feel completely worthless. In order to overcome this pervasive shame, she should change her whole perception and image of herself. When the therapist proposes this reading, Zaira acknowledges that it makes sense to her.)

Transformations of shame

Shame can be transformed into either pride or indignation. The goal of our therapy, however, is not to achieve some specific transformation. It is rather to understand the emotions the person feels, and help her to experience them differently. Sometimes, in the course of therapy, the patient discovers in themselves something to be proud of; at times, they get indignant at something that happened and made them feel ashamed. We elaborate on these new feelings, of course, and try to give them some more meaning. Unavoidably, sometimes we actively favour some transformation—e.g., when a woman who has been subjected to abuse gets outraged by it after having been ashamed for a long time. Being neutral is impossible, and not even advisable in many cases; we feel, anyway, that an excess of directionality on the part of the therapist risks going beyond the frame of therapy as we see it.

(For Zaira, the process of working through her shame has just begun. She is able to face her shame, and rationally to understand it, but that feeling comes back again from time to time, in most areas of her life, and she is unable to stop it. She is processing it, though: at the following session she reports feeling much better, although she confesses that she could not face Boris without being ashamed and afraid of him. At the same time, some symptoms, including her eating disorders, seem to have currently disappeared. The therapy is going on.)

Clinical examples

Cassandra: abuse, humiliation and shame

The interweaving of shame, guilt, and humiliation with each other and with other emotions, and the way it is played out in the context of people's lives should be considered very carefully by therapists. We will try to illustrate such process with a case vignette portraying an episode within the course of a long-term therapy.

Cassandra is a 45-year-old married woman whose marriage has been dull and tired for some years. She finds her husband Giulio detached and distant from her, feeling that she is continually trying to inject some life in their relationship, to little avail. Their sexual life is presently frozen, and it has been like that for some time. She does not consider the perspective of a divorce, though. She sought individual therapy to find a way out of this conundrum.

Recently, she met Aldo, a 75-year-old retired man, during a seasonal event in the little town they live in. They go on seeing each other in cafes and other social events. Initially he appears to be very welcoming and paternal toward Cassandra. She begins to see him on a more or less regular basis. There are no sexual or romantic subtexts on her part. He gradually shows that he does not agree: Aldo is a man born in another, much more patriarchal world. He boasts a long history of sexual exploitation toward countless young women he met at the heyday of his job.

He begins to get closer and closer to Cassandra. At first she accepts his attention, also because she feels their huge age difference to be a shield against any possibility of a sexual encounter. Slowly, she gets more and more annoyed by his increasingly obvious innuendos. She discusses the state of things with Giulio, who does not take them seriously, suggesting simply that she get rid of him with a few dismissive jokes.

Cassandra is apparently unable to take such simple measure. She feels trapped in a situation where she feels obliged to follow Aldo's directives: she is ashamed at the idea of saying "no" after having accepted him—although, questioned, she says she never did anything to openly encourage his advances. One day, she finds him in his car on the road home. He offers her a lift, and suddenly kisses her. She is shocked and disgusted by the episode. Initially she cuts him off, blocking him on the phone and social networks, then steps back and starts seeing him again, "against my own will". There are more wanton advances, that she seems unable to simply refuse. She appears subdued: "I feel I cannot refuse to see him, after compromising so much!" To the therapist, it is clear that he is harassing her, yet he is apparently unable to help her get out of that relationship.

The therapist is the only one to know the extent of this stalking: initially she had confided in some women friends, who gave her the sensible advice to stop seeing and contacting him once and for all; having failed in doing this, she is ashamed to let them know. In a session, she recognises that her shame is much deeper: she is ashamed of her own behaviour, as if she were responsible for his actions (Chapter 7). This prevents her from seeking help from her husband—he could judge and blame her, she fears—or from her friends. Her shame seems so deep to paralyse and isolate her.

The tangle of her emotions, the therapist reflects, originated from a humiliation, that she suffered and made her own, turning her experience of being harassed by Aldo into her own responsibility, which made her feel ashamed and guilty at the same time. In the therapist's hypothesis, shame has the effect to isolate her from all social support, transforming the relationship with Aldo in a one-to-one interaction, where she feels bound to lose.

"Do you feel ashamed in talking about all this?" the therapist asks.

"Yes, it's hard simply to mention it. I had to force myself to even talk to you about it."

"Why do you feel ashamed, in a situation where he was the only perpetrator?"

"I'm afraid I encouraged him, so now I have no right to turn him down…"

"What do your female friends say about this?"

"I don't know. After I betrayed their advice I don't feel entitled to tell them anything anymore."

"So you're ashamed of them too?"

"Yes!"

"Try to see your situation from the outside," the therapist says. "If a friend of yours were in the same position, would you be willing to help her?"

"Yes, of course!"

"What would you do?"

"I'd tell her to block him immediately on all media, and then I'd prepare her to face him in person. I'd be together with her in all this."

"When you say 'together', you turn on a light in my brain. You are terribly ashamed, and maybe what you need to face your shame is to face it together with somebody else. Have you got a female friend close enough not to be ashamed of her?"

"Yes, I have the right person in mind."

"If your friend had been in your situation, you would talk to her and prescribe her a conduct. At this point, if I could, I'd suggest you to open up to her. Then she'll be able to prescribe you the steps you need in order to get your life back."

Here the therapist can make a prescription without becoming strategic, because he is simply prescribing her to do what she herself was imagining doing with a fictional friend. So he is simply taking what she said and feeding it back to her: he is prescriptive and non-prescriptive at the same time. He acknowledges her humiliation. In the remains of the session, he offers a (different) male perspective, based on his knowledge of elder patriarchal men, who took for granted that women were inherently subdued (Chapter 2). He offers an interpretation of Aldo's patriarchy that shifts the focus from Cassandra's supposed faults to his actual responsibilities. Cassandra's sense of shame seems to diminish in the course of the session, also because the mere idea of sharing her feelings with another woman is comforting in itself. The next step of the therapy will have to deal with the roots of her submission: her relationships with an authoritarian father and a depressed, submissive mother in her early life was already a major theme in her therapy. The subsequent sessions will revisit part of those experiences.

Nicoletta: shame and the body

Sometimes, shame is so pervasive in a person's life that the whole of a therapy can be characterised by it. Let us take a look at one such situation.

Nicoletta, 59, is a knowledgeable, cultivated woman, from an affluent Italian family: her father came from Italy to London after World War II, and created a very successful business there. Ten years ago Nicoletta underwent a surgical operation for a mammal tumour, with the complete removal of one breast. She is divorced, living with her 16-year-old daughter, Sue. Nicoletta brings to therapy her problems with Sue, a girl that she describes as extremely seductive and sexualised, and who was involved in a possible sexual assault by some male peers. Sue remembers she awoke, completely drunk, in a room of a girlfriend's house, with no memory of what had happened. For Nicoletta, the discovery of Sue's issues came exactly at "the end of a very intense love story". She had been working for several years in London, in the field of theatre, coming back to Italy only seven years ago, because she wanted to change her life after her divorce, and wanted Sue to study in Italy. She describes herself as "Anglo-Saxon" in her culture. Sue's father remained in London, where he married a much younger woman and had another daughter, Sue's half-sister, who is now about two years old.

One year ago, Nicoletta encountered—casually, in an airport—Graham, a former high-rank public officer. They began a very discreet courting, made of afternoon teas and visits to galleries. Graham came, in turn, from a divorce, and was currently on leave from his work, wanting a year off to reorganise his life. He is passionate about art and ballet, and Nicoletta describes him as very elegant. During the past year they met more or less fortnightly. Nicoletta felt both love and danger, in exiting her affective anaesthesia, and the long period when she had devoted herself to her daughter. After the end of her marriage and the operation, she only had a fleeting sexual relationship with a former fiancé; it had been important for her to realise that she could still attract a man even with a breast missing. She defined that relationship as "a laboratory". With Graham she fell in love. After a long time they finally have their first kiss, but the morning after Graham writes her that the only future he sees for them is being friends. Nicoletta is struck by the news, and feels utterly depressed. At this point Sue begins to show problems at school—possibly, Nicoletta reflects, to draw her mother's attention.

When she comes to therapy, Nicoletta is destabilised by her love failure. She had found herself imagining a possible future with that man. She says: "I guess I lost him because I didn't tell him my secret, the absence of a breast." Apparently, she is both proud of having survived her illness, and ashamed of her aesthetic appearance. She dreads the idea of not being attractive to men because of her "mutilation". In turn, she is ashamed of such superficiality, but at the same time she knows that this shame for her body distances her from the world of men. The (woman) therapist makes her see the documentary film *Il corpo delle donne* ("The body of women"),[15] about the way in which Italian women accept for themselves the male gaze in viewing their own bodies (Chapter 2). At the following session she appears very resentful of the therapist: "I'm not one of those Italian women who can see themselves only through the eyes of men!" she declares—although she acknowledges that in her family of origin both her father and her brother, her first male role models, belong to that very same Italian male standard of which she disapproves. She reflects on how she has been influenced by the male gaze in her life.

When she comes back the next time, she has done some quite obsessive, almost stalking research about Graham on the Internet, finding images and videos 15 years old, where Graham appears as a simple, ordinary bureaucrat, far from the elegant, posh, cultivated persona he has developed in later years. She could even access images of his home, since he decided to put it on a rental platform, discovering that the furniture is stylish but cheap. What emerges from the therapeutic conversation is that both she and Graham hold some secret, they are both ashamed of something: she is ashamed of having only one breast, he is ashamed of his humble origins, and this is why their relationship had become impossible.

The therapist works on her shame: why is it so difficult for her to accept being seen as she is, as the body she is now, rather than the past perfect body that she remembers? She could put her present body into the open: what would happen if a garment shop assistant, a friend, would see it? At the same time, she can also accept having a superficial gaze on herself, to be subjected to the same internalised standard. There is a double shame here: being ashamed of being seen, and being ashamed of being ashamed of being seen; shame, and shame of shame. She has consciously internalised a moralising gaze, but without being aware she has internalised a more superficial, male-oriented gaze too. Watching the documentary has been a moment of truth, also because she is deeply influenced by visual media, whereas she is less impressed by talking, since her dialectics makes it easy for her to protect herself. The video went right to her feelings, and she could react in a more authentic way.

Shame here is transformed first into indignation (negative), then into pride (positive). First she is indignant at watching the video, then she can shift to be proud of herself. The therapist allows her to see herself from an external standpoint. In this way, she is enabled to identify no longer with a part of herself, the woman without a breast, nor with the indignant one, but with a woman that wants to be seen by anybody and desired by men. In this way she can be proud of herself, and also accept her own ambivalence. She can identify with the proud woman or with the weak, mutilated woman, but she can also maintain an interlocutory position for a long time in her inner dialogue, until maybe a unified vision can emerge. She can be free from the dichotomy, "either my mutilation denotes me, or it doesn't exist". She can choose a complex, manifold view of herself.

Conclusion

What we do with shame we do with any other emotion. From time to time, we check the dominant and tacit emotions emerging in the therapeutic dialogue, and we focus on one of them. Sometimes, a change of the emotional tone in a session is a therapeutic goal in itself. More often, though, we integrate our work on emotions with the consideration of our—and the patient's—positioning in the course of the session. The resulting process is one of the main characteristics of our approach, namely what we define as finding one's place.

Notes

1 Darwin (1998) noted that blushing is one of the few emotional expressions to be strictly human, not shared with any other animal.

2 This list was proposed by Sylvan Tomkins (1963), who also included guilt as part of the continuum. We prefer to keep a clear distinction between shame and guilt.

3 "There is no interaction in which participants do not take an appreciable chance of being slightly embarrassed or a slight chance of being deeply humiliated" (Goffman, 1959, p. 243).

4 In her famous study of Japanese society, *The Chrysanthemum and the Sword* (1989), cultural anthropologist Ruth Benedict introduced a distinction, that became quite commonplace, between societies of guilt and societies of shame: archaic and Eastern societies would be characterised by shame as dominant emotion, whereas modern and Western societies would be dominated by guilt. Japanese psychoanalyst Takeo Doi (1971) links the Japanese tendency to shame with dependency: in Japanese society shame is strong because of strong feelings both of belonging and dependency, whereas in Western—especially Anglo-Saxon—societies the emphasis lies on independence and assertiveness, that favour clarity in communication. In Japan, apparently, ambiguity, that can be a way of avoiding shame, is instead well-tolerated. (Shame and guilt, actually, are usually intertwined in any society, and quite difficult to disentangle from each other.)

5 James Gilligan (1997) maintains that "the emotion of shame is the primary or ultimate cause of all violence. ... The different forms of violence, whether toward individuals or entire populations, are motivated (caused) by secret shame" (pp. 110–111). Websdale's (2010) study of 211 cases of familicide supports such a thesis. Retzinger (1991) observed, in conflictual couples, shame/anger loops, with a tendency to escalate, once again with a potential development of violence.

6 "If shame is evoked but not acknowledged, irrational aggression of withdrawal is generated by spirals of unacknowledged shame or shame and anger ... Being ashamed that one is ashamed leads to withdrawal, and can continue indefinitely. Being angry that one is ashamed, and ashamed that one is angry, results in irrational aggression" (Scheff, 1998, p. 107). This is what Helen Block Lewis (1992) defines as "the feeling trap".

7 Goffman (1961) described "degradation" (humiliation) rituals at the admission to mental hospitals. A ritual of the same sort is visually presented at the beginning of Stanley Kubrick's movie *Full Metal Jacket*. T.E. Lawrence's (1955) memoir *The Mint* shows how a former—and repentant—war hero submitted himself to humiliation by enrolling in the Air Force under a disguised name—a proper form of self-humiliation.

8 In regard to poverty, see Walker (2014), to race issues see Kaufman (1989), to gender see Mereish and Poteat (2015). For internalised racism, see Speight (2007); for internalised homophobia, see Rossell (2016).

9 Philosopher Thomas Hobbes saw indignation as the anger we feel from an intentional damage done to us by another—stronger when that damage brings some undue advantage to the perpetrator. Indignation generates a contempt for unfair power, and as such it has become a strong weapon for all movements against authority (Watt Smith, 2016b).

10 Following a path originally traced by Darwin (1998), Paul Ekman (Ekman et al., 1969) maintains that the recognition of basic emotional expression is independent of culture, and that it can be considered as a species-specific human trait. Despite being the standard view of basic emotions, Ekman's claims of universality have been repeatedly challenged (e.g., by Russell, 1994). We will not deal with that dispute here.

11 In many non-Western societies, the central importance of shame is taken for granted (Wong & Tsai, 2007). As we have seen, Ruth Benedict considered Japan a

"shame culture" (1946, pp. 222–223; see also Lebra, 1971). In the Maori society, shame (*whakamaa*) is also considered as a key emotion (Metge, 2004).

12 An interesting view on this topic is presented by Tarishi Verma (2022). In her online investigation on the shame experienced by victims of sexual assault, she found that social media appeared to help victims to react to perpetrators through a "campaign to name and shame" them (p. 482). The emphasis, thus, tended to shift from the shame of victims to the shaming of perpetrators.

13 Frye argues that, against public shaming, a stricter attitude towards social media is advisable, especially toward massive shaming of individuals.

14 For a very thorough description of this process, referring to three very relevant founders of therapeutic approaches—namely Carl Rogers, Albert Ellis and Fritz Perls—see Carol Magai and Jeannette Haviland-Jones's book (2002) *The Hidden Genius of Emotions.*

15 "The body of women: The image of the female in Italian TV" (by Lorella Zanardo, 2009), was the first Italian documentary focused on the critique of the exploitation of women's images for commercial, ideological and political purposes.

References

Averill, J.R. (1974). An Analysis of psychophysiological symbolism and its influences on theories of emotion. Reprinted in: Harré, R., & Parrot, W.G. (Eds.) (1996), *The Emotions. Social, Cultural, and Biological Dimensions* (pp. 204–228). Sage.

Bateson, G. (1936). *Naven.* 2nd edition. Stanford University Press, 1958.

Becvar, D.S. & Becvar, R.J. (2013). *Family Therapy. A Systemic Integration.* 8th edition. Pearson Education Limited.

Belpoliti, M. (2010). *Senza vergogna.* Guanda.

Benedict, R. (1989). *The Chrysanthemum and the Sword.* Houghton Mifflin, (original edition 1946).

Bertrando, P. (2015). *Emotions and the Therapist.* Karnac.

Bertrando, P. & Toffanetti, D. (2003). Persons and hypotheses: The use of the therapist in the therapeutic process. *Australian and New Zealand Journal of Family Therapy,* 24 (1): 7–13.

Boscolo, L. & Bertrando, P. (1993). *The Times of Time. A Perspective on Time in Systemic Therapy and Consultation.* 2nd edition. Routledge, 2020.

Cooley, C.H. (1922). *Human Nature and Conduct.* Scribners.

Damasio, A.R. (1994). *Descartes' Error: Emotion, Reason and the Human Brain.* Putnam.

Darwin, C. (1998). *The Expression of Emotion in Man and Animals.* London, Murray. 3rd edition, with an Introduction, Afterword and Commentaries by Paul Ekman, HarperCollins (original edition 1872).

De Sousa, R. (1987). *The Rationality of Emotion.* MIT Press.

Doi, T. (1971). *The Anatomy of Dependence.* Kodansha America, Inc., 2001.

Dumouchel, P. (1995). *Emotions: Essai sur le corps et le social.* Institut Synthélabo.

Ekman, P., Sorenson, E.R., & Friesen, W.V. (1969). Pan-cultural element, in facial display of emotions. *Science,* 164: 86–88. DOI:10.1126/science.164.3875.86.

Fredman, G. (2007). Preparing our selves for the therapeutic relationship: revisiting "Hypothesising revisited". *Human Systems,* 18: 44–59.

Fredrickson, G.M. (1996). *Black Liberation: A Comparative History of Black Ideologies in the United States and South Africa*. Oxford University Press.

Frye, H. (2022). The Problem of Public Shaming. *Journal of Political Philosophy*, 30: 188–208. DOI:10.1111/jopp.12252.

Ge, X. (2020). Social media reduce users' moral sensitivity: Online shaming as a possible consequence. *Aggressive Behavior*, 46: 359–369. DOI:10.1002/ab.21904.

Gergen, K.J. (1991). *The Saturated Self*. Basic Books.

Gilligan, J. (1997). *Violence: Reflections on a National Epidemic*. Vintage Books.

Goffman, E. (1959). *The Presentation of Self in Everyday Life*. New York: Doubleday Anchor.

Goffman, E. (1961). *Asylums*. Doubleday.

Goffman, E. (1963). *Stigma: Notes on the Management of Spoiled Identity*. Prentice Hall.

Haley, J. (1973). *Uncommon Therapy: The Psychiatric Techniques of Milton Erickson, M.D.* Norton.

Han, Byung-Chul (2017). *Psychopolitics: Neoliberalism and New Technologies of Power*. Transl. by Erik Butler. Verso (original edition 2014).

Hatfield, E., Cacioppo, J.T., & Rapson, R.I. (1994). *Emotional Contagion*. Cambridge University Press.

Hawthorne, N. (2003). *The Scarlet Letter*. Harmondsworth: Penguin (original edition published 1850).

Heller, A. (1976). *The Theory of Need in Marx*. St Martin's Press (original edition 1974).

Jacquet, J. (2015). *Is Shame Necessary?: New Uses for an Old Tool*. Knopf.

Kafka, F. (2009). *The Trial* (English Translation: Mike Mitchell). Oxford World Classics (Original edition 1925).

Kaufman, G. (1989). *The Psychology of Shame: Theory and Treatment of Shame-Based Syndromes*. Springer.

Kleckner, T., Frank, L., Bland, C., Amendt, J.H., & duRee Bryant, R. (1992). The myth of the unfeeling strategic therapist. *Journal of Marital and Family Therapy*, 18: 41–51. DOI:10.1111/j.1752–0606.1992.tb01737.x.

Krause, I-B. (1993). Anthropology and family therapy: a case for emotions. *Journal of Family Therapy* 15, 35–56. DOI:10.1111/j.1467–6427.1993.00739.x.

Lawrence, T.E. (1955). *The Mint*. Jonathan Cape.

Lebra, T. S. (1971). The Social Mechanism of Guilt and Shame: The Japanese Case. *Anthropological Quarterly*, 44 (4), 241–255. DOI:10.2307/3316971.

Levi, P. (1986). *The Drowned and the Saved*. Translated by Raymond Rosenthal. Simon & Schuster.

Lewis, M. (1992). *Shame: The Exposed Self*. Free Press.

Lewis, M. (2000). Self-conscious emotions: embarrassment, pride, shame, and guilt. In M. Lewis & J.M. Haviland-Jones (Eds.), *Handbook of Emotions* (2nd ed.) (pp. 623–636). Guilford Press.

Lewis, M. & Haviland-Jones, J.M. (Eds.) (2000). *Handbook of Emotions*. 2nd edition. Guilford Press.

Lini, C. & Bertrando, P. (2020). Finding one's place: emotions and positioning in systemic-dialogical therapy. *Journal of Family Therapy*, 42, 204–221. DOI:10.1111/1467–6427.12267.

Lutz, C.A. (1988). *Unnatural Emotions. Everyday Sentiments on a Micronesian Atoll and Their Challenge to Western Theory*. University of Chicago Press.

Magai, C. & Haviland-Jones, J. (2002). *The Hidden Genius of Emotion. Lifespan Transformations of Personality*. Cambridge University Press.

Mereish, E.H. & Poteat, V.P. (2015). A relational model of sexual minority mental and physical health: The negative effects of shame on relationships, loneliness, and health. *Journal of Counseling Psychology*, 62 (3): 425–437. DOI:10.1037/cou0000088.

Metge, J. (2004). *Rautahi: The Maoris of New Zealand*. Routledge. DOI:10.4324/9781315017921.

Miller, G. & de Shazer, S. (2000). Emotions in solution-focused therapy: A re-examination. *Family Process*, 39: 5–23. DOI:10.1111/j.1545–5300.2000.39103.x.

Nussbaum, M. (2004). *Hiding from Humanity. Disgust, Shame, and the Law*. Princeton University Press.

Pandolfi, A.M. (2002). *La vergogna. Un affetto psichico che sta scomparendo?*. Franco Angeli.

Planalp, S. (1999). *Communicating Emotion: Social, Moral, and Cultural Processes*. Cambridge University Press.

Pocock, D. (2010). Emotions as ecosystemic adaptations. *Journal of Family Therapy*, 32: 362–378. DOI:10.1111/j.1467-6427.2010.00517.

Retzinger, S. (1991). *Violent Emotions*. Sage.

Rigotti, F. (1998). *L'onore degli onesti*. Feltrinelli.

Rober, P. (2005). The therapist's self in dialogical family therapy: some ideas about not-knowing and the therapist's inner conversation. *Family Process*, 44: 477–495. DOI:10.1111/j.1545–5300.2005.00073.x.

Ronson, J. (2015). *So You've Been Publicly Shamed*. Riverhead Books.

Rossell, N. (2016). Fear of Knowing: Homophobia, Shame and the Repercussions. *Australasian Journal of Psychotherapy*, 34 (1): 43–59.

Russell, J.A. (1994). Is There Universal Recognition of Emotion From Facial Expression? A Review of the Cross-Cultural Studies. *Psychological Bulletin*, 115 (1): 102–141. DOI:10.1037/0033–2909.115.1.102.

Salmela, M. (2019). Shame and its political consequences in the age of neoliberalism. In: C. Sun (Ed.), *Interdisciplinary Perspectives on Shame: Methods, Theories, Norms, Cultures, and Politics*. Lexington Books.

Sartre, J.P. (2001). *Sketch for a Theory of the Emotions*. Routledge (original edition 1938).

Scheff, T.J. (1998). Therapeutic alliance. Microanalysis of Shame and the Social Bond. In: W.F. Flack & J.D. Laird (Eds.), *Emotions in Psychopathology*. Oxford University Press, pp. 99–113.

Speight, S.L. (2007). Internalized racism: One more piece of the puzzle. *The Counseling Psychologist*, 35 (1): 126–134. DOI:10.1177/0011000006295119.

Stratton, P. (2003). Causal attributions during therapy I: Responsibility and blame. *Journal of Family Therapy*, 25: 136–160. DOI:10.1111/1467-6427.00241.

Tomkins, S. (1963). *Affect, Imagery, Consciousness*, Vol. 2. The Negative Affects. In: *Affect, Imagery, Consciousness. The Complete Edition*, pp. 289–545. Springer, 2008.

Tracy, J.L. & Robins, R.W. (2007). The psychological structure of pride: A tale of two facets. *Journal of Personality and Social Psychology*, 92: 506–525. DOI:10.1037/0022-3514.92.3.506.

Turnaturi, G. (2016). *Vergogna. Metamorfosi di un'emozione*. Feltrinelli.

Turner, W.B. (2000). *A Genealogy of Queer Theory*. Temple University Press.

Verma, T. (2022). Investigating Shame in the Age of Social Media. *Women's Studies in Communication*, 45 (4): 482–496. DOI:10.1080/07491409.2022.2136895.

Walker, R. (2014). *The Shame of Poverty*. Oxford University Press.

Watt Smith, T. (2016a). Pride. In *The Book of Human Emotion*. Profile Books, pp. 150–152.

Watt Smith, T. (2016b). Indignation. In *The Book of Human Emotion*. Profile Books, pp. 203–205.

Watzlawick, P., Jackson, D.D, & Beavin, J. (1967). *Pragmatics of Human Communication*. Norton.

Websdale, N. (2010). *Familicidal Hearts: The Emotional Style of 211 Killers*. Oxford University Press.

Wong, Y. & Tsai, J. (2007). Cultural models of shame and guilt. In J.L. Tracy, R.W. Robins, & J.P. Tangney (Eds.), *The Self-Conscious Emotions: Theory and Research* (pp. 209–223). The Guilford Press.

Chapter 6

Finding one's place

The third pillar—and probably the pivotal one—of systemic-dialogical therapy concerns the awareness of our own position in the context we are embedded in. We have called this process finding one's place. From this point of view, our first therapeutic goal is to evaluate contexts and systems together with the patient. The second is to understand our own emotions in that situation. The third is to connect these two kinds of awareness, and, by so doing, to find our place in the system, so to help the patient to find their place in turn.

The nature of finding one's place

Systemic therapists originally dealt with positioning by focusing on the therapist's position within a therapeutic system (Cecchin, 1987). Such a perspective, though, was later widened. According to Bateson (1972), everything we do or say gets meaning only within a context. Awareness of our position in the different contexts we inhabit may increase our ability to choose and act in our lives. We discovered, however, that cognitive awareness is inadequate to such a task, since emotions are the most powerful motivation forces for human beings (Krause, 1993): only getting a sense of how we feel in any specific position enables us to make meaningful choices. This entails a twofold activity, consisting both in evaluating one's position, and becoming aware of one's emotions. This is the process that we define as "finding one's place".

Finding one's place, as we see it, is the equivalent of a snapshot, an emotional position caught on the map (one of the possible maps) of an existential situation. The therapist uses their ability to find their place in order to help patients, too, to find their places within the significant systems of their lives. Once they are enabled to find their place, people may see themselves in several different snapshots, that will allow them to find an orientation in the flux of their experience, giving them a better sense of their possibilities and choices. In order to introduce the subject, we will present a clinical example.

DOI: 10.4324/9781003381754-7

Clinical example: the burden of illness

Martin is a business manager of 40, married and childless. He suffers from a congenital condition that, although neither severely impairing nor immediately risky, forces him to keep his health under constant control. When he comes to therapy, he says that his mood is becoming more and more bleak, despite the fact that he feels both his job and his couple relationship are fully satisfactory.

It is agreed that the therapy will be held both in person and online. Martin says this is due to his work engagements but, in the course of the first sessions, the therapist discovers that it also depends on another health problem. In the past two years, he suffered from both foot pain and a meniscus injury, that led to a minor operation. After that, Martin says, his life has changed. The pain in his legs and feet never fully subsided, with a twofold consequence: on the one hand, the past year has been repleted with follow-up visits, X-rays, magnetic resonances, and, all in all, illness-centred thoughts; on the other, he can neither run nor walk as freely and thoughtlessly as he used to. This is another major trigger for his depressive feelings. The therapist observes that Martin seems to feel crippled, although no difficulty is immediately visible to an outside observer.

"You know," Martin comments, "I've been forced to pay attention to my health literally from when I was born, and now it's an obsession. I'm young but I feel old!" At night, he often dreams of trekking or running.

In the following sessions, the therapist learns more about Martin's life. He is the only child of a divorced couple. His father, who is now 80, is a business owner, his mother, 76, a doctor. He has a good enough, albeit slightly distant and now further loosened, relationship with his father, but a very difficult one with his mother: in the past it had been overtly conflictual, now it is distant and shallow. He considers her as self-centred and manipulative, and once even states, to the therapist's perplexity: "I never had any esteem for my mother!"

He describes his liaison with Beatrice, his wife, as good enough, although in the past it had been troublesome, and led to a previous three-year couple therapy. Workwise, he likes his job, although he still thinks about a PhD that could have advanced his career, but that he left unfinished, just lacking the completion of his PhD thesis.

The therapy proceeds for several sessions. The therapeutic relationship appears good, but the sessions bring little change. Martin appears thoroughly focused on his actual and perceived impairment, and reflecting on it does not offer any relief.

One day, as he reiterates his feelings of loss, the therapist begins to notice the overall structure of all their therapeutic dialogues so far: Martin expresses some degree of hopelessness, and the therapist is apparently obliged to offer some alternative view, that Martin finds unconvincing from the start, and so on. This time, the therapist elaborates: "Maybe the issue is exactly this: I feel as if you wanted to restore a condition of the past, and nothing could be worthy of your interest apart from it. The problem is, it is impossible to recreate that past, and so you experience the same sense of disappointment and betrayal every time. I wonder what could happen if you accepted that the present situation is your situation, and tried to accommodate to it."

In subsequent sessions, Martin brings some changes: he decided not to focus on his lost sense of well-being anymore, and to centre his attention on what is left to him—the pleasant sensations he may get from a good walk or an easy trek, the fact that despite his pain he is still able to walk significant distances, and so on. His general mood is one of relief. Slowly, however, he reverts to his usual sadness, this time, it seems, without any possible reason.

During an online session, the dialogue drags on without enthusiasm and with long pauses, until Martin, annoyed, addresses the therapist: "Are you listening or are you checking messages on your phone? You are absent, distracted…"

The therapist realises that, albeit not looking at his phone, he was actually distracted. He apologises, but now feels completely stuck. He has to reflect on his positioning in the course of the therapy. There are two main questions: "Why was I distracted? Am I bored?" and "How is it that Martin is always so unhappy?"

"Where am I?"

"Where am I?" is the first question we ask ourselves in therapy. When the therapist encounters a patient, they must understand first the reciprocal positioning of themselves and their patient, then their position within the different systems they inhabit. The analysis of positions is associated to that of contexts, that we consider as liquid and mutable.

In the history of systemic thinking, the reflection on the therapist's position has had a twofold aspect. The very word "position" has at least two different meanings for the therapist: on the one hand, it refers to the therapist's attitude toward their patients and other actors within the therapy; on the other, to their place—and their awareness of it—within the metaphorical space of the therapeutic system (Bertrando, 2007, Chapter 5).

The attitude of the therapist was one of the main focuses in Milan-inspired therapies.[1] The original Milan team reflected on it in their final article, "Hypothesising-Circularity-Neutrality" (Selvini Palazzoli et al., 1980a). Neutrality was a requirement, a prescribed position for the therapist. Family members were supposed to be unable, if asked, to state whether the therapist was taking sides with any member of the family. Karl Tomm (1987a) then rephrased neutrality as an inner attitude of the therapist's, who, besides not siding with any family member, was also supposed not to favour any specific theory of change.

The notion of neutrality implied an omniscient, dispassionate and detached therapist. If we consider the therapist as one of the stakeholders in therapy, inextricably connected to their patients, neutrality is but a myth. An even fiercer criticism came from feminist authors who argued that neutrality inadvertently legitimises a status quo characterised by male supremacy, gender stereotypes, and even, albeit implicitly, violence and abuse (Goldner et al., 1990; see also Chapter 2). As a possible remedy, Gianfranco Cecchin (1987) proposed curiosity as an alternative therapeutic disposition, that at its heart captured the stance, implied in Milan systemic hypothesising, of treating the therapist's perceptions and ideas as provisional. Constantly moving from one vantage point to the other, the therapist avoided the pitfalls of a one-sided and unbalanced position, without trying to be "neutral".

Cecchin later conceptualised the idea of irreverence (Cecchin, Lane, & Ray, 1992). The therapist should not just avoid attachment to a single vision of the other(s), they should also distrust a theoretical position that could imprison them in a Procrustean bed. The irreverent therapist neither subscribed to positions coming from their patients and other members of the therapeutic systems, nor were they forever committed to their own theories, relevant as they might be. To this end, it was useful for the therapist to be as aware as possible of the prejudices they would unavoidably bring into therapy (Cecchin, Lane, & Ray, 1994).

If position as stance implies the active positioning of the therapist, we must remember that the therapist is also positioned by others: patients, families, groups, services, institutions, society, culture. The therapist is always positioned in several possible ways within the significant system. In the article "The problem of the referring person" (Selvini Palazzoli et al., 1980b) the original Milan team analysed the impact of different kinds of referring persons on the therapist's activity, showing how it could be governed or distorted by an event—the referral—apparently peripheral and irrelevant in the therapeutic process. A "prestigious" referring person could lead the therapist to lose their authority, whereas a referring person who was an actual or metaphoric "member of the family of the patient" could enmesh the therapist in the family system. In this context, when speaking of the position of the therapist, the team were clearly alluding to its twofold meaning: the therapist always takes an active position (a stance) toward others during therapy, but at the same time they passively occupy a position (a place) that they are given by other actors within the system.

Building on this insight, Boscolo and Bertrando (1993) developed the concept of "significant system", i.e., the whole set of people and institutions involved in the patients' lives, beyond their families. It includes, apart from nuclear, original, and extended family, the referring person(s), workplaces, school, friendships and peer groups, and, most of all, any public or private institution involved, such as health, social and psychiatric care, as well as the judiciary and police. The very therapist who defines and circumscribes the significant system is, in turn, embedded in it, and should be aware of their own relationships with all the other actors, individuals and institutions. Their position in this virtual space is the overall constellation of those relationships.

In the same period, Harry Goolishian's group in Galveston, Texas, created the concept of "problem-determined system". According to Goolishian and Winderman (1988),

> Problem Determined Systems are linguistic systems composed of intersecting domains of linguistic experience continually evolving and changing with increasing or decreasing numbers of actors. [...] The treatment system is defined independently of any a priori socially defined convention, boundary or grouping of individuals (e.g., couple family, extended family, community, colleague, etc.). Thus we say, systems do not make problems; languaging about problems makes systems.
>
> (p. 135)

More radical than Milan therapists in undermining classic family therapy categories, these authors re-define human systems as sets of discursive practices, at the same time depriving them of any "naturalistic" underpinning. No human system is a "given", existing outside specific historical and cultural conditions (see Bertrando, 2000).

We reflected on positioning and the therapist's position for the whole course of our practice, first each one of us on his own, then jointly. Our experience in public mental health—short-lived for Paolo, longer for Claudia—was seminal in fostering the understanding of where we stood in relation to an array of different systems. We needed a more comprehensive framework that could help us in this process, elucidating both our passive positioning in the system(s), and our active stance within it.

A possible way of unifying the two notions of position we have described lies in positioning theory (Harré & van Langenhove, 1999; see also Bertrando, 2015, Chapter 4). Originally aimed at substituting the rigid concept of social role with the more flexible and pliable one of position, positioning theory is concerned with "how people use words (and discourse of all types) to locate themselves and others" (Moghaddan & Harré, 2010, p. 2). When we position ourselves in relation to another, we are implying certain possibilities for action and asking the other to respond. The other may, in turn, either accept our position and counterposition themselves accordingly, or refuse it and take a discordant position, which we then react to, and so on. Depending on the position we take (or that is attributed to us), certain actions will be legitimate, and others denied. Positioning is always reciprocal, and evolve in time, sometimes very rapidly.

From a therapeutic perspective, positioning theory offers a good description of the reciprocity between the therapist's own positioning and the patient's one, as well as their interaction with other members of the system, thereby bridging the gap between the active and passive meanings of position. One possible limitation of this theory lies in its basic discursive nature, that neglects pre-discursive and extra-discursive interactions that are usually omitted from discourse analysis, but are certainly part of dialogues. When we were defining our dialogical approach, we quickly realised that those non-discursive aspects were essential parts of the dialogue.

A theory that shows substantial similarities to positioning theory, without overlooking nonverbal interaction, is quite familiar to systemic therapists: Watzlawick, Beavin and Jackson's (1967) pragmatics of human communication. Their second axiom states that the relational level classifies the content level of any communication, thus regulating the relationship between the actors in the system. In emphasising reciprocal performative power, the pragmatics of communication is akin to positioning theory, but with an emphasis on nonverbal interaction, since most relational level messages are transmitted through nonverbal (analogical) channels. Despite this difference, the pragmatics of human communication appears, like positioning theory, unconcerned with emotions. We believe, instead, that emotions are central to the understanding of human systems (Chapter 5).

"How do I feel?"

The second question we ask ourselves in a therapeutic encounter is "How do I feel?" Whereas the first question has been a cornerstone of our practice for a long time, and it has been explored in depth at the time of the previous book (see Boscolo & Bertrando, 1996), reflection of emotion is, as we have stated in Chapter 5, much more recent. Initially, with the discovery of emotions in systemic practice, we simply considered them as one of the many aspects of therapy; then we began to consider how emotions interacted with positioning (Bertrando, 2009a).

The most important driving force toward the notion of finding one's place stemmed from Claudia's experience within the public mental health sector. She began to reason about the discomfort she was feeling in that context. It became clear to her, and later to both of us in our discussions, that the mere analysis of her position lacked something, and never brought a proper understanding of the situation and of its consequences on her. What was lacking was the full consideration of her emotions.

At the time, we already saw human systems as networks of emotions, conveyed partly through discourse, partly through nonverbal interaction (Chapter 5). The therapist's and the patient's emotions, as well as the emotions of significant others, were beginning to play a key role in our therapies, with the attention we paid both to the more apparent (dominant) emotions, and to the emotions that seem to be hidden in interaction (tacit emotions). In this perspective, understanding emotions became as essential as hypothesising on alliances and coalitions, or determining which stories are being narrated about whom. The emphasis on verbal language and discourse was complemented by a renewed attention to pre-verbal and extra-verbal exchanges, more easily linked to emotional interaction.

Such evolution also allowed a different concept of positioning. As we have seen before, from a systemic-dialogical perspective, what we see in a given situation depends on our position within that situation (see Bertrando, 2009a). This implies that what we can feel, too, may be considered as a function of that very same position: our emotions are modified by any change within the system. What we feel depends both on our personal history and on the interpersonal processes we are involved in. We do not only experience the emotional effects of our position in the system: if we can change it, we can also change our affective state, and thus maybe have an effect on the overall emotional tone of that system. Working within an emotional position is at the heart of the therapeutic process.

In a systemic-dialogical perspective, emotions are influenced by and in turn influence context and reciprocal positioning. In other words, our position in the system is inextricably connected to our feelings. At the same time, what we feel within the system leads us to take specific positions in it, e.g., getting closer to somebody and more distant from somebody else. If movement within the system becomes restricted or even impossible, our emotional state will readily be characterised by discomfort and distress.

If we connect emotion and positioning, we must also remember that what we feel when we enter the therapy room is also conditioned by the way in which our patient wants us to feel. If we admit that emotions may be strategic, this implies that each of us wants the other to feel the emotion better suited to our desires. We could discuss at length to what extent we are aware of such strategies; probably there is a wide range of possibilities, from accurately planned strategies to wholly unconscious movements.

In Chapter 5 we saw the relevance of our and the patient's feelings in shaping dialogue within therapy. Here we can observe how our position is connected to our emotions. When we learned to balance in our practice positioning with emotion, we discovered that many of the patient's actions, that previously seemed not to make sense, or needed complex circumstantial explanation, are dictated by the person's emotional state. The reciprocal influence of position and emotions quickly became the trademark of our work.

Finding one's place

According to Zygmunt Bauman (2000), contemporary (liquid) society, in contrast to modernistic (solid) society, is characterised by an intrinsic fluidity (Chapter 1). One of the many implications contained herein concerns personal identity, that cannot be considered as fixed and stable anymore. In the nineteenth-century German middle classes, as described in Thomas Mann's novel *Buddenbrooks* (1994), the position attained in the process of building one's life was not a given, once and for all, rather it required a constant revision of oneself. But:

> The situations of the Buddenbrooks and our situation is not the same, they knew damn well what they had to do in order to remain respectable middle-class people, because all the world was a world of prescription and proscription. You could virtually have a list of what you must do and what you must avoid or desist from doing. Nothing comparable today, and that's a problem: and leads to instability. Instability of norms, instability of values.
>
> (Bauman, in Bauman, Bertrando & Hanks, 2010, pp. 45)

In the contemporary world, we need to find criteria for survival that are not dictated by external agencies. To make sense of our position in the world, a structural explanation is not enough, since all references are continually changing. Here our emotional state may help. Regarding the reciprocal relationship between members of a human system, an emotion, considered as a pre-logical and pre-categorical event, provides news of the overall state of relationships. At the same time, the sense of our emotions is better understood if we get a notion of the different systems and contexts we are embedded in.

To speak of finding one's place, therefore, means to connect position and emotion. The essence of such a process had been foreseen many years ago by Gregory Bateson, in his commentary to Pascal's famous sentence:

> "The heart has its reasons which the reason does not at all perceive." Among Anglo-Saxons, it is rather usual to think of the "reasons" of the heart or of the unconscious as inchoate forces or pushes or heavings— what Freud called *Trieben*. To Pascal, a Frenchman, the matter was rather different, and he no doubt thought of the reasons of the heart as a body of logic or computation as precise and complex as the reasons of consciousness.
>
> (Bateson, 1972, p. 148)

We can really know where we are only if we know how we feel. At the same time, "where we are"—our awareness of the relational network we are part of—changes the very nature of "how we feel". Finding one's place means developing an emotional awareness of our being within complexity. It is not only a way of knowing, but also a disposition to action. Integrating position and emotion allows us to choose a course of action in full awareness.

In her work on the therapist's emotional postures, Fredman (2007) recommends a pre-session ritual, where the therapist and the therapeutic team discuss the ways in which the therapist's emotions may influence their stance during the session. We prefer to emphasise what happens during the actual session, reducing or eliminating pre-session activities. We therefore rely on the therapist's internal dialogue, where they can check both their emotion and their positioning along the way (see Rober, 2005). The therapist may then re-evaluate their dispositions and actions after the session, together with a team when present, or in supervision, or in self-reflection.

Briefly, the process of finding one's place may be seen as organised in the following phases. Once again, they do not imply a succession in time, but rather a set of simultaneous events, that are sequenced here for the sake of clarity:

- Understanding our feelings in a given moment and situation, the well-being or discomfort we experience, the emotions that become more evident and the ones that retract from the horizon of consciousness;
- Acquiring awareness of our attitudes toward other actors, both in the here and now of the situation, and in the overall context, and of the way in which such attitude leads us to act in one way or another toward them;
- Evaluating our position within the context: "Therapeutic responsibility begins with seeing your own position in the system" (Cecchin, 1987, p. 409);
- Acting in accordance to our analysis of both positioning and feeling, so as to get to a synthesis and an integration of them.

Finding one's place concerns any person in any situation, rather than just the therapist in the therapeutic relationship. One of the goals of therapeutic work is helping people to become aware of their position within the system, where they are and how they act, their emotions in relation to these, and becoming able to integrate such knowledge in their responses to situations and contexts.

This process bears some resemblance to other ways of dealing with emotions in therapy, the most obvious being transference and countertransference analysis (Esman, 1990; Michels et al., 2002). Within the family therapy field, there are similarities with Mony Elkaïm's (2004) concept of resonance, that extends the transference idea to whole relational configurations and, more distantly, Murray Bowen's (1972) work on the differentiation of self. Finding one's place is different from such perspectives in at least two respects. First, it goes beyond the dyadic focus of all psychoanalytic models—including inter-subjective psychoanalysis (Stolorow, Atwood, & Orange, 2002)—and deals with the whole relational and contextual environment of the therapy, looking both at the immediate feelings within the session, and at the network of relationships that encompasses the patients' lives. Second, it does not necessarily emphasise the re-activation of past patterns: consistently within a systemic-based epistemology, we centre instead our considerations on present relationships, contexts and events.

One could interpret finding one's place as a static concept, which might immobilise us in one position. We believe rather that it allows the creation of a map that orients the person in their metaphorical moving through human systems. Having a map does not make anyone static, no more than for an explorer using a physical or electronic map to get her bearings during an excursion. In the process of finding one's place, moreover, any movement recursively changes the map, in a continuous activity of re-positioning.

Clinical example: the sad therapist

Finding one's place is a snapshot that connects the patient's inner world to their external lives. As such, it is an instantaneous event. The changes that are brought by it, though, are comparatively slow and gradual. Both therapist and client must find their places again and again in the course of therapy. Let us give an example. Annalisa is a psychotherapist. She seeks personal therapy to overcome a persistent sense of sadness and gloom that periodically haunts her, bringing her back to her difficult childhood, spent in a small village in southern Italy, with a psychiatrically diagnosed mother and a father whom she experienced as passive and listless. She has fought this feeling for years, undergoing a first personal therapy, but she feels she is not out of it yet.

The therapy goes on for a couple of years, with several ups and downs: Annalisa sometimes appears attached to her feelings, and in those moments her grimness feels like a challenge to the therapist. On an occasion, she tells of a surprise party that her friends organised for her birthday. Her response to it was, as usual, sad and sulky. The therapist feels compelled to push her out of her sadness, becoming unusually challenging: "How can you be so sad and feel so abandoned when your friends bothered to use their free time just to prepare a party for you?" The session becomes a fight. The therapist has to find her place: how does she feel in this challenging position? Quite uncomfortable, and angry. That anger is a clue: where does it come from? The therapist feels that Annalisa is displaying a posture of aggressive sadness: she is angry too.

> "I have a feeling, and I have to ask you: are you angry right now?"
> Annalisa answers, surprised: "Yes, when you tell me, I realise I'm angry!"
> "Where does this anger come from?"
> "I don't know, I felt again excluded by them, as if they were the lucky ones who wanted to help the poor, marginal girl…"

The dialogue now brings her to retell her story, her feeling of being marginalised and left to live with her unhappy parents in the past. She begins to perceive that her sadness gets her stuck in her distant past, preventing her from seeing the many changes she has made in more recent years. Looking back to this session in the course of the therapy, she will always remember it as a pivotal moment: a tell-tale snapshot. Many more sessions will be necessary, however, to consolidate that change.

A time comes when both patient and therapist begin to feel that the therapy should come to an end. Annalisa realises that, in order to treasure the changes fostered by the therapy, she needs moments—she says—to "exercise" her ability to find her place. Moments to get out of herself, to look at her situation like a drone that produces an extreme, panoramic wide-angle. If she can see the events of her life from outside, she can reconnect her feelings to events in the here and now. If she cannot, those feelings would bring her back, despite herself, to the past. This generates a meaningful difference. Feelings located in the past cannot be remediated: they already happened, and nobody can change them, therefore they make her helpless. Often they are related to her childhood, bringing her back to moments when she truly could not influence what happened to her. What she feels in the present, instead, gives her back agency. She can act upon what is happening in the present, instead of being overwhelmed.

When she realises this, Annalisa negotiates a new contract with the therapist:

"I find such reasoning easy when I talk to my patients," she says.

"What would happen, then, if you tried to consider yourself as one of your patients?"

The result is a new format for her therapy, with less frequent sessions, and a second-order therapeutic work, where the subject is not her life events anymore, but rather her way of dealing with them. For her "training" Annalisa chooses to find one hour per week, where she takes her time to get away from her daily routine, and find her place: she can wonder how she feels, where she is, and how she can modify her feelings or her position.[2] The session ends with Annalisa pacified and relaxed. The therapy will go on for a few sessions, then it will end satisfactorily for both patient and therapist. Annalisa, in the end, commits herself to go on with her care of herself indefinitely.

Annalisa shows us that the immediate snapshot of finding one's place can create a connection between what is happening in the here and now and long lasting emotional patterns. This is not a typical insight that produces an instantaneous, discontinuous change, after which the person is once and for all different (see Boscolo & Bertrando, 1993). Finding one's place may be—albeit not necessarily—an epiphany. But it then becomes part of a continuous process of care of oneself, a diachronic process that stabilises the discontinuous change, transforming it in a life practice.

Domains in finding one's place

There are domains in finding one's place. Finding one's place is an exacting activity. It requires the ability to focus on different variables, quickly shifting from one to another in a short time. To make things easier, we propose to distinguish different domains in finding one's place: the therapist can focus on them one at a time, highlighting different aspects of the process in an orderly fashion without getting lost in complexity. We do not conceive reality itself as ordered in different domains, though. Domains are a product of our knowing activity, and therefore they are methodological, rather than ontological (Eco, 1968). We can consider each domain as a conceptual set of premises and prejudices, emerging from the activity of people and institutions, and internalised by individuals. We have defined four of them:

1. *Macro-contextual (political) domain.* It deals with the wider cultural and political context, and the premises and prejudices deriving from it, our awareness of their influence on us, and the opinion we form of them. An example may be the idea of "family" (Chapter 1). Let us imagine a situation where, as it often happens, the macro-context is conservative, promoting a stereotyped way of being in the family: mass media, educational agencies, city planning, economy, all support the traditional family model, anticipating its needs so as to control its structure and its consumptions (Foucault, 2004). Has our hypothetical patient developed any thoughts about this belief system they are part of? Do they feel conditioned in their needs and desires by such ideas, or do they feel things are right as they stand? Do they feel represented by them? Closeness or distance from the dominant values within the macro-context may generate distinct feelings: shame or pride in feeling "different", well-being or boredom in feeling "the same" as the majority, distress or anger in not being able to choose, and so on.

It is important for the therapist not to neglect dimension such as economical conditions and race, even when it may be uncomfortable to face them in the session. What is the economical condition of the patient? And what is their way of coping with it? Is the patient privileged? If so, are they aware of it? Is the patient subjected to racism? Are they showing signs of being—maybe subtly—racist themselves?

And what about the therapist? How, and to what extent, are their premises conditioned by such a macro-context? To what extent do they diverge from it? Are they similar or different compared to their patient's? The therapist's feelings can be the same as their patient's, with possible additional distress or interest if their premises are discrepant from their patient's, and so on. The therapist must reflect on whether and how they may show their disagreements with the patient, especially in regard to issues like race or class, where there is a risk of becoming confrontational: the first duty of the therapist is to understand their patients on their own terms, in order to be able to put differences into the dialogue afterwards, and make them reflect on their invisible assumptions.

2. *Group domain.* It deals with positioning and feelings within social groups in general, from community to school or work, and the family itself. For example: how does the patient feel in their work group? What are their

ideas regarding organisation, competition, money, recognition? How do they react to their colleagues' gender in connection with their jobs? How do they position themselves in regard to tasks and authority?

Concerning the therapist; do they work on their own? Are they working in co-therapy or in a team? Are they part of an institution, which entails some subjection to authority and, at the same time, also as part of a group of colleagues from whom they may ask for advice, or a multidisciplinary team? How do they feel in their present situation? How is it influencing their relationships to patients?

3. *Mutual (intimate) domain.* According to Lyman Wynne (1984), "mutual" relationships, characterised by closeness and emotional intensity, usually include partner, parents, children, close friends, etc. For example: is the patient close to somebody they really want to be close to, independently of conventions, categories and social obligations? If they are, how did they choose to be there? If they are not, how are they still there?

Intimate relationships obviously do not concern the therapist within the therapeutic relationship: intense as it is, it is defined and limited by rules of the setting, which safeguard against the possibility of inappropriate intimacy or mutuality, that would interfere with the detachment needed for therapeutic activity. If the therapist feels that the relationship with a specific patient is becoming intimate, supervision is urgently required. Apart from such extreme occasions, here the most pertinent question regards the therapist's premises about intimacy: What is the meaning of intimacy for the therapist? How was and is it played out in their past and present life? How does this affect their attitude toward patients when they deal with intimacy issues?

4. *Intra-relational (internal) domain.* It deals with the way in which the context influences the internal dialogue within the dialogical self (Chapter 1). As such, this is the domain where we reflect upon the answers to the questions posed in all three of the other domains. For example, a specific macro-context, with its premises, negatively influences the way in which the patient stays in a specific group, and therefore also her relationships with other group members. Why? Therapeutic hypothesis: because the context's relational requests contrast with ancient internalised emotional and relational patterns. The therapist's task is to bring forward the contrasts and reflect them back to patients, making the process more visible. In turn, the therapist may consider whether their own ancient patterns could be reactivated by the therapeutic situation. This is the activity, in our practice, that most resembles counter-transference or resonance analysis (see above).

Distortions in finding one's place

Finding one's place can be distorted in the life of some patients. We often observe in them a tendency to position themselves in one way only, without changing in response to the demands of different contexts. We may consider such attitudes as ways of finding—or not finding—one's place, both for individuals and couples or families. They concern contradictions and distortions in the evolution or harmony of a system in its different domains (inter and intra-personal). We have not developed yet a comprehensive theory of such dispositions; we provisionally define them as "distortions in finding one's place". This section will analyse four possible variants of them: fixity of past patterns, identification of a part for the whole, discrepancy between domains of finding one's place, and mismatch of ends and means. Here is a brief description of them.

1   *Fixity of past patterns.* The person finds their place according to coordinates that made sense in the past, but have now been left behind by events, a way of acting reminiscent of Freud's (1920) repetition compulsion. In couple or family relationships we can see the most diverse combinations: our patient may be the person who stays in the past when the other is evolving, thus feeling mystified in the present; or the patient may be the other one, who cannot tolerate the other's stillness; both members of a couple inhabit different time coordinates, with a resulting inability to communicate; our patient may be the only person who progresses within a whole family that is stuck in time: the patient becomes deviant in the eyes of other family members because of a better orientation toward the external world; and so on (see also Boscolo and Bertrando, 1993).

2   *Identification of a part for the whole.* According to the theory of dialogical self, relationships activate in each person multiple self positions, in accordance with the relational moment. The dialogical self is seen as fluid and mutable, albeit with some internal consistency (Chapter 1). When unable to find her place, the person identifies with only one of the possible self positions within their dialogical self: they identify that part with the whole. We may then assume that they are unaware of their own inner multiplicity and are therefore unable to organise it. They will easily stick to that one position, that they will use in any context. For example, a mother comes to therapy with her 25-year-old daughter. In the first session, the mother insists she is doing all she can to help the daughter to be happy, devoting her whole life to care for her. The daughter, though, feels controlled and overwhelmed by the mother, and repeatedly asks her to leave her alone. Subsequent questions show that the mother is actually positioning herself only as a mother, without being able to adopt any different position in life. She has turned one of her many possible self positions into her own identity.

3   *Discrepancy between domains.* The person knows where they are, but not how they feel, or they know how they feel but not where they are. In both cases, they will produce inappropriate behaviours. For example, a woman develops relevant depressive symptoms and a persistent feeling of anxiety and restlessness that she is unable to connect to any external

event. In therapy, she realises that she began feeling that way when both her elderly parents became ill, and she felt that all responsibility for them fell on her; until that realisation, though, she was well aware of her sadness and anxiety, but completely unaware of how these feelings were related to her position.

4 *Mismatch of ends and means.* Sometimes the person does know where they want to get, but they do not know how to get there. Here usually the person has some emotional awareness of their own condition, but they struggle to face the hardship of dealing with their feelings. Therefore, they insist on postponing any decision, finding themselves in a sort of stalemate position, where they cannot move, despite all the suffering they feel.[3] Charles is on the verge of retiring, after a fulfilling and satisfactory professional life. After retirement, he can go on with his profession as a consultant, receiving at the same time a good pension. Despite this, he feels perplexed and anguished. He struggles to realise and express his feelings: he knows perfectly well that he wants to have a good life after retiring, but feels completely stuck. His therapist hypothesises that he cannot accept the passing of time, that brings new life practices, but brings others to a closure. She tries to foster in him a set of new micro-practices for his new phase of life. This happens through a process of micro-analysis of Charles's current practices.

In all of these cases, the therapist should, first of all, find their place in the system, then, from this place, ask questions which may create the possibility of patients finding more fluidity and a different place, both in the therapeutic relationship and in their relevant systems. It is also useful to adopt a developmental perspective, bearing in mind how people, systems and contexts change over time.

Clinical example: mothers and children

Maura is 35 and works as a waitress in a restaurant, as does her partner. She is the mother of a six-month-old child. Taking care of him is difficult for the parents, who mostly work times when childcare institutions are unavailable. They have to seek the help of grandparents, especially Maura's mother, who unfortunately has very different ideas about child rearing, using means that her daughter strongly disapproves, such as putting the child in front of a TV to get some respite. Maura gets mad at her, and comes to therapy in distress and great sadness.

The therapist tries to connect these emotions, clear and strong as they are, with Maura's and her mother's positions. Maura's mother had been an anxious, over-performing mother, in her daughter's recollections. Now Maura feels a difference in her mother's attitude—she has become more relaxed and easygoing—that she cannot accept.

"I cannot see her as a mother anymore!" she says.

"And that's right, because you're the mother now," answers the therapist. "And this means that it's a problem if you want to be the daughter as well."

Her new position as a mother is at odds with her (preferred) daughter position, where, she explains, she can be a little girl again, and forget about the excess of responsibility inherent in her being a mother. If she finds her place she can choose the position to take. In the end, she chooses to face her mother as a younger mother, seeking care and understanding in her partner instead.

In Maura's case, the basic distortion lies in a fixity of past patterns. In the presence of her mother, she becomes a (small) daughter again, and seeks a kind of mothering she cannot get any longer. This is also at odds with her new position as a mother, producing in her a dissonance that in turn enhances her anxiety. Realising this process helps her to find her place, and to feel better in accepting her mother as she is in the present.

The burden of illness (reprise)

While he feels stuck, the therapist tries to reflect on how the domains in finding one's place operate both in Martin's life and in the therapist's conduction of therapy:

Domain 1. The therapist first reflects on himself. What kind of therapist is he in this therapy? Thinking about himself and the relationship he established with Martin, he feels he got close to what Cecchin, Lane, and Ray (1994, p. 10) define as "the missionary therapist"—a therapist who feels he is more lucky that his patient, and therefore must share his luck with him and help him. Another prejudice he is playing out is the typical position of the systemic therapist, who must provide smart hypotheses that make a difference and change the patient's situation. The therapist felt much better when he was able to address one of Martin's distortions in finding one's place—since his tendency to go back to his lost physical well-being could be seen as a typical fixity of past patterns.

Apparently, Martin is not asking his therapist to provide any solution. He simply reacts to the therapist's discouragement, and interprets it as distraction (which it partially is, by the way). As far as the macro-contextual domain is concerned, anyway, the relevant distortions come from the therapist's side.

Domain 2. Martin says that he is well-liked in his workplace, where he constructed in the past decade quite a solid position. He is apparently not particularly interested in getting a better-paid job, or to try anything different. The PhD he left behind, he considers simply as something incomplete that he could complete or not, depending on the circumstances. What is curious, for the therapist, is that he talks more or less in identical terms of his relationship with Beatrice, his wife. The therapist reflects on his own prejudices in this regard: he feels that one should always strive to do their very best in any field, and that renouncing this aspiration involves a major loss. He wonders whether, inadvertently, he began to see Martin in such light, as a man who renounces and by so doing loses important opportunities. Most of all, he wonders whether this impression may have led to his inattentiveness when Martin displays such behaviour, with no idea of changing it.

Domain 3. Some of Martin's premises seem to contradict what the therapist finds obvious, i.e., that adult children should arrive to a balanced enough relationship with their parents. Such premise is also reinforced by family therapy literature, that tends to emphasise this point. Here there is some distance between patient and therapist. Martin spent his early life with a nurturing—but not overly nurturing—father, and a mother whom he felt was mostly preoccupied with herself. It makes sense that he expects a sustained attention and interest from his (male) therapist. The therapist realises that Martin's comment about his own mother gave him the idea that he was more detached and less needy than he probably is.

Domain 4. Possibly, Martin's apparent lack of enthusiasm makes sense if one thinks about his life: he grew up in a family that, while not overly unsupportive, did not provide him with a secure environment. This was probably complicated by his medical condition, that made him feel unstable and insecure. Little wonder that he has always preferred not to run risks: risk could—and in his perception probably would—lead to the worst result, unbalancing him and leaving him exposed.

The therapist's reflection helps him to understand his own reaction: he was getting bored, which means, therapeutically, that he was feeling that any intervention on his part could not make any difference (Bertrando & Arcelloni, 2009). From this feeling of uselessness came his inertia, that ultimately led to inattention. The feeling of boredom was related to his perceived duty to "make a difference" and, in some way, to provide Martin a solution that does not exist.

Having found his place, the therapist can now move from the position of striving to make something happen to the position of Martin's companion in understanding his situation. The therapist can begin to address Martin's choices and fears without the risk of judging them—he understands now that his own passivity was also due to the clash between his own prejudice ("one must do all he can, and maybe more") and his patient's ("one must first of all protect himself and reduce risk"). The therapy becomes now a journey through Martin's life, where the therapist has recovered his curiosity, and can thus help Martin develop his own. Together, they begin to review Martin's story and his choices, considering them from an interested but dispassionate viewpoint.

They discover that Martin made many attempts to get something better from his extended family, but to no avail; that he is now open to talk with Beatrice and re-examine their situation, in order to make it more involving for both. Ultimately, Martin is beginning to consider the possibility of getting back to his PhD and completing it, also because lately he has felt limited in his stable, but somewhat stagnant, work position. There are still moments when his mood darkens without apparent motives, but all in all both patient and therapist have the feeling that the therapy is proceeding.

Finding one's place in institutions

Finding one's place always means understanding multiple contexts. For therapists, the contexts to consider depend on the conditions of their work. A private practitioner has to deal—like anybody else—with the macro-contextual level, understanding the cultural, social, economical and political underpinnings of their practice. Nor can they forget the intimate and intra-relational levels, that are obviously relevant in their profession. The therapist who works in an institution must have an additional sensitivity to what we call the group, or micro-social level: they must consider the organisational dimensions of the institution they are operating in, their position and sense of well-being in it, and often also the additional power they have for the very fact of being part of an institution—especially a public one, that may decide about the social welfare of a person, or even their possibilities to keep their children. Let us see some examples.

Nora

Nora is a 29-year-old psychologist who works as a freelance professional for two different mental health public institutions, besides maintaining some private practice. She is comparatively satisfied with her position, but also worried by its instability. When one of the services announces recruitment for a stable post, she applies and is hired. She brings for supervision her new restlessness: the perspective of changing her work life is interesting and challenging, but she cannot help feeling some regret and some reservations about it. Nora must choose between the manifold (liquid) identity of a freelance consultant and part-time private practitioner, and the monolithic (solid) identity of an employee of the NHS. She is uncomfortable in both positions and must find her place.

During the supervision, she realises that she must change her priorities and the kind of relationship she is accustomed to: she was comparatively free, albeit precarious; now she is subjected to a boss and her authority. In Bauman's terms, she chose to trade freedom for security. She must understand whether the security she was seeking is worth the effort. After some reflection, she feels she is inclined to accept the post, but she keeps in her mind the possibility of quitting whenever she may decide it is the case.

At the following supervision, she arrives with a relieved face. She has finally made her decision. She realises that what made it so hard was the necessity to abandon her private practice mindset: private practice is a technology of the self that she needs to overcome in order to adapt to her new context. At the same time, she cheerfully describes one of the novelties she made in her new office: "I took away the desk, and substituted it with a round table: this creates a new environment, where both I and the others may enter a more open, dialogical dimension." She is trying to bring dialogue—her preferred way of working—within her new environment.

Virginia

Virginia, a psychologist of 35, works as a therapist in a Child and Adolescent Service. She has been working there for two years. When she arrived, she found an already established, all-female multidisciplinary team led by a quite experienced midwife. Within the larger team, Virginia found herself closer to two other, much more senior female psychologists. In time, the team has undergone many changes, not always for the best: three midwives and a psychologist have left, and have been substituted by new colleagues, while three more educational therapists have been recruited. Lately, the team leader has gone on maternity leave, and has been substituted by a less expert colleague. Despite her alleged absence, the original team leader sometimes visits them, and Virginia feels she is acting as a sort of unrecognised supervisor. All in all, Virginia is feeling angry.

"At whom?" the supervisor asks.
"At all of them. The whole context has changed for the worse!"

She notices that she is beginning to feel restless with patients too, as if they were causing the lower quality of her intervention, although she realises this cannot be the case. Her closer colleagues do not help in this respect: they are much angrier than her, and keep comparing the present situation to older times when "everything was working much better".

The supervisor points out a potential emotional contagion, where her colleagues' anger contributes to her uneasiness; it is also possibly an identity issue for the other two: they have been in that service from the very beginning.

"Maybe," the supervisor reflects, "they consider the service as 'their own' service, and maybe even the original team leader consider it as 'her own' service. Is there a possibility that you have begun to think that you could organise it better yourself?"
"Perhaps it's true," Virginia admits.
"In this case, you could be sharing their prejudices, that a professional working responsibly in a service is entitled to appropriate it."

Possibly, Virginia fell into a distortion of finding her place: thinking that she can change the rules of a larger system, when she is not officially appointed to do it. A position of *hybris*, that leads to discomfort, anger, and sometimes folly (Chapter 5).[4] In order to escape such folly, Virginia must find her place: if she is able to see institutional rules as something that she cannot change, she can then find the course of action that may help to do her job in the best possible way within the circumstances.

When she comes back to supervision, Virginia seems definitely less angry: she reports that she is actually feeling better after abandoning the idea that the system must change. At the same time, she also feels disillusioned, and thinks that working there is not interesting to her as it used to be. She is considering the possibility of quitting. Here the consequences of her finding her place are twofold: on a first, immediate level realising her helplessness is a relief; on a deeper level, it leads to a progressive disengagement, and to the possible end of her very relationship with that work context.

Institutions, race, culture, and class

Race, culture, and class play an important part in many cases that involve institutions, since therapy for low-income classes is mostly provided by state or non-governmental agencies. This example is taken from a supervision that happened in Australia.

Jessica, 66, is married to an older man, who now is no longer self-sufficient and needs full time care by her. They are both indigenous Australian and live in a traditional Aboriginal community, where they have the status of respected elders. They have grown around 40 children, theirs or from other parents, in the community. The presented situation regards the custody of two children: Dexter, eight, and Eileen, six. They are two of the children of Clarissa, who in the past had been brought up by Jessica herself. The local Department of Child Safety (DOCS) gave custody to Jessica, after the assessment to an Aboriginal elder, who decided she was fit to have them in custody, despite the destructive habits of the first-born Dexter.

After placement Dexter has become even more destructive, with temper tantrums, on one occasion setting the grandparents' house on fire, and so on; he changed three schools, being thrown out from all three. Many agencies were involved in Dexter's care, with enormous expense. In the meantime, the family moved, passing from one DOCS to another, that now considers Jessica unable to care for these children. They give our therapist, a white Australian, the task of evaluating Jessica's parental ability.

The therapist brings to supervision her dilemmas: "I feel that Jessica is not really able to properly care for Dexter and Eileen. At the same time, she is very loving and very amiable with me, and I feel like betraying her if I don't leave the children with her. I'm afraid to be influenced by my condition as a white mother, and I wonder whether I can understand exactly what's like for her; also, I feel that there has been a lot of institutional confusion, and I don't feel right to be the one that gives this judgement. I must do it, though."

Therapist and supervisor draw a map of the different institutions involved in Jessica's case. There are a lot of them: Jessica's family, of course; the local Aboriginal community; an agency for the elderly, that helps with James's care; the two DOCS; three different schools; IFACSS (a natives' agency); a psychiatrist; possibly in the future, a court; potentially, at all times, media and politics.

Then the supervision group discusses some additional information. First of all, Jessica's initial assessment had been positive on the basis that "she loves the children, she's done the right thing with the others, she will make it"; Jessica shares the same belief. Somebody guesses that the elder who performed the evaluation could not afford to give her a negative evaluation in the face of the native community. The therapist has talked to the psychiatrist, who thinks the boy is lost, and she should concentrate on saving his sister. The new DOCS seems unable to simply take the children away from Jessica, but keeps making things difficult for her—e.g., making mandatory for her to travel 50 km for a visit, and she doesn't drive—in order to make her resign of her own initiative.

The therapist interviewed Jessica too, of course. She does not seem very troubled by the whole process, but sometimes she feels tired by her age and worries, and is beginning to think she could as well see the children on weekends, simply as a grandma. The therapist feels she has been brought in by DOCS with a hidden agenda: she should encourage Jessica to withdraw, with the pretext of therapy.

(In the course of this dialogue, the supervisor reflects on his own positioning, too. He is attuned to the therapist's dilemma, because he feels the risk of playing out inadvertently his racial prejudices—he is a European white man, after all. At the same time he cannot avoid hypothesising that Jessica is too tired to go on. Relying on his own discomfort, he can mirror the therapist's indecisiveness, so that she can look at herself from the outside.)

At this point, the supervision group finds it is possible to discuss some hypotheses. First of all, who is the therapist's client? Clearly, it is DOCS. The therapist should be professionally loyal to DOCS and its prejudices, except that they clash with her own prejudices about being sympathetic with the persons involved—especially Jessica. Who is the therapist's patient? The therapist is appointed as an evaluator rather than a therapist, so strictly speaking she should have no patient. If she could, she should probably consider Dexter and Eileen as her patients. During the supervision, though, she talked as if her patient were Jessica. To a participant, this process impinges on the therapist's identity: is she an assessor or a therapist? Her task appears unclear both to herself and to DOCS.

There is a strong influence of broader political and cultural issues. The therapist cannot forget the tradition of social mistreatment of native Australians, something that is still present in the way institutions deal with them: native agencies tend to be patronising and subtly racist. The therapist is actively resisting the temptation to give in to white Australian racism. Another participant points out the social sense of guilt that she sees in all the institutions involved: the problem of removing children from Aboriginal families after what happened in the past. They would be relieved if Jessica stepped out of her own counsel, freeing them from the responsibility of choice.

Another participant reminds a concurrent re-organisation of DOCS, at state level, that plays a role in increasing confusion. Different cultures and perspectives are involved: the first DOCS trusted Jessica, whereas the second is sceptical; the Aboriginal community trusted Jessica's love; the psychiatrist is totally (medically) distrustful. The whole situation brought to an accretion of interventions, to no avail. A participant also observes a process of scapegoating going on: everybody is blaming Dexter for what is happening. The supervisor also points out an apparent dichotomy: the therapist apparently can only answer yes or no, with no other possibility; hence her sense of becoming an external, unsympathetic, cold judge to Jessica.

(In this part of the process, the supervisor feels at ease. He feels he has gained some understanding of the position of the main actors in the case. At the beginning he had been an extraneous observer; now he is more participant, and his questions to the group and feedback to the therapist reflect his finding his place.)

After this dialogue, the therapist feels she is able to find her place. She can recognise the social sense of guilt that was evoked in the supervision as her own. It led her, in turn, to want to be a therapist in a situation where she cannot maintain a therapeutic position. It is now clear that she must be an assessor, and her range of motion is limited by her passive positioning by DOCS.

At the same time, she now feels that she can go beyond the yes/no dichotomy. If she cannot be a therapist, she can be a sympathetic assessor, with the possibility of talking: she can open different dialogues. She can talk to Jessica in order to explain her choice, and maybe discuss with her whether she is ready to become at last a proper grandma, seeing them at weekend; but she can also talk with DOCS, articulating more clearly her assessment, maybe giving some indication for treatment.

Here finding her place means, for the therapist, to accept first of all the limitations of her position, conditioned as it is by the institutions involved; then to become more aware of her own prejudices in the situation. Only at this point can she take action, using the interstices between the prescriptions and prohibitions coming from people and agencies, and finding the best course of action available in the present conditions.

Conclusion

Our main idea is that, when we enter into any relationship, an instant network is activated within us and around us, linking various elements on several planes—emotional, rational, internal, relational. At the same time, different positions are (internally) activated in us, that we may (relationally) adopt toward the others, both in actual and imagined interaction. Such a network extends both in space—family, social systems, institutions—and time—family of origin, past relationships, personal history. Its elements exist both as memories of the past, presence in the present, and projection into the future (Boscolo & Bertrando, 1992). All knots in the network reciprocally relate to each other. Activating one puts others in motion, e.g., any present relationship necessarily activates knots rooted in the past.

Finding one's place means, to the therapist, shifting to a different emotional position, from which they may be more able to engage patients in questions and hypotheses involving new, freer frames of reference, that may then make the initial knots recede into the background: in the main case presented, for example, bringing to the fore issues related to intimacy and family. Within these frames it should be possible for patients to find their place in a way that allows more consistency between their thinking and feeling, and between their inner and outer world. If a person knows where they are and how they feel, their responses can be properly dialogical, integrating different domains of the relationships they are embedded in.

The clinical consequences of finding one's place are manifold. Our ability to find our place as therapists may be played out, from time to time, in one or another relational domain. We may find our place in relation to patients, to the overall therapeutic system, and even to macro-contextual variables, such as gender or culture. The therapist may thus facilitate a dialogical environment, where patients can create new ways of being in relationship. This does not mean to reduce complexity, but rather to find new ways to inhabit it. If the therapist helps patients to see different levels in a dialogical relation with one another, they can develop a three-dimensional view of their lives. What is more, once a person has found their place, they can take full responsibility for their actions, as we will see in the next chapter.

Notes

1 Actually, the Milan therapists were neither the only ones nor the first to deal with it. As is the case in any form of psychotherapy, in family therapy too, attention has been paid toward the therapeutic relationship, first implicitly (Minuchin, 1974), then explicitly (Flaskas, Mason, & Perlesz, 2005).

2 This reminds us of a therapy session, of course, but is also somewhat similar to the "care of oneself" of ancient Stoics, as it was interpreted by Michel Foucault (1990).

3 The opposite, paradoxical case—not knowing where we want to go, but knowing how to get there—could be defined as the "rebel without a cause" position, well epitomised by Johnny Rotten's famous line, "don't know what I want but I know

how to get it", meaningfully followed by the statement "I wanna destroy" (from the song "Anarchy in the UK", by Sex Pistols, 1976).

4 Hybris was, in ancient Greek tragedy, the condition of humans when they try to defy the gods: it inevitably brings them to ruin. This concept was first applied to systemic therapy by the original Milan group in their book *Paradox and Counter-paradox* (Selvini Palazzoli et al., 1978).

References

Bateson, G. (1972). *Steps to an Ecology of Mind*. Chandler Publishing Company.

Bauman, Z. (2000). *Liquid Modernity*. Polity Press.

Bauman, Z., Bertrando, P., & Hanks, H. (2010). Liquid Ethics—psychotherapy in a time of uncertainty. *Human Systems*, 20 (1): 42–56.

Bertrando, P. (2000). Text and context. Narrative, postmodernism, and cybernetics. *Journal of Family Therapy*, 22 (1): 83–103. DOI:10.1111/1467–6427.00139.

Bertrando, P. (2007). *The Dialogical Therapist*. Karnac.

Bertrando, P. (2009a). Emotional positioning and the therapeutic process. *Context*, 107 (December 2009): 17–19.

Bertrando, P. (2015). *Emotions and the Therapist*. Karnac.

Bertrando P. & Arcelloni, T. (2009). Anger and boredom. Unpleasant emotions in systemic therapy. In: C. Flaskas & D. Pocock (Eds.), *Systems and Psychoanalysis*. Karnac, pp. 75–92.

Boscolo, L. & Bertrando, P. (1992). The reflexive loop of past, present, and future in systemic therapy and consultation. *Family Process*, 31: 119–130. DOI:10.1111/j.1545–5300.1992.00119.x.

Boscolo, L. & Bertrando, P. (1993). *The Times of Time: A Perspective on Time in Systemic Therapy and Consultation*. 2nd edition. Routledge, 2020.

Boscolo, L. & Bertrando, P. (1996). *Systemic Therapy with Individuals*. Karnac.

Bowen, M. (1972). On the differentiation of the Self. In: *Family Therapy in Clinical Practice*. Jason Aronson, 1978, pp. 467–528.

Cecchin, G. (1987). Hypothesizing-circularity-neutrality revisited: An invitation to curiosity. *Family Process*, 26: 405–413. DOI:10.1111/j.1545–5300.1987.00405.x.

Cecchin, G., Lane G., & Ray, W.L. (1992). *Irreverence: A Strategy for Therapists' Survival*. Karnac.

Cecchin, G., Lane G., & Ray, W.L. (1994). *The Cybernetics of Prejudices in the Practice of Psychotherapy*. Karnac.

Eco, U. (1968). *La struttura assente*. Bompiani.

Elkaïm, M. (2004). The feelings of the psychotherapist: systemic approach and resonance. *Psychotherapies*, 24: 145–150.

Esman, A.H. (1990). *Essential Papers on Transference*. New York University Press.

Flaskas, C., Mason, B., & Perlesz, A. (2005). *The Space Between: Experience, Context, and Process in the Therapeutic Relationship*. Karnac.

Foucault, M. (1990). *The History of Sexuality Volume 3: The Care of the Self*. Penguin (original edition 1984).

Foucault, M. (2004). *Naissance de la biopolitique. Cours au Collège de France 1978–79*. Gallimard.

Fredman, G. (2007). Preparing our selves for the therapeutic relationship: revisiting "Hypothesising revisited". *Human Systems*, 18: 44–59.

Freud, S. (1920). *Beyond the Pleasure Principle*. English translation by James Strachey. *The Standard Edition of the Complete Psychological Works of Sigmund Freud*, Volume XVIII (1920–1922): 7–64.

Goldner, V., Penn, P., Sheinberg, M., & Walker, G. (1990). Love and violence: Gender paradoxes in volatile attachments. *Family Process*, 29: 343–364. http://dx.doi.org/10.1111/j.1545-5300.1990.00343.x.

Goolishian, H.A. & Winderman, L. (1988). Constructivism, autopoiesis and problem determined systems. *The Irish Journal of Psychology*, 9 (1): 130–143. DOI:10.1080/03033910.1988.10557710.

Harré, R. & Van Langenhove, L. (Eds.) (1999). *Positioning Theory*. Oxford: Basil Blackwell.

Krause, I-B. (1993). Anthropology and family therapy: a case for emotions. *Journal of Family Therapy*, 15: 35–56. DOI:10.1111/j.1467–6427.1993.00739.x.

Mann, T. (1994). *Buddenbooks: The Decline of a Family*. (English translation by John E. Woods). Everyman's Library (original edition 1901).

Michels, R., Abensour, L., Eizirik, C. L., & Rusbridger, R. (2002). *Key Papers on Countertransference*. Karnac.

Minuchin, S. (1974). *Families and Family Therapy*. Harvard University Press.

Moghaddam, F. & Harré, R. (2010). Words, conflicts and political processes. In F. Moghaddam & R. Harré (Eds.), *Words of Conflict, Words of War: How the language we use in political processes sparks fighting*. Praeger.

Rober, P. (2005). The therapist's self in dialogical family therapy: some ideas about not-knowing and the therapist's inner conversation. *Family Process*, 44: 477–495. DOI:10.1111/j.1545–5300.2005.00073.x.

Selvini Palazzoli, M., Boscolo, L., Cecchin, G., & Prata, G. (1978). *Paradox and Counterparadox*. Jason Aronson.

Selvini Palazzoli, M., Boscolo, L., Cecchin, G., & Prata, G. (1980a). Hypothesizing-circularity-neutrality. Three guidelines for the conductor of the session. *Family Process*, 19: 3–12. DOI:10.1111/j.1545–5300.1980.00003.x.

Selvini Palazzoli, M., Boscolo, L., Cecchin, G., & Prata, G. (1980b). The problem of the referring person. *Journal of Marital and Family Therapy*, 6: 3–9.

Stolorow, R.D., Atwood, G.E., & Orange, D.M. (2002). *Worlds of experience: Interweaving philosophical and clinical dimensions in psychoanalysis*. Basic Books.

Tomm, K. (1987a). Interventive Interviewing: I. Strategizing as a Fourth Guideline for the Therapist. *Family Process*, 26: 3–13. DOI:10.1111/j.1545–5300.1987.00003.x.

Watzlawick, P., Beavin, J. & Jackson, D.D. (1967). *Pragmatics of Human Communication*. Norton.

Wynne, L.C. (1984). The epigenesis of relational systems: A model for understanding family development. *Family Process*, 23: 297–318. DOI:10.1111/j.1545–5300.1984.00297.x.

Chapter 7

Responsibilities

The fourth pillar of our approach is responsibility. We believe that taking responsibility for one's actions is an essential factor for therapeutic change. Individuals should be able to take responsibility both toward relevant others in their lives (relational responsibility), and in regard to the position they take (positional responsibility). To help the patient in such effort, the therapists must, in turn, take their responsibility for the development of the therapeutic process.

Taking responsibility

Although responsibility is a relevant concept in psychotherapy at large,[1] it got scant attention within the field of systemic therapy. This is probably due to systemic therapy's very nature, initially centred solely on superindividual systems, such as the family: a family as such cannot be responsible for anything, only individual family members can. Bateson (1972) maintained that, if we consider the wider system, we find no trace of responsibility or power—hence his well-known disregard of the concept of power itself. Only within a renewed focus on the individual, and on the dynamics of power that are ubiquitous in real life, are we drawn toward acknowledging responsibility.

If we put ourselves in this position, the landscape dramatically changes. We cannot escape our responsibilities. The only possibility is to decide whether we want to follow a code of action or take personal, moral responsibility (Bauman, 1993; see below). Adherence to a code may make us uncritical. Moral responsibility, instead, makes us consider, case by case, our relationships with others, and therefore the consequences that our actions have upon them.

It is now clear to us that many of the changes we see in our clinical activity are related to the dark sides of the postmodern condition (Bauman, 2000; see also Chapter 1 and Appendix A). The link to responsibility, however, was initially mysterious to us. We saw it when we began reflecting on the relationship between responsibility and positioning in systems and contexts, as they have evolved in our times. When we realised the extent of the

DOI: 10.4324/9781003381754-8

connections between responsibility and social changes, we felt that, by addressing this issue, we could make our therapy both more effective and a better fit to the present cultural climate. In order to do that, we had to distinguish the multiple meanings that the concept of responsibility can have.

Individual responsibility

First of all, let us consider the easiest meaning of responsibility in liquid modernity (Chapter 1). According to the neoliberal creed, each individual should be responsible for everything that happens to them. In this perspective individual responsibility is a form of passive positioning. Let us tell a story. Steve is 23, with a BA in communication. After some uncomfortable experiences in a firm, he decided to take advantage of his skills on YouTube, by the use of platforms that allow him to sell his videos. At the same time, he subscribed to another platform that helps him to work as a photographer, another ability he developed at the university. He has to stay up extremely late every evening in order to complete the videos he must upload and put online every day. His workday almost coincides with the whole of his time. Even his holidays are turned into videos that must be edited and put online.

Steve cannot reflect on his position. He accepts the position that the context puts him into and, within that position, he feels fully responsible for his actions. Born subject to these rules, he cannot question them. They are his reality because the context of his life is shaped in such a way as to offer no alternatives. He can only do the best he can. As a "digital native", he does not even see the process and takes these harsh environmental conditions for granted. He feels—despite his fatigue, his weariness, his anxiety about being able to complete all his tasks by the end of the day—that he is free, creative, and autonomous.

Is Steve free? He certainly is—to this extent, neoliberal apologists tell the truth. Is he completely free? He certainly is not—he is free only to move within a boundary. This is the neoliberal deception. We are put into a position we cannot escape, and must take responsibility without actually having the power to make decisions. In a word, Steve is positioned by the context, imprisoned by a thousand inescapable micro-practices of power (Foucault, 1977).

Actually, passive positioning is by no means a new condition. According to positioning theory (van Langenhove & Harré, 1999), not only do all of us position each other during our daily interaction, but contexts, too, position everybody inside them. In times of "solid modernity", our position was mostly established by rigid hierarchies: the army would position us as executors of orders; the church, as subject to spiritual rules; the family, as affective agents. In the first instance, we were expected to obey orders; in the second, to conform to strict ethical prescriptions; in the third, to be affectionate and caring toward members of our family. In all cases, positioning entailed a strong performative drive. If we did not conform, we not only underwent social disapproval, we would easily feel guilty.

The present condition of liquid modernity led to a loosening of accepted social bonds and chains of command. Passive positioning still exists, but it is acted out more subtly. Steve is not forced to do anything, yet he acts as if he were. The neoliberal practice of living makes most obligations and prohibitions implicit. Everyone may ideally do what they prefer—therefore they are responsible for their actions. Actually, desire must be contained within narrow limits. We can do whatever we want, provided that the context is not put in doubt. The subject is positioned in such a way as to become responsible to fulfil tasks without questioning their sense—because they are not legitimised to. Freedom is granted only within the imposition "you are responsible": "No rights without responsibility" (Giddens, 1998, p. 72).

> Consider, for instance, health risks. Many people get ill through no fault of their own. But a large proportion of illnesses are related both to life-style practices and to wider conditions of the "created environment". It doesn't make any sense to suppose that liability in these circumstances can remain wholly with the collective, whether this be government or an insurance company. The active assumption of responsibility, as in attempts to reduce levels of smoking, becomes part of the very definition of risk situations and therefore the attribution of responsibility.
>
> (Giddens, 1999, p. 9)

This kind of individual responsibility produces both anxiety (at not being able to reach one's goals for the future), and guilt (at not having reached them in the past or present). A script thus emerges, in which we are implicitly but forcefully invited to participate, without discussing rules or criteria. These very rules, however, both make us responsible and make us wish to escape such responsibilities.

Active positioning

An alternative option to passive positioning can be to discuss and review our position in the system. This would entail a different kind of responsibility, that involves active positioning: a positional responsibility. We think that, even before being responsible for what we do or we do not do, we are responsible for the position we take.

How does positional responsibility differ from individual responsibility as it appears in public dominant discourse? First of all, in avoiding over-estimating our possibilities as individuals (Shotter & Katz, 1999). All of us have the possibility to act only within the limits posed by the systems we are embedded in, and by the contexts we inhabit. Understanding the shape of the context we are in, together with our position within them, allows us to take the right level of responsibility toward tasks, obligations, and requests contained within those contexts. This means that we are responsible for the relationship we create, or, at least, for the way we stay in those relationships.

Contexts generate implicit codes that we tend to take for granted. Bauman (1993) contrasts "ethical code" with "moral responsibility". The first is the adherence to a set of rules posed by social agencies, whereas the second is a responsibility we take individually. In solid modernity, ethical codes prevailed. It was possible to appeal to an authority—a book, a teacher, a hierarchy—to justify one's actions, or to resort to a strong belonging—a structured group—that could take a collective responsibility, thus lifting the burden from the individual.

Adherence to a code, however, makes us uncritical (Gergen, 1999), particularly if the ethical code is undeclared, and so impossible to discuss. The participants in Milgram's (1974) famous experiments, who believed they were administering electrical shocks to innocent victims out of mere obedience to authority, accepted a technical responsibility. They were trying to do what the authority was asking in the best way they could, according to established criteria which they embraced without doubts, even at the cost of providing pain and suffering to their "experimental subjects".

According to Bauman (1989) the Holocaust (the Shoah) was made possible mainly by obedience to authority. Many if not all of the people involved accepted their role in inhuman actions because they were only part of the cog and did not feel responsible for the end result. In the light of Milgram's research, this is only the extreme case of a general tendency: if we entrust the authority with the responsibility of deciding what is the "right" goal and what are the procedures we must follow, we will feel exempted from evaluating time by time what we are doing and we will only feel the responsibility to do it well. In other words, Bauman says that the mechanisms proposed by Milgram make it possible to understand how the full acceptance of an authority leads to the discharge of responsibility on authority. This, Bauman (1989) says, is a formal description of Hannah Arendt's (1963) "banality of evil".

If the ethical code "strives to define 'proper' and 'improper' actions [and] sets for itself an ideal of churning out exhaustive and unambiguous definitions" (Bauman, 1993, p. 11), moral responsibility is based on "erratic and unreliable moral impulses" (Bauman, 1993, pp. 248–9), on emotional, rather than rational, factors. One can find it "in insubordination toward socially upheld principles, and in action openly defying social solidarity and consensus" (Bauman, 1989, pp. 177–8).

Moral responsibility, in other words, makes us consider, case by case, our relationships with others, and the consequences that our actions have upon them. We substitute a preoccupation with the future consequences (on others) of what we do—Max Weber's (1919) "ethics of responsibility"—for an ethics based on a decontextualised adherence to "what is right"—Weber's "ethics of principles". We build such responsibility together. Nobody is fully responsible for a relationship and nobody is fully exempt from responsibility either. We are responsible both for our position and for the way we position the others.

We must try and understand what the responsibilities are that are entailed in each relationship. (With some differences, though: our responsibility is different in informal conversation compared to therapeutic dialogue; parents' responsibility is different if their children are newborn or adult, and so on.)

The therapist's responsibility

What is the therapist's responsibility in therapy? We consider the therapist as responsible only for the therapeutic process, rather than for the final outcome: we do not have to achieve the end result, which is up to the patients.[2] We try to act in such a way that patients are able to increase their awareness and agency. This means that we are responsible to foster a therapeutic process that constantly maintains therapeutic characteristics: our is a process responsibility. Process responsibility means to guarantee that, in our therapies, every moment is ethically as well as technically acceptable, and aimed at maximising the possibilities for patients to develop their own positions and take action in their lives. This is our personal responsibility.

All in all, we, as therapists, cannot know what is best for our patients. The therapist who tries to act on behalf of them, who—moved by a wish to help them, or by a more or less unavowable feeling they cannot make it by themselves—suggests or even tries to impose directions or solutions, enters a distortion in finding their place: they mistake a part for the whole, seeing mostly the limits and unresolved issues of the patient, rather than their resources and strengths.

We prefer, if necessary, to put ourselves in our patients' shoes and then tell them how we would feel in their place. That does not mean explaining to patients what they are feeling (we do not know that better than them), nor prescribing how they should feel; we just state our vision of what is happening. It is up to them to confirm or disprove our assumptions according on their experience, and then make their choices. This does not eliminate our responsibility, but rather accentuates it, because we are personally responsible for what we carry in dialogue and our part in it. Ours, again, is a positional responsibility.

The patient's responsibility

If therapists guarantee a good enough therapeutic process, patients have the biggest share of responsibility regarding the outcome, in terms of increased awareness, understanding of social context, disappearance of symptoms, or solution of problems. They are responsible for their choices. However, the final result of therapy is uncontrollable, both by patients and therapists.

The patient's responsibility lies mostly in the future. The meaning of responsibility changes in relation to time. The emphasis may be either on the past ("I am responsible for what I have done") or the future ("I am responsible for what I am going to do"). Responsibility in the past implies facts that have already happened, and are therefore irretrievable. In this case, "I am responsible" means "I have acted well", or, more often, "I did it wrong". An internal dialectic, which concerns our relationship with ourselves, and our judgement about ourselves, easily generates guilt: "What have I done?" "What haven't I done (and should have done)?" If it centres on others, it may easily produce blame (stigmatisation of the other) and a position of victim. If we feel ourselves to be the victims of others, we will blame them (Stratton, 2003). Responsibility in the present tends to be associated with yet another emotion, shame ("How do others judge what I am doing or not doing?"), or, if we feel ourselves to be in the right, its opposite, pride (Chapter 5). Here, we create a community, actual or imaginary, that can judge our actions or even our personal worth. Such a judgement takes place in the present.

Of course, to understand past or present responsibility can be important. In many cases, such as violence or abuse, it is absolutely necessary. In therapy, though, entering the interplay between guilt, blame and shame, can be risky. We are mostly interested in responsibility toward the future: the responsibility for what we will do. Emotionally, this kind of responsibility may take the form of anxiety. "What should I do and how?" etc. For the same reason, however, responsibility for the future gives back to people their own relational agency. Unlike past responsibility, future responsibility is on the verge of happening, and, therefore, it can always be changed. If the person takes responsibility for what they can do in the future, they also have the possibility to change.

Distortions of responsibility

As in the case of finding one's place, responsibility has its distortions, too. They emerge when responsibilities are avoided or, on the contrary, are taken on excessively. We provisionally distinguish four varieties: undue responsibility, sacrifice, shifting responsibility, and victim position. We will describe these distortions, and exemplify them through clinical vignettes.

Undue responsibility ("I'm responsible for what I can't control"). In previous pages, we have seen several instances of this kind, when people take on responsibilities, especially at work, which go beyond what is necessary. This process is definitely fuelled by neoliberal practices.

Maria is a 35-year-old chef. She is quite successful in her job, but she is apparently unable to enjoy her own achievements. She feels responsible for anything that happens not only in her kitchen, but in the whole restaurant, believing she has to amend any shortcomings, to the point of bringing her own cooking devices from home when the restaurant's ones are broken. She is unable to negotiate with the owners, and, at the same time, she is asking too much from her colleagues. Everybody, in her view, should participate in the enterprise as she does. Her anxiety often becomes unbearable, and it affects her relationships both with her colleagues and her partner.

Sacrifice ("I'm wholly responsible for somebody else's well-being"). In this case, the person takes responsibility not only for the consequences of their own actions, but also for the happiness of others, even when it entails events in which the person is not involved in any way. Such a dynamic is easily associated with guilt. Sacrifice, in extreme cases, becomes a full-fledged pathology of responsibility: I sacrifice myself, I even become a scapegoat, and by so doing I take upon myself all responsibilities within the relationship. Sacrifice relieves others of their responsibilities, and thus makes the relationship unbalanced.

Lisa is a 30-year-old researcher. She migrated from Italy to France after her graduation because her country did not offer good possibilities in her field. Afterwards, she transferred to Switzerland to follow her Geneva-born boyfriend, who left her soon after finding a job. Now Lisa is deeply despondent. She feels betrayed, thinking, "He did this to me, after all I did for him!" They probably got together, she says, because they were both alone and precarious in a strange land. Gradually, she became his supporter, to the point of sacrificing a very good position in order to follow him to his homeland. The end of his existential precariousness was also the end of their couple relationship. Reflecting on this, Lisa realises that she first played out this attitude in her relationship with her own mother, whose unhappiness she always felt responsible for. It was through her mother's sacrifice that she was able to study. Such a tangle of sacrifices made her life burdensome and almost devoid of joy.

Shifting responsibility ("It's not up to me"). This is the basic form of irresponsibility. It entails a refusal to acknowledge one's personal responsibilities. Sometimes it takes the form of blame (onto others), which is a complete devolution of responsibility. Other people, or our parents, or society at large, are responsible for our distress or even our hurting others. On other occasions, it appears in the form of a symptom, since a symptom is, by definition, something we are not responsible for.

Alice, 40, is unemployed after an impairing car accident that triggered a depressive phase, accompanied by a loss of self-confidence, anxiety and panic attacks. She arrives at the session after missing a lesson of the professional course she is attending because she feared a panic attack, which makes her feel a total, hopeless failure. Therapist and patient reflect on how she ended up missing her lesson: is it possible she simply did not wish to go? If she tells herself she cannot, she does not face the responsibility of choosing, adopting a passive attitude. If she tells herself she does not want to go, she takes responsibility, which is harder, but makes her in charge of her own decision. Of course, if she is choosing, she must take the neoliberal blame for her lack of will. This is not easy for her. After the session, she has a violent panic attack, and misses the two following therapy appointments. Afterwards, therapist and patient work together to get her out of her guilt. In the end, she manages to find a job, although rather modest (in the past she wanted a qualified one): she feels uncertain and slightly anxious, but ready to begin all the same.

Victim position ("Somebody else is responsible for my troubles"). When taking responsibility is too painful, one may unwittingly choose the position of a victim (Giglioli, 2014). To be a victim is the opposite of being responsible. Of course, we do not deny that there are real victims, many of whom we find in our daily practice. The woman subjected to domestic violence, the abused child, they are obviously victims, and we must consider them as such. But if we see ourselves only as victims, and we show others just that side of us, our very identity ends up being founded on our passivity, on what made us victims in the first place, rather than on our ability to hold an active position in our lives.

In this way we identify, once again, a part with the whole: "victims are victims because they are helpless" (Giglioli, 2014, p. 89). As victims, we can only be victimised or saved by somebody else, thus assuming a wholly passive role. The therapeutic issue is how we can help our patients to escape such perverse dualism, where they are either responsible for everything, or (irresponsible) victims.

Dante, a 40-year-old employee, seeks therapy after separating from his partner, Beth, who he decided to leave due to her "impossible" demands. Since that moment, Beth has made it hard for him to meet their two-year-old daughter, accusing him unrelentingly for the failure of their relationship, and creating unceasing obstacles to father-daughter encounters. Dante is furious with Beth. He states he is the victim of her abandonment and he is now vexed by her. And he appears truly surprised when the therapist reminds him that he was the one who decided on separation. With this reminder he is now ready to discuss his role as a father and his actual responsibilities for the evolution of family relationships.

Clinical example: choosing one's ethnicity

Teresa is 39. After many difficult couple relationships, she has found a man, Roberto, that she trusts. They are planning to have a child. Apparently it was an easy decision, until one day she comes to therapy anguished about a recent talk they had. They were discussing where to live with their future newborn: she comes from northern Italy, he comes from the south. At some point, he flatly declares that he does not want his child to be born in the north. He does not like the presumed coldness of people. She is of course upset, but there is more: she realises that there is something in the subject that is profoundly disturbing to her.

The part of northern Italy she come from is actually the region at the border with Austria, that Italians call Alto Adige, Austrian Südtirol. It is a bilingual region, where everybody is required to speak both Italian and German. Teresa is the daughter of divorced parents of different descent. At the age of 15 she had to make a final choice about her ethnicity. The youth at that age are presented with a questionnaire that requires to indicate their ethnicity, that can be Italian, German, or "Other", and this is of some importance, since most social institutions are separate. When this happened, Teresa was torn between two identities, since her father describes his ethnicity as German, her mother as Italian. Moreover, the choice is not exactly neutral. Italian speakers are regarded by the whole of the population as slightly—if not officially—second class compared to German speakers: for example, German speakers usually also speak fluent Italian, but not vice versa. She already had to choose between an Italian and a German school, and she chose the Italian one, which made her feel ashamed of herself.

Feeling overwhelmed, she finally decided for the "Other" option. This in turn made her German-speaking father feel outraged—he already felt the same when she chose the Italian school—which led to a difficult relationship between them ever since. She bursts into tears when she recalls that time. The therapist comments that probably she felt too big a responsibility for a 15-year-old— deciding something as deep and essential as her own ethnic identity, as if that identity wholly depended on her. She elaborates: her responsibility is all but obvious: the necessity of choosing was created by the regional administration, which in turn responded to a political climate complicated by the historical vicissitudes of the land.[3] By highlighting the macro-contextual level, the thera-pist aims at freeing Teresa from a personal responsibility that was unduly put on her—a distortion of responsibility due to social and political conditions.

Teresa now is able to elaborate on the guilty feeling that accompanied her for most of her life. She also realises that now she is torn by contrasting feelings again: on the one hand, she would like her child to live a continuity with her past and her places, that she still deeply loves, and maybe to recover some closeness with her family of origin, especially her estranged father; on the other, she does not want her child to be forced to the same decision. The therapist reminds her that in any case her children would come from a dif-ferent situation and would not be subjected to the same pressures she had to endure. In the end, Teresa seems to feel relieved from the burden of her past responsibilities.

Clinical example: Diana, making the others happy

Dealing with responsibility during the therapeutic process requires the therapist to engage in a complex and painstaking work. In our practice, this means to follow a series of steps that, albeit not being rigidly sequenced, tend to remain constant. We will try to illustrate them through a clinical example. It is just a fragment from a single session, but it can give a sense of the process.

During Christmas holidays it is easy to detect the re-emergence of implicit family rules and rituals that exert a powerful prescriptive force on all family members. This is what Diana is referring to when she comes back to therapy after the Christmas pause stating, "I hate Christmas!" and showing clear signs of sadness and frustration. It is natural, for the therapist, to ask why. Diana is a professional woman of 40, divorced, with two sons of 12 and 10 and a fledgling relationship with a new partner. Christmas generates for her an abundance of contradictions. Her parents and brother ask her to be present at the family dinner, as she has always been; her sons—together with her former husband—wish to see a temporary reunion of the original nuclear family and her new partner, in such a configuration, feels left alone. The families of her son's friends also appear to claim her presence during Christmas holidays, or so she feels.

"And the fact is, everything went really well!" she says, on the verge of tears. "Yet, I can't be happy, I feel horrible, I'm distressed for no reason!" Although it may appear a completely unimportant event, this (successful) Christmas seems to undermine all the well-being she has laboriously achieved after two years of separation.

Focusing on facts seems useless. Diana appears well aware of both the facts and their value. So the therapist focuses on emotions. In the beginning, Diana just repeats that she feels bad, while the therapist cooperates by pointing out the sadness she perceives in her. The dialogue slowly brings forth the many emotions that surround the nucleus of her sadness: anguish, nostalgia, melancholy, shame, restlessness, fatigue. Reflecting on the sense of those emotions within her family of origin, her couple relationships, and other relations, Diana describes a recurring pattern: "Everybody considers me as the provider of welcoming, of care, of dedication. Everybody, my parents, my ex-husband, my sons, my friends, my partner... and Christmas worsens everything. I become the vestal virgin of the feasts."

She describes the small apartment where she went to live after her divorce. For Christmas it was cosy and decorated, "like a mountain chalet". She prepared presents and Christmas cards for everybody, organised dinners and cocktails, up to the climax of the big dinner, where her parents, brother, sons, ex-husband, all gathered to celebrate. "Did you feel good at this dinner?" the therapist asks. "No! I was where I didn't want to be, and I wasn't with the person I wanted to be with. I would have felt guilty if I hadn't done it, and I still felt guilty after doing it. I guess I was raised to be always loving and caring."

While the dialogue helps her to give meaning to the jumble of emotions she brought to therapy, Diana begins to position herself: she notices that she allows (induces?) others to hold very definite expectations towards her: "Everybody thinks I like to take care of others without expecting anything in exchange." She realises, in other words, that she holds at least some responsibility for her position within the systems of her intimacy. The therapist can now point out how the roles she accepts contradict each other. Diana takes pride in being an independent, working woman—and her job is also necessary to safeguard her own and her children's well-being. At the same time she feels a strong, gendered pressure toward the care of the (mostly male) members of her extended family. The therapist proposes that these contradictions may be deeply connected with two conflicting ethical codes, the patriarchal and the neoliberal. Being a working woman has always been important to Diana, but this is also true for being a good mother, a good caregiver, a good wife or partner, and so on.[4]

Now the issue is how she can change, if possible. During the session, Diana experiences another emotion, which beforehand was completely tacit, that is, her anger toward the others. She wonders whether she is entitled to ask everybody why they cannot see her for who she feels she is, why they go on behaving as if she has no needs of her own. "Most of all," she muses, "why are they all thinking I must be the grown up, responsible one? Why do they expect it? Even my mother insists on telling me I must act mature!"

As yet Diana has no solutions to her problems, but at least she has attained some awareness. She must be the one to state her position to the others, including her dearest ones. She must set some limits. It cannot be an all-or-nothing process—she cannot simply forget the customary rites and roles of her life. But she can find, step by step, by trial and error, a way to stand up for herself.

Practice of responsibility

We will now try to follow the steps the therapist had to take to bring forth the implicit dynamics of the session, and help Diana in the process of taking positional responsibility.

Emotionality. The therapist gets to work, first focusing on the dominant emotions that appear in Diana's immediate presentation. Then she turns to hidden and implicit, tacit emotions. In Diana's case, the therapist senses, beyond her evident feeling of discouragement and humiliation, some hidden and ill-defined anger Diana is not aware of, although she appears to be strongly influenced by it. Being a woman herself, the therapist can easily single out Diana's tacit feelings. The therapist tries to give names to emotions in order to help Diana process them.

Emotional information. Now the therapist widens her horizon, looking at relational networks. She connects Diana's immediate feeling to her own and the others' positions within the complicated relational tangle she is embedded in. Diana reports she feels bad, but she still stays there. The therapist tries to help her discover the sense all this makes for her. This leads her to consider both her proximal and wider environment, as well as the culture she and the therapist participate in. Diana's emotions here have the function of guiding an investigation of the whole field of her experience. What is the meaning of work for her, what is the meaning of care, why care (of her family of origin, especially) is so important, what are her role models within and beyond the family?

Finding one's place. As the session unfolds, the therapist tries to help Diana move from a position of passive acceptance toward finding her place. Diana begins to get to a balance between emotional and cognitive levels, shifting from a mere acknowledgement of her emotions to a positional awareness of them. Progressively, she is enabled to give meaning to her emotions by working on her position in the family system. This also encourages her to wonder how she positions herself with regard to traditional family values, on the one hand, and, on the other, the affections she has for the members of her family of origin, and of her past nuclear family. She can now question her passive positioning, that made her accept the individual responsibilities the family rules put on her. She has been inducted by others—or perhaps by herself—to accept a traditional gender role (patriarchal values), and, at the same time, a relevant working role (neo-liberal values). Such roles take their toll on her, but she is driven to fulfil them both. She is passively positioned, yet her responsibilities are doubled. She actively embraces a sacrificial distortion of responsibility, but at the same time she loathes it. Her ambivalence towards both old and new roles was one of the reasons she sought therapy in the first place.

Taking positional responsibility. Now the therapist can work on positional responsibility. Like many of the patients we have reviewed in the previous pages, Diana is not responsible for the passive position she is put in, both by her family members and by social and cultural rules; but she is responsible for the active position she takes in regard to them. The therapeutic process brings this to her awareness, and therefore enables her to take responsibility for her positioning. Thus the position that Diana felt as a necessity, an obligation, a mere "being like this", begins to be conceived as her own choice—albeit dictated and favoured by a series of embedded social codes and cultural rules, such as the ones regarding a woman's role in a family. We always choose, even when we do not choose: we choose not to choose. Diana, after giving a new meaning to the obligations that she feels, can decide either to change, or to stay where she is, but with a different feeling and a different meaning.

Clinical example: the right to grumble

Taking responsibility does not necessarily mean to take action and change one's actual (factual) situation. Sometimes the patient may prefer to maintain their present position, but consider it as a choice rather than an obligation. In such cases, an increased awareness is the change we can obtain. This happens with patients who simply want a place where they can freely complain about their lives.

Alina, a woman in her 40s, comes to therapy because of her son Richard, a pre-school boy with a probable diagnosis of ADHD. She does not accept the therapist's suggestion of family therapy, and settles for an individual therapy that is, from the very beginning, saturated by her complaints about Richard, apparently unmanageable both at school and at home. The therapist tries to intervene with questions and hypotheses, but Alina appears almost uninterested in them. The more the therapy progresses, the more extreme become her feelings against Richard: "I hate him!" she shouts once; at the same time, she appears ashamed and guilty for her own thoughts and feelings. She never confessed the extent of her distress to anybody else.

After many sessions, Alina abruptly interrupts therapy and disappears. She reappears almost a year later. When questioned about the reason of her withdrawal, she simply states that "things with Richard were getting better," and she felt no more need of therapeutic encounters. She comes, now, for a quite different reason: her relationship with her aged father. She feels he does not bother to even see her—he lives two hours away and never came to see her new house. She feels abandoned, and again confesses she hates him, before entering again in a series of complaints. "I think that you have a peculiar idea of therapy," the therapist interrupts her. "You don't want me to help you get out of your dilemmas. Maybe you just want a right to grumble."

The therapist explains. In the late Middle Ages and early Renaissance, Genoa was one of the most important marine republic in the Mediterranean, with a powerful navy. Apparently, the recruitment of seamen in the Genoese navy could happen under two quite different contracts, with or without the "right to grumble" (in Latin: *ius murmurandi*): the first one provided high pay and no grumbling, the second one reduced pay and a right to complain (Pettinotti, 2017).

Some patients are in the same position of those ancient mariners: they feel that their present position, uncomfortable as it is, is the only possible for them in their condition. They feel compelled to maintain that position, but at the same time they are dominated by unpleasant emotions—in Alina's case, an overwhelming anger. They need some relief, and they find it in grumbling. Complaining becomes a way of maintaining some balance in their emotional lives. Usually, they feel this situation as a necessity. If they find their place, they may begin to consider it as a choice: nobody can force them to stay there, if they really do not want to. If it is a choice, it may become acceptable, also introducing the possibility of actual change in the future—after all, one can always choose something else. For the time being, anyway, the change is limited to a new awareness.

Alina accepts the therapist's reading. What she needed—and got from therapy—was a sympathetic space where she could complain without getting either disapproval or well-intended suggestions. The therapeutic attitude we practice offers her such acceptance, at the same time presenting her hypotheses about her relationships with the others: her son, her father, her husband, her sisters, thus enabling her to experience different viewpoints and lessening her anger.

Conclusion

Briefly, our approach entails a responsibility accepted by both therapists and patients as a free choice, rather than tied to a rigid code; a relational responsibility, centred on the care of relationships rather than internal rules; a positional responsibility, with awareness of one's position in the context; a responsibility directed to the future, since we consider it necessary to take responsibility for our past choices, but, at the same time, we project responsibility to the future choice of possible actions.

Positional responsibility means to feel responsible toward any person within the systems we belong, and for the stance we take toward each of them. This awareness may also allow us to criticise the system, or what we find unsettling in it. Of course, this comes at a cost: the cost of leaving a comfortable (passive, conformist) position, and embracing a more challenging, difficult one.[5] Taking responsibility means also acknowledging the extent of the expectations we have toward ourselves and the others, as we will see in the next chapter.

Notes

1 Several theorists have put in the foreground the concept of responsibility in therapy, from the point of view of both therapists and patients (e.g., Erba et al., 2014; Gantt, 1994; McNamee & Gergen, 1999).
2 At the beginning of systemic and strategic therapy, therapists were considered directly responsible for the outcome of therapy (see Haley, 1986). This implicitly required patients to accept uncritically the therapists' actions, delegating them to decide what was right. This has long been debunked in most systemic therapies of today.
3 Alto Adige was annexed to Italy after World War I, in 1918. Beforehand, it had been part of the Austro-Hungarian Empire. During the fascist dictatorship, a great effort was made in order to render it "more Italian", exacerbating the resentment between the two linguistic communities.
4 In Nancy Fraser's (2016) words, she is experiencing the demands and contradictions both of productive and reproductive work (Chapter 2). In Judith Butler's (1990) conception, she is acting according to conflicting scripts.
5 "For the denizens of modern society in its solid and managed phase, the major opposition was one between conformity and deviance; the major opposition in modern society in its present-day liquified and decentred phase, the opposition which needs to be faced up in order to pave the way to a truly autonomous society,

is one between taking up responsibility and seeking a shelter where responsibility for one's own actions need not to be taken by the actors" (Bauman, 2000, p. 213).

References

Arendt, H. (1963). *Eichmann in Jerusalem: A Report on the Banality of Evil*. Viking Press.

Bateson, G. (1972). *Steps to an Ecology of Mind*. Chandler Publishing Company.

Bauman, Z. (1989). *Modernity and the Holocaust*. Polity Press.

Bauman, Z. (1993). *Postmodern Ethics*. Blackwell Publishing.

Bauman, Z. (2000). *Liquid Modernity*. Polity Press.

Butler, J.P. (1990). *Gender trouble: feminism and the subversion of identity*. Routledge.

Erba, S., Di Prima, S., Semola, E., & Serra, P. (2014). *Psicoterapia: un pensiero, un metodo, una pratica*. Franco Angeli.

Foucault, M. (1977). *Discipline and Punish: The Birth of the Prison* (translated by A. Sheridan). Allen Lane (original edition 1975).

Fraser, N. (2016). Contradictions of capital and care. *New Left Review*, 100: 99–117.

Gantt, E.E. (1994). Truth, freedom and responsibility in the dialogues of psychotherapy. *Journal of Theoretical and Philosophical Psychology*, 14 (2): 146–158. DOI:10.1037/h0091139.

Gergen, M. (1999). Relational responsibility. Deconstructive possibilities. In: S. McNamee & K.J. Gergen (Eds.), *Relational Responsibility. Resources for Sustainable Dialogue*. Sage, pp. 99–109.

Giddens, A. (1998). *The Third Way: The Renewal of Social Democracy*. Polity Press.

Giddens, A. (1999). Risk and responsibility. *The Modern Law Review*, 62 (1): 1–10. DOI:10.1111/1468–2230.00188.

Giglioli, D. (2014). *Critica della vittima*. Nottetempo.

Haley, J. (1986). *The Power Tactics of Jesus Christ and Other Essays*. 2nd edition. Triangle Press.

McNamee, S. & Gergen, K.J. (Eds.) (1999). *Relational Responsibility. Resources for Sustainable Dialogue*. Sage.

Milgram, S. (1974). *Obedience to Authority*. HarperCollins.

Pettinotti, P. (2017). *Storia di Genova dalle origini ai giorni nostri*. Biblioteca dell'Immagine.

Shotter, J. & Katz, A.J. (1999). Creating relational realities. In: McNamee, S. & Gergen, K.J. (Eds.), *Relational Responsibility: Resources for Sustainable Dialogue*. Sage, pp. 151–161.

Stratton, P. (2003). Causal attributions during therapy I: Responsibility and blame. *Journal of Family Therapy*, 25: 136–160. DOI:10.1111/1467-6427.00241.

Van Langenhove, L. & Harré, R. (1999). Introducing positioning theory. In: Harré, R., & Van Langenhove, L. (Eds.), *Positioning Theory*. Basil Blackwell, pp. 14–31.

Weber, M. (1919). *The Vocation Lectures* (translated by R. Livingstone and edited by D. Owen & T. Strong). Hackett Books, 2004.

Chapter 8

Expectations

Taking responsibility also means recognising one's own expectations as processes that originate in the individual, rather than characteristics of the other (s). Our work on expectations stems directly from our consideration of responsibility. Expectations, in the end, became almost an additional pillar of the approach. This chapter addresses both therapists' and patients' expectations, and the different ways in which they influence the course of therapy.

Some distinctions

When we began to focus on expectations in our clinical work, we discovered that they are essential for getting oriented in our daily life. Expectations are unavoidable: we always expect other people, institutions, nature itself to behave in a predictable way. When—as the whole world recently experienced, for example with the Covid-19 pandemic—life events become unpredictable and betray our presumedly reasonable expectations, we get disappointed, scared, distressed. At the same time, we found that the subject was less obvious than we had originally thought. This is why we want to start from basic definitions: what exactly is an expectation? And how can we distinguish it from a desire, a hope, a premise, a prejudice or a hypothesis?

In dictionaries, the definition of expectation is usually simple. According to the Oxford Dictionary, it is "a belief that something will happen because it is likely". The Merriam-Webster Dictionary is even more tautological: "the act or state of expecting: anticipation". The Cambridge Dictionary, beside a similar definition—"the feeling of expecting something to happen"—adds a different nuance: "the feeling that good things are going to happen in the future". They all share the idea that an expectation is the anticipation of a predictable event. When an expectation seems to concern positive events, its semantic field overlaps with that of desire and hope, although with more moderate characteristics: an expectation does not have the strength of desire nor the consolatory power of hope (see Flaskas, 2007). It basically concerns events that we take for granted.

DOI: 10.4324/9781003381754-9

There is also another relevant difference. Sometimes we expect events that we consider probable, but we would like others to happen, less probable, but emotionally charged with desire. Houser (2005) defines the former expectations as predictive, based on the regularity of events, the latter as prescriptive, based on what we would like to see achieved. We tend to highlight the desiring component of some expectations (see Lini, 2014), so we will call the former "rational" or "realistic" expectations, with a general form that can be expressed as: "this is what generally happens, so I expect it will happen this time too"; the second "desiring" or "desired" expectations, whose general form could be: "I would like this to happen, so I imagine (hope) it will happen".

In the systemic field, concepts close to expectation are premises, prejudices and hypotheses. Premises, as they have been interpreted by Bateson-influenced systemic therapists, are implicit, socially constructed, culturally standardised, and largely unconscious conceptions or practices. Bateson's original definition of premises was proposed within his anthropological description of the Iatmul culture in New Guinea:

> When a mother gives food to her child, we can see implicit in this cultural act a number of structural assumptions: that mothers feed children; that children are dependent on their mothers; that mothers are kind; that taro is edible; etc. etc.

Bateson's idea is that in any culture several structural assumptions may be found in "a large number of its details. [...] Thus a premise is *a generalised statement of a particular assumption or implication recognisable in a number of details of cultural behaviour*" (1936–1958, p. 24, italics in the original).

A premise is therefore a basic assumption that is valid for a culture—or at least a subculture. There are premises accepted by an entire society, easily shared by all or almost all of its members; and specific premises of much more restricted communities: a definite social group, a therapeutic school, a family, a therapeutic team, and so on. The latter include the "family premises", a concept favoured by the Milan school: a set of premises shared by all members of a family, usually considered as dysfunctional, which the therapist challenges by introducing different premises in the course of the therapeutic dialogue (see Boscolo et al., 1987, p. 125).

The case of prejudices, theorised by Cecchin, Lane and Ray (1994), is different. They are more likely to be personal and idiosyncratic, rather than shared like the premises. In many cases they are conscious, so much so that they are often expressed in words, and one can use them as justifications for their actions:

> When we talk about prejudices we mean all the sets of fantasies, ideas, accepted historical facts, accepted truths, hunches, biases, notions,

hypotheses, models, theories, personal feelings, moods, unrecognised loyalties—in fact, *any* pre-existing thought that contributes to one's view, perceptions of, and actions in a therapeutic encounter.

(Cecchin, Lane & Ray, 1994, p. 8)

To give an example, is the idea of "family" a premise or a prejudice? It contains very profound, social and cultural premises; at the same time, it can become a prejudice when it takes on specific characteristics for a given individual, a family or another more or less organised social group (see also Chapter 6). Perhaps it is possible to say that a prejudice is an individual's or a family's interpretation of a premise.

As we have seen in the case of desire and hope, an expectation has something in common with both premises and prejudices. It is an assumption that is easily taken for granted, like a premise, and it can be either conscious or unconscious. It generally is quite personal, and still determines our behaviour, like a prejudice. What is specific is the temporal dimension: expectation is the act of expecting something, therefore of waiting, and as such it is always directed to the future, whereas both premises and prejudices tend to be implicit or explicit descriptions of what is going on in the present. An expectation can be based on a premise or a prejudice, but with a different time horizon (Boscolo & Bertrando, 1993).

From this point of view it is easy to make another distinction, between expectations and hypotheses. In particular, if we make a hypothesis about the future, we imagine something that could happen, but we do not necessarily expect it to happen. The hypothesis is not yet an expectation but rather constitutes its foundation. Furthermore, a hypothesis is generally thought out, explicit and well-articulated, while an expectation can have implicit foundations that are unknown even to those who have them: it is impossible not to have expectations, but it is possible to be unaware of them.

An example may clarify the relationship between premise, prejudice, expectation, and hypothesis. Nina is 29, an employee who lives with her boyfriend. She comes from a troubled family: her mother abandoned her father without letting him know that she was pregnant. Nina was originally told that he was dead, and learned the truth only when she was an adolescent, to discover that his father had actually died in the meantime. She grew up with her mother and grandmother in an apartment contained in an old country house, that was the joint property of her extended family.

When her grandmother and then her mother died, Nina found herself broke. She turned to her aunts and cousins, wanting to sell the family house, where now only herself and one ageing great-aunt were living, in order to secure some money from her share. She met a barrier: it was impossible to get an agreement that encompassed all family members.

"Nobody cared about me," she says, "and I'm the one who suffered most. I thought we were a family where everybody cares for each other, and I discover that each of them stick to their own business and don't care the least about me!"

"The fact is," the therapist answers, "that you expected them to share your view of your family, or, better, your view about what a family is. They apparently don't feel an obligation toward you. It was your expectation, but you can't make them behave according to what you expected."

Here the therapist is trying to sort out the different levels: Nina's basic premise is that in a family—and she does not distinguish between a nuclear and an extended family—there is a commitment to reciprocal care. Her prejudice is that this care obligation applies to her extended family, and involves also money issues. The therapist proposes that money is just part of the picture—and not even the most important: she expects love from her relatives, but they refuse to give it. Her expectation becomes a request, as if they had the duty to love her. All of them should do what she feels is the right thing to do, i.e., putting her needs first. The therapist hypothesises that possibly her relatives apply such reasoning to their respective nuclear families, but not to the whole of the extended family, so they can reject Nina's desires without feeling guilty at all. She expects instead them to feel guilty because of her own prejudice.

The therapist works carefully with Nina, helping her to take responsibility for her expectations. If she realises that her expectations come from herself, she might also accept that her extended family is entitled not to satisfy them. If she becomes less demanding, there is also a possibility that the stuck family situation loosens up a bit.

Kinds of expectation

There is more than one kind of expectation. What we have defined above as "rational expectations" have been widely theorised, especially in economics, where they have attracted attention since the time of John Maynard Keynes. John Muth (1961) proposed a theory in which individuals are considered as fully rational actors, capable of using all the information available in a given economic system, the Theory of Rational Expectations. Since information is a rare and therefore valuable—and expensive—commodity in economics, economic operators optimise its use through proportionate expectations. In other words, all actors place themselves in a perfectly rational perspective and, on average, always make choices based on the most reasonable expectations. This position is quite similar to the one proposed by Jay Haley (1963) in his strategic understanding of therapy: in a human system, each member pursues their own benefit—that, for Haley, means to secure a position of power, i.e., the ability to define the rules of relationship. This is done by evaluating circumstances in a purely rational way (see also Haley, 1973).

Leaving economists (and strategic therapists) aside, the most interesting expectations from a therapeutic standpoint are those that we have defined as prescriptive or desiring. They can in turn be divided into generic expectations, which concern work, society, and the many possible situations in life, and relational expectations. The general form of the latter is "I expect (desire) something from someone else". These are the expectation we mostly work with, as we have seen in Nina's case.

The fact is, it would be tiresome and disorienting to see other people's behaviour as subjected to random variations. For this reason we try to anticipate possible patterns: a relational expectation is a "stable pattern of expected behaviour" (Burgoon, 1993, p. 31). According to Edward E. Jones, "it is essentially impossible to conceive of a participant who approaches social interaction without some series of expectations, hypotheses or predictions about how the other participant will probably behave in different circumstances" (1986, p. 43). We calibrate ourselves to others according to the expectations we have of them. Expectations are frames (Goffman, 1974) that give shape and meaning to our interactions with others. Anthropologist George Herbert Mead (1932) thought that the Self was shaped (also) by the powerful influence of significant others, therefore by the expectations we have towards them and they have towards us. The interplay between the expectations we have towards others and the expectations of others towards ourselves influence us, our perception of ourselves and our choices.

Expectations toward others

Expectations toward others are often relevant in therapy. Let us see an example. Chiara's parents decided to have their sick dog put down. Chiara is passionate about animals, she has great veterinary experience, but her parents did not involve her in the decision, making—she says—the dog suffer unnecessarily. A violent argument ensues. Chiara goes to bed anguished over the issue, but does not call her parents. She will only speak to them on the following day. She is disappointed mainly because she, considering herself an animal expert, expected that the parents of an adult daughter (she is 35 years old) would regard her as a reliable interlocutor.

The therapist brings her to wonder whether her disappointment may be due to a violation of her adult expectations: she expected them to see her as an adult daughter, even better equipped than them to take care of the family dog; but they probably had a different view, as if she were much younger—it can happen to parents, reflects the therapist. When her adult expectation was disproved, however, a childhood expectation of hers came into play: she often felt neglected in childhood, building a narrative of abandonment on top of it. There is a clash of different expectations from her parents: disappointed in her positive, adult one, she has now the negative expectation (certainty) that they will not care about her, therefore it is useless even to check what is actually happening. In the end she discovers that her parents had not had the dog put down, and were simply waiting for her phone call once her anger had cooled.

The expectations that we create towards others have to do with what Möllering (2005) defines as "the trust/control duality": the possibility of trusting another person, accompanied by some degree of control over their actions, allows us to have positive expectations towards them—keeping in mind that trust is in itself a form of expectation (Möllering, 2001). Duality means that trust must be guaranteed by some constraint on the other accomplished through control. The less we trust the other, the more our expectations will depend on control.[1]

When what actually happens turns out to be very different from our expectations, there is a violation of expectations. According to Judee Burgoon (2015), such a violation can be experienced as positive or negative: a negative violation (parents who unexpectedly do not involve Chiara) is obviously experienced worse than conformity to expectations; but a positive one—which would have occurred if they had involved her more than expected or had completely delegated the dog's well-being to her—leads to far better feelings than mere compliance.

Expectations from others

Expectations from others toward ourselves are even more important. Clio, 31, claims to suffer greatly from the enormous expectations that everyone has on her. Such a distress in turn magnifies them, transforms them into obsessive thoughts that paralyse her and prevent her from doing anything. The therapist observes that Clio actually holds opposite expectations towards herself, compared to the ones she attributes to others: she expects to be basically incompetent in doing things. It is as if these two sets of expectations were constantly fighting within her: the expectations from others, that foster her performance anxiety, and her own expectations toward herself, who feels incapable of accomplishing anything. In the therapeutic dialogue the therapist reflects with her on how she spent her life carrying the weight of these colossal expectations, and how perhaps they were not possibly real—how she suffered for the ghosts of other people's expectations. Being able to transform her own expectations of herself into realistic ones, no longer influenced by such ghosts, becomes an important point of improvement for her.

Kemper (1966) observed, in an experimental study, that the expectations of significant others influence the concept of oneself up to full adulthood, and above all in the negative: like Clio, his subjects often felt they were not up to par of the expectations of others. As Clio illustrates well, the image we have of ourselves also influences the relationships between our expectations toward others and the expectations of others toward us. Cerase (1974) interviewed a group of Italian migrants to the United States who returned to their homeland, finding that their expectations for their new life in their country of origin depended on their and the others' perceptions of success. Migrants who felt they had failed in the USA expected and desired to rediscover their old knowledge and habits, thus easily reintegrating into village life; those who instead thought they had been successful in America expected to change the structure of their village organisation by bringing innovations, and were disappointed to find very strong structural resistance to change: the expectations of those who remained at home were very different from theirs.

Expectations in clinical work

Everything we said about expectations in everyday life can be applied to our clinical activity. Reading Edward Jones's statement above, any therapist with some systemic training probably found an echo of Watzlawick, Beavin and Jackson's (1967) famous first axiom of communication: "It is impossible not to communicate". Likewise, it is impossible for us not to have expectations. So far, we have extensively dealt with the many and different expectations of our patients; therapists, though, have their expectations too, and we must remember and consider them.

Patients' expectations from therapy

Patients' expectations influence the course of therapy. This has been a commonplace observation since the days of Hans Eysenck (1952) and Jerome Frank (1968): the majority of people seek therapy because they are demoralised, and positive expectations, accompanied by trust and hope, are among the first requirements for therapeutic success. Michael Lambert (1992) proposed a hypothetical percentage weighting of the factors of change in therapy, regardless of the model. Putting aside an overall 40% that can be attributed to extra-therapeutic factors, such as the personal characteristics of patients or the environments from which they come, he ascribes 30% to common or nonspecific factors of therapy (therapeutic relationship, genuineness, empathy, etc.), and a paltry 15% to the specific techniques of each approach. If all these factors have been widely cited in subsequent literature, the remaining 15% is much less considered. Lambert attributed it precisely to the patients' expectations toward therapy. Expectations, therefore, would be at least as important as the actual therapeutic model used.

To clinicians, these percentages are not so relevant, although they have fuelled a still active debate about common factors in therapy (see Asay & Lambert, 1999). What interests us is the confirmed fact that patient expectations are a necessary part of therapy.[2] In short: expectations, desires, hope and trust toward therapy and the therapist have a role not unlike the one we have observed with expectations toward family and friends. And those expectations generate similar problems if they are disappointed: as therapists, we will never be too careful in understanding the expectations our patients have from us, and also in clarifying how much and how we can or cannot satisfy them.

Playing with expectations

Playing with expectations may also be a (forbidden) game for the therapist. The more experienced the therapist, the more standard hypotheses are created about each type of patient. The therapist risks to see types rather than persons: the typical panic case, the typical obsessive-compulsive, the typical anorexic. In this way, patients become apparently predictable: we see a problem, we expect a precise set of behaviours related to it. A more or less restricted range of possible hypotheses is thus created, that fosters a hierarchy of expectations, ordered on the basis of probability, from the most probable to the least likely. It is almost inevitable that, in the absence of open contradictions, the therapist would tend to choose the expectation they feel as most probable, which will generally also be the most familiar.

Such mechanism closely resembles what happens to professionals who operate within a normative system, for example medical diagnostics: if a patient coughs, the doctor evaluates whether the cough is dry or wet, then whether there is fever or not, then possibly requests a chest X-ray in order to progressively narrow the field of possible diagnoses and treatments. In any case, from the beginning the doctor will expect a problem with the respiratory system, then with the lungs, and so on. Therapy is different from medicine because the latter is grounded in a vast corpus of accepted notions (aetiology, pathogenesis, pathological anatomy), whereas in psychotherapy there is no common standard, so what each therapist does is partly based on their own favourite theoretical frame, partly—much more—on their own personal experience.

Be that as it may, when therapeutic hypotheses become recurrent, they take the form of more or less rigid expectations. If we apply a psychiatric or psychoanalytic framework, we will expect a patient diagnosed with obsessive-compulsive disorder to display not only the relevant symptoms, but also a personality profile similar to the "obsessive character" originally described by psychoanalysts (see Freud, 1909; Reich, 1980). In classic family therapy, it was expected that the presence of a certain symptom corresponded to a precise relational (family) configuration. For example, in the case of anorexia one could expect, depending on the theoretical orientation, an enmeshed family where hierarchies proved ineffective (Minuchin et al., 1978), or a family with hidden alliances accompanied by difficulties in acknowledging both family games and individual suffering (Selvini Palazzoli, 1974, part IV).

Today family typologies have become more sophisticated and multi-dimensional, taking into consideration variables such as attachment patterns and personality disorders (Selvini Palazzoli et al., 1998). Still the results, in terms of creating expectations, remain very similar.

Expectations in a systemic-dialogical frame

If we put expectations in a systemic-dialogical frame, we may wonder: How do expectations arise? From what needs do they emerge? The observations and theories we listed above tell us that we could also describe expectation as a way of managing unpredictability, and the anxiety that is connected to it. Bateson (1967a), in his famous essay on primitive art, maintained that humans always look for redundancies, that he elsewhere defines as the "patterning or predictability of particular events within a larger aggregate of events" (Bateson, 1967b, p. 414). A work of art simply creates more and more complex patterns of redundancy, but redundancy is necessary to any form of more or less advanced communication.

Expectations work on redundancies. In this way, we create a sort of heuristic of unpredictability: we imagine a range of possible situations, then we choose one. At that point we "know" (we believe we know) what the future holds for us, and this, at least apparently, makes it easier for us. At the same time, however, that very expectation also fosters a sense of necessity: the moment we expect something, we prepare ourselves as if that something were to happen. If it does not happen, we get frustrated. As one of our patients said, referring to his partner, "expectations pave the way to disappointment". Our patient concluded that the ideal condition was to have no expectations at all, and he believed he was able to achieve it. But, as we have seen, it is impossible not to have expectations. The mechanism that produces them is always at work. This is all the more true in the case of prescriptive or desiring expectations—our patient clearly referred to them—since we want them to be fulfilled.

The question now becomes: to what extent are we aware that we ourselves conceive our expectations, and therefore that we are responsible for them? Or do we instead feel that our expectations are "out there", as if they were part of the environment, objective, therefore independent of us? Many of our patients—but sometimes even ourselves as therapists—take the latter position. The expectation becomes reality, precisely because it is the most convenient possibility for us. When we apply such expectations to people, when we conceive prescriptive relational expectations, we constantly risk falling into what Bateson would call an epistemological error: confusing (our) expectations with the actuality of the other. In this sense, it is true that our disappointments are the result of our expectations. We are disillusioned when the other—the others, the world—puts us face to face with a reality different from the expected one, as in Nina's or Chiara's case.

At the same time, we also risk disappointing the others' expectations, or bending ourselves to the expectations of others so as not to disappoint them, as happened to Clio. Every time we encounter relational expectations, upon closer inspection, the expectation is not a desire, but the anticipation that someone will make our desire come true. If this does not happen, we are disappointed, and often angry with the disappointing other. Let us reflect on that disappointment: if we are disappointed by others, does it depend on their wrong actions, or rather on the expectations we have of them?

Let us then try to read the expectations in the light of positioning theory. Our relational expectations necessarily position the other as the one who should fulfil them, or simply as the one who cannot help but arrange themselves in the way we have expectantly foreseen; the same happens to us, when we are positioned by the expectations of others, as we have seen in the case of Diana from Chapter 7, who was expected by her family to be caring and nurturing, demanding nothing in return. We often fail to understand the contexts we live in, because we fail to read (locate) our expectations, which lead us to prefer one view over all the others. The view we favour is usually the one that allows us, in a fantastic way, to make a wish come true.

The issue, then, is to find our place with respect to expectations. If we find our place, we can become more aware of the expectations we have built for ourselves. Realising that we were the ones who created those expectation, we take responsibility for them, and we can compare them with alternative visions of ourselves and others. This process, in therapy, involves first of all the therapist; we must learn to distinguish our patients from the expectations we have of them. Once again, having found our place, we may then help the patients to position themselves toward their own expectations. This means recognising expectations as such, understanding the emotions they arouse in us, whether they are fulfilled or disappointed, and then taking responsibility for them. We will try to illustrate this process by means of a microanalysis of a clinical situation.

Clinical example: Delia, "what I expect from my father"

Delia is a 35-year-old woman, with a good job, a steady heterosexual relationship and a child. Others view her as a satisfied and self-confident person. Nevertheless, she comes to therapy in order to better deal with some upcoming, challenging decisions about her future. During therapy, some important issues emerge regarding her family of origin: Delia describes her parents as strong couple, but too focused on their own indissoluble bond. She feels that both of them have always been centred, above all, on the needs of her father, for many years afflicted by an apparent subclinical depression, which has always attracted most of her mother's attention.

Delia's father decides to write a sort of autobiographical narrative, a book to describe his life and tell his story. He then sends a draft to his daughter.

Delia, upon reading it, is seriously disappointed: she expected the book to be about her too, she imagined to be one of the main characters, but she discovers that she has not even been mentioned. Her father talks about his encounters, the many strangers he met, his work and travel vicissitudes, as well as, naturally, his beloved wife. Delia had instead thought, up to that point, that her father's gaze was basically focused on her.

A big intergenerational unresolved issue emerges in Delia. When she discloses it in therapy, she realises that she has always sought recognition from her father, who instead constantly placed himself at the centre of the family world, asking for confirmation—among others—from her. This time too, he apparently did not send his manuscript to offer something to his daughter; he was basically asking her for a stylistic opinion on his work. He wants to know if it is a well-written book, if it can be offered to others, and so on. Rather than a daughter to take care of, Delia is seen as a reviewer.

At this point, the therapist tries to investigate the interplay of expectations: what premises, prejudices, desires and expectations emerge in this fragment of a session?

First of all, there is an important cultural premise: for parents, especially in Italy, their children should be the most important thing in the world. It is a premise that has the value of a strong behavioural prescription, which positions anyone within the culture, unless they openly question it—as Delia never did.

Her interpretation of this premise generates a prejudice: if a parent (her father) has to talk about his own life, he should always focus on his children (in this case, on her). From this emerges, inevitably, the prescriptive expectation that Delia creates towards her father: "He will certainly write about me, because he's been necessarily interested in me above all." Behind it, of course, lies a desire that Delia wants to be satisfied: "Show me that you love me!"

Delia fell into a typical daughterly epistemological error: from the day her father became a father, she imagined him living his entire life first and foremost as a father. It is difficult for her to accept that her father may be also a man with his own life, who does not always contemplate Delia's presence—although, when the therapist offers her this possibility, she cannot help but agree. There is a discrepancy between her unconfessed desires and her reasoning, and the discrepancy was highlighted by an unpredictable event such as receiving that unexpected manuscript. The surprising situation in which Delia found herself exposed an expectation that usually remained hidden and subterranean. As it happened to Chiara, the unfulfilled expectation brings to light emotions dating back to a much earlier age and relational configuration.

The therapeutic dialogue brings out that Delia even today positions herself in relation to her father in a way that is incongruent with her age and the degree of evolution of their relationships. If she were eight years old, she would certainly expect to be the centre of her father's life, but in that case the expectation would be more than justified by the level of maturity in the relationship. The problem here arises because, albeit being an adult daughter, she is somewhat fixed on a childlike relationship, without evolving it toward a relationship between two adults. She now has to correct a distortion in finding her place.

When Delia manages to reflect on her own expectations, she realises and accepts that her father wanted to be recognised for his artistic and literary merits, rather than give her a gift. She is neither happy nor satisfied, but manages, with some difficulty, to accept it. Her father will never be the parent she always wanted.

(During their dialogue, Delia and the therapist also make some hypotheses about the father's expectations. The latter expects his daughter to evaluate her work in a dispassionate and professional way, therefore putting her in a supervising, "superior" position. If we want to describe the process in traditional family therapy terminology, here the father seems to parentify his daughter: he expects from her a type of evaluation that, according to commonly accepted cultural premises, would rather be a parent's responsibility. This puts Delia in a particularly difficult situation. Therapist and patient wonder whether such a process already happened in the past, and has something to do with her present-day difficulties. This small episode set in motion a new phase of therapy.)

As for the therapist, her work was facilitated by not expecting anything different from Delia: in an individual therapy it is easy to expect regressive experiences to be revealed and patients to react in a way that is not congruent with their chronological age. The therapist wonders what would have happened if she had, instead, confirmed Delia's mature and competent image, thus being positioned by a different set of Delia's expectations.

It was important for the therapist to raise a series of questions. They were not necessarily questions the therapist asked Delia (although she did ask some), but rather questions she encouraged Delia to ask herself: "Where does this desire come from? Can I move on, get over it, not expect it to be satisfied? Can I look for something else besides this recognition that I crave so much? Can I make peace with what I haven't had and will never have? Can I accept that, on the other hand, I've had something else, maybe much more: encounters, friends, partners, jobs, a child...?"

The questions led her to find some provisional, tentative answers: "At this point I can accept my father, and expect from him what he can give me. And at this point I can also tell him 'well done', which is what he wants to hear. I can give him the attention he requires of me. Which is not my spontaneous reaction, it is certainly filtered by my reflection, but at the same time it is not a false position, and it allows our relationship to become more comfortable."

Within this process, the therapist in turn asked herself another series of questions, less specific and more general, linked to the many dimensions of expectations. The therapist uses them to create questions she can ask her patient directly, of course taking into account the particular case and its characteristics: What are the expectations that I can see? What are the basic premises they are founded upon? What prejudices has the patient created for herself? What are her underlying desires? Who is asked to satisfy them? How can we, at this point, detach ourselves from those expectations, conceptualising the fact that any expectation is a product of the person who create it and, therefore, like a hypothesis, it is only one among many possible?

Interestingly, here our work on expectations meets our interest in needs and desires (Lini, 2014). Delia felt a need for recognition. Feeling a need implies that the other must absolutely satisfy it: a need cannot remain unanswered. Again, in childhood such a position is justified, and the need for recognition is a proper need, as it probably was for Delia in her past. In adults, however, being recognised is not a need but a desire. Desire, unlike need, can be deconstructed: a desire is something we wish, but without the urgency and cogency of need. Desires can also be artificially induced: after all, a lot of advertising, so pervasive a force today, consists in creating desires, then transforming them into needs that must be satisfied at all costs.[3] Satisfaction of desires can be postponed, or put aside for good if necessary. It is always possible to review desires and change them.

Reading expectations in the framework of desire—therefore as something that can always be reviewed and revalued—allows us to master the emotions that accompany it instead of being subjected to pure emotionality. Delia's disappointment contained several emotions: anger, wariness, fear of abandonment, sadness, despondency. Similar emotions, and others equally strong, often emerge in the case of unfulfilled relational expectations. The person who experiences them feels them in all their strength, but often struggles to find their place toward them, relating them to their own expectations.

In such cases, we question the emotions that emerge in the session and connect them to the patient's positioning, in order to give them back a (relational) meaning and with it a possibility of mastering them. When patients succeed in reviewing the emotional tangle that accompanies a prescriptive or unfulfilled expectation, they no longer are its victims. They move from emotionality to emotional information, thus taking responsibility—among the rest—for their own expectations (Chapter 7). An alternative story can then be constructed (see White, 1993), in which the person is responsible for their own expectations, but at the same time can master them: they become active protagonists (heroes) of their story, through the hermeneutics of expectations— and therefore of desire.

Notes

1 According to Locke (2005), each of us expects from others reactions similar to those we would have ourselves, which in turn suggest plans of action. For example,

he has observed that active and assertive people—who tend to easily criticise others—will in turn expect criticism and contempt from others, and therefore prepare themselves to react with anger.

2 These ancient considerations have been repeatedly, albeit not outstandingly, supported by empirical studies too. Constantino et al. (2011) carried out a meta-analysis of 46 independent studies, finding a weak but still significant correlation between expectations towards therapy and its results, a fact also confirmed by a series of less systematic reviews (Greenberg et al., 2006; Constantino et al., 2012; see also Duncan et al., 2010).

3 According to Marx—and likewise to Italian critical psychiatrist Franco Basaglia, who was not by chance a Marxist—a theory of desire is not possible, since desire is easily induced, and therefore it can be false or belong to false consciousness, to ideology (Heller, 1976).

References

Asay, T.P. & Lambert, M.J. (1999). The empirical case for the common factors in therapy: quantitative findings. In: M.A. Hubble, B.L. Duncan, & S.D. Miller (Eds.), *The Heart and Soul of Change: What Works in Therapy*. American Psychological Association.

Bateson, G. (1936/1958). *Naven*. 2nd edition. Stanford University Press.

Bateson, G. (1967a). Style, grace, and information in primitive art. In: *Steps to an Ecology of Mind* (pp. 128–156). Chandler Publishing Company, 1972.

Bateson, G. (1967b). Cybernetic explanation. In: *Steps to an Ecology of Mind* (pp. 407–418). Chandler Publishing Company, 1972.

Boscolo, L. & Bertrando, P. (1993). *The Times of Time: A Perspective on Time in Systemic Therapy and Consultation*. 2nd edition. Routledge, 2020.

Boscolo, L., Cecchin, G., Hoffman, L., & Penn, P. (1987). *Milan Systemic Family Therapy: Conversations in Theory and Practice*. Basic Books.

Burgoon, J.K. (1993). Interpersonal Expectations, Expectancy Violations, and Emotional Communication. *Journal of Language and Social Psychology*, 12: 30–48. DOI:10.1177/0261927X93121003.

Burgoon, J.K. (2015). Expectancy Violations Theory. In C.R. Berger, M.E. Roloff, S. R. Wilson, J.P. Dillard, J. Caughlin and D. Solomon (Eds.), *The International Encyclopedia of Interpersonal Communication*. DOI:10.1002/9781118540190. wbeic102.

Cecchin, G., Lane G., & Ray, W.L. (1994). *The Cybernetics of Prejudices in the Practice of Psychotherapy*. Karnac.

Cerase, F.P. (1974). Expectations and Reality: A Case Study of Return Migration from the United States to Southern Italy. *The International Migration Review*, 8 (2): 245–262. DOI:10.1177/019791837400800210.

Constantino, M.J., Ametrano, R.M., & Greenberg, R.P. (2012). Clinician Interventions and Participant Characteristics That Foster Adaptive Patient Expectations for Psychotherapy and Psychotherapeutic Change. *Psychotherapy*, 49 (4): 557–569. DOI:10.1037/a0029440.

Constantino, M.J., Arnkoff, D.B., Glass, C.R., Ametrano, R.M., & Smith, J.Z. (2011). Expectations. *Journal of Clinical Psychology*, 67: 184–192. DOI:10.1002/jclp.20754.

Duncan, B.L., Miller, S.D., Wampold, B.E., & Hubble, M.A. (Eds). (2010). *The Heart and Soul of Change: Delivering What Works in Therapy* (2nd ed.). American Psychological Association. DOI:10.1037/12075-000.

Eysenck, H.J. (1952). The effects of psychotherapy: An evaluation. *Journal of Consulting Psychology*, 16: 319–327. DOI:10.1037/h0063633.

Flaskas, C. (2007). Holding hope and hopelessness: therapeutic engagements with the balance of hope. *Journal of Family Therapy*, 29: 186–202. DOI:10.1111/j.1467-6427.2007.00381.x.

Frank, J.D. (1968). The influence of patients' and therapists' expectations on the outcome of psychotherapy. *British Journal of Medical Psychology*, 41: 349–356. DOI:10.1111/j.2044–8341.1968.tb02043.x.

Freud, S. (1909). Notes on a case of obsessional neurosis, English translation by James Strachey. *The Standard Edition of the Complete Psychological Works of Sigmund Freud, Vol.* X: 155–318.

Goffman, E. (1974). *Frame Analysis: An Essay on the Organization of Experience.* Northeastern University Press, 1986.

Greenberg, R.P., Constantino, M.J., & Bruce, N. (2006). Are patient expectations still relevant for psychotherapy process and outcome? *Clinical Psychology Review*, 26: 657–678. DOI:10.1016/j.cpr.2005.03.002.

Haley, J. (1963). *Strategies of Psychotherapy.* Grune and Stratton.

Haley, J. (1973). *Uncommon Therapy. The Psychiatric Techniques of Milton Erickson, M.D.* Norton.

Heller, A. (1976). *The Theory of Need in Marx.* St. Martin's Press (original edition published 1974).

Houser, M.L. (2005). Are We Violating Their Expectations? Instructor Communication Expectations of Traditional and Non Traditional Students. *Communication Quarterly*, 53 (2): 213–228. DOI:10.1080/01463370500090332.

Jones, E.E. (1986). Interpersonal behavior: the effects of expectancies. *Science*, 234: 41–46.

Kemper, T.D. (1966). Self-Conceptions and the Expectations of Significant Others. *The Sociological Quarterly*, 7 (3): 323–343. DOI:10.1111/j.1533–8525.1966.tb01697.x.

Lambert, M.J. (1992). Psychotherapy outcome research: implications for integrative and eclectic therapists. In: J.C. Norcross & M.R. Goldfried (Eds.), *Handbook of Psychotherapy Integration.* 1st edition. Basic Books, pp. 94–129.

Lini, C. (2014). Bisogno e desiderio nel processo terapeutico. *Terapia Familiare*, 104: 23–45. DOI:10.3280/TF2014–104002.

Locke, K.D. (2005). Interpersonal problems and interpersonal expectations in everyday life. *Journal of Social and Clinical Psychology*, 24 (7): 915–931. DOI:10.1521/jscp.2005.24.7.915.

Mead, G.H. (1932). *Mind, Self and Society.* University of Chicago Press.

Minuchin, S., Rosman, B.L., & Baker, L. (1978). *Psychosomatic Families: Anorexia Nervosa in Context.* Harvard University Press.

Muth, J.F. (1961). Rational Expectations and the Theory of Price Movements. *Econometrica*, 29: 315–335. DOI:10.2307/1909635.

Möllering, G. (2001). The Nature of Trust: From Georg Simmel to a Theory of Expectation, Interpretation and Suspension. *Sociology*, 35 (2): 403–420. DOI:10.1177/S0038038501000190.

Möllering, G. (2005). The Trust/Control Duality: An Integrative Perspective on Positive Expectations of Others. *International Sociology*, 20: 283–305. DOI:10.1177/0268580905055478.

Reich, W. (1980). *Character Analysis*. 3rd edition, enlarged. (Engl. Transl. by Vincent Carfagno.) Farrar, Straus & Giroux (original edition published 1933).

Selvini Palazzoli, M. (1974). *Self-Starvation. From Individual to Family Therapy in the Treatment of Anorexia Nervosa* (Trans. by A. Pomerans). Jason Aronson.

Selvini Palazzoli, M., Cirillo, S., Sorrentino, A.M., & Selvini, M. (1998). *Ragazze anoressiche e bulimiche. La terapia familiare.* Raffaello Cortina Editore.

Watzlawick, P., Beavin, J. & Jackson, D.D. (1967). *Pragmatics of Human Communication.* Norton.

White, M. (1993). Deconstruction and therapy. In S.G. Gilligan & R. Price (Eds.), *Therapeutic Conversations* (pp. 22–61). W. W. Norton & Co. (reprinted from the *Dulwich Centre Newsletter*, 3, 1991, 1–21).

Epilogue

Conscientious individualism

CLAUDIA: Closing this book, and looking back to what we have written, do you find there is any emerging pattern that maybe we did not see at the beginning, and now has taken a shape?

PAOLO: We have described both a way of looking at people, relationships and situations, and a way of working with them to help them out of the mires of their problems, regardless of whether they are symptoms or not. We have shown how we take care of their existential situation, of their gender, race, class, of their emotions and their positions within relevant systems. We had some success—not always, but in many instances. I think it is important to understand not simply the outcome rates, but most of all the kind of successes we had.

CLAUDIA: Success depends on the issues brought to therapy. I think we found more and more cases that—besides symptomatic issues—brought what we can call existential issues. Some of those issues require togetherness in order to be faced, as we have seen in most intersectional cases, beginning with gender to end with economics. This creates an insoluble problem: therapy—any therapy, independent from its approach or its setting—doesn't allow a collective dimension, although that dimension is probably necessary to go beyond the shortcomings of postmodernism, with its individualised, and therefore basically neoliberal, view. Therapy cannot be an alternative to open political positioning. So, what can we actually achieve in therapy? What is the task of a systemic-dialogical therapist who does not want to deny their basic presuppositions?

PAOLO: We can add an additional complication. In present-day postmodern liquid modernity, the individual has gained a central status. We cannot avoid such individualism in dealing with our patients. The collective dimension is often outside our patients' horizon. We must accept the current individualism, because the historical, social, economic and political forces that have shaped it and keep it alive are too strong for us to challenge in the therapy room. The fact that we cannot change them in therapy doesn't mean, of course, that we cannot try to change the state

DOI: 10.4324/9781003381754-10

of affairs politically. But this is not directly related to our therapeutic activity.

CLAUDIA: There is something I have observed at least in many of our patients. At the end of the therapy they remain focused on their own individuality, but in a different way. We could call their position conscientious individualism. We can say that conscientious individualism means to pay attention to the individual—ourselves as individuals, the others as individuals—and pay simultaneous attention to wider systems and contexts.

PAOLO: You mean that our task, as therapists, could be to promote, not by preaching or by pushing patients, but through our very practice, a different way of living one's individuality?

CLAUDIA: Yes. The individuals, therapists as well as patients, should not only be aware of relational networks—this was already daily business for all systemic therapists in the Milan tradition—but also of the fact that any private action is political: the personal is political. We could adopt this position as a guideline for our own therapeutic practice, and by doing this that kind of personal positioning may become acceptable to the people we are working with. This does not substitute political activity, of course. It makes people responsible for the political dimensions of their choices. Of course, patients might, at this point, choose to take a political position, or they might choose not to: this is not a therapist's concern.

PAOLO: Let us go back to our concept of positional responsibility: we are responsible towards all the people who are part of the systems to which we belong, and we are responsible for the positions we take towards them. This implies that finding one's place is the preliminary step towards positional responsibility: a responsibility that is above all oriented towards the future, and concerns positions and expectations. If we are not aware of contexts and systems, we cannot even strictly speaking take a stand, because we have no idea who we should be responsible for, nor how we should take responsibility.

CLAUDIA: This also means that, once we have considered all the elements which we can access, we also have the possibility of criticising the system—or what, in it, generates discomfort for us. In this process, our emotions can be a good enough guide, as long as we are able to reconsider and reevaluate them, rather than being dominated by them. If we can apply a systemic view to our emotions, we can use them to understand our situation and motivate ourselves to action.

PAOLO: Hence: we can take full responsibility only if we find our place in the landscape of our life; at the same time, we take personal and moral responsibility, but remain aware of the relationships of which we are but a part.

CLAUDIA: If we find our place in relation to systems, contexts and our expectations, we can maintain our ideals, even if we are aware that they will probably not be reciprocated.

PAOLO: This is similar to Bauman's moral responsibility: even if the prevailing ethical code is utilitarian, competitive and performance-oriented, we can still maintain a different perspective; at the same time, we need to know and understand the prevailing ethical code thoroughly, to help people find their place in it, take responsibility for themselves and develop realistic expectations for their lives.

CLAUDIA: From the patients' point of view, this could mean: I am not—and cannot be considered—entirely responsible for my conditions, but I am fully responsible for the positions I take within them. There is therefore the possibility of exercising—assuming, if necessary, the responsibility for it—a double refusal: refusal to see oneself as the "entrepreneur of oneself", and refusal to behave according to the rules of competition.

PAOLO: As therapists, in this perspective, we should be clear about our political position, at least in our inner dialogue. I think that it's not mandatory to disclose our political positioning to patients, unless openly questioned about it. Otherwise, there is a risk of indoctrinating them. Political activism is something for our daily life, but not for the therapy room. The risk of becoming social engineers is always present.

CLAUDIA: So we can say: successful therapy may help our patients to develop a form of conscientious individualism, where they can examine and revise their own individual positions in the light of their relational network, and find their place in it, developing relational responsibility toward others.

PAOLO: As we have said, this does not happen every time. We make proposals to patients, and they answer according to their own possibilities, sensitivity and wishes. I found that it happens many times, though, and when it happens, patients are more satisfied, and they leave therapy with a sense of fulfilment.

CLAUDIA: That is, I feel, the best we can expect from our therapies.

Appendix A

The evolution of an approach

Systemic-dialogical therapy evolved from the Milan systemic approach to family and individual therapy (see Selvini Palazzoli et al., 1980a; Boscolo et al., 1987, Cecchin, 1987, Cecchin et al., 1992; Boscolo & Bertrando, 1996), in turn grounded in the systemic perspective outlined by Gregory Bateson (1972).

A long journey

We came a long way to get where we now stand. Or, better, our journey has been long and winding, yet to some extent it led us to arrive where we started and know the place for the first time, as Eliot would say. When the two of us began working together, we were still using the kind of advanced Milan systemic model described in the book *Systemic Therapy with Individuals* (Boscolo & Bertrando, 1996). The Milan model, in turn, was the result of an evolution that began in the 1950s with the emergence of systemic thinking and of family therapy (Bertrando & Toffanetti, 2000).

At the beginning, systemic therapy was but one of the several competing models of family therapy. The specific term "systemic therapy" did not even exist: it was first used by Lynn Hoffman (1981), to describe the work of the original Milan team. Usually, therapists who followed that approach qualified it as "family systems therapy". It was mainly based on Gregory Bateson's (1972) interpretation of cybernetics principles: relationships were considered the foundation of human life, and individuals seen as emerging from their interactions rather than vice versa; systems as a whole were more than the sum of than their parts; from human interaction, rules emerged, that spontaneously regulated any system (Guttman, 1991); the family was the paramount example of a human system, and so it became the main target of systemic therapeutic interventions (Haley, 1959).

When family systems therapy was born, the only relevant psychotherapeutic model was psychoanalysis, extremely inner-oriented, not yet showing the relational and intersubjective evolutions of years to come. Family systems therapy, instead, focused on observable interactions and patterns, offering a

DOI: 10.4324/9781003381754-10

viable alternative to psychoanalytical understanding, especially in complex cases, such as families with a psychotic member, or with maladjusted children and adolescents. It proposed, however, a totally external view of the person, losing sight of individuals' inner lives, to favour a systemic holistic perspective. The clinical cases of Jay Haley (1973), the Mental Research Institute group (Watzlawick et al., 1974), and the Milan team (Selvini Palazzoli et al., 1978) gave a rich view of family relationships, but a schematic, one-dimensional conception of family members, exemplary types rather that complex individualities: family systems could change their rules, but family members remained, more or less, the same. Moreover, cybernetics had been created by mathematicians and engineers, and this gave the model a very rationalistic, cognitive flavour (Heims, 1991).

Systemic theory was born within solid modernity. When it was created, the family as an institution was living its heyday (Bertrando, 1997): it was considered as the place where both each person's well-being and each person's problems originated and evolved. The family was taken for granted, as if it were a universal feature of humankind. Bateson's notion of the double bind (Bateson et al., 1956; Bateson, 1971), originally seen as a family-based etiological theory for schizophrenia, was completely ahistorical, like the laws of genetics his father William Bateson had introduced in British biology at the turn of the twentieth century (Lipset, 1980). Salvador Minuchin (1974) considered the family from a more sociological perspective, but mostly referred to Talcott Parsons's (Parsons & Bales, 1956) normative view of the patriarchal, heterosexual American family. Systemic therapy aimed at universals, yet such universals were dangerously similar to American parochial values. Consideration of wider political or economic contexts were scant—Minuchin himself was one of the very few to attempt some social critique in his *Families of the Slums* (Minuchin et al., 1967)—which was ironic for the very people who had introduced the notion of context into psychotherapy. Gender issues were all but neglected, since gender differences and roles were uncritically accepted, or at least minimised (Appendix B).

These somewhat simplistic models were all the same successful, so much that—for example—the MRI systemic-strategic therapeutic model (Watzlawick et al., 1974), once established, remained substantially unchanged for decades. The Milan approach, instead, underwent continuous changes, first through the rediscovery of Bateson's original ideas (Selvini Palazzoli et al., 1980a), then by incorporating constructivist (von Foerster, 1982; von Glasersfeld, 1987) and social constructionist (McNamee & Gergen, 1992) perspectives.

It was in that period, around 1990, that some attention toward individuals reappeared. On the one hand, the individual became again relevant as the observer that defines the boundaries and characteristics of the system (Maturana & Varela, 1980) or as the narrator of their own story (White,

1989); on the other, the attention to larger systems, other than the family, grew (Anderson et al., 1986, Boscolo et al., 1987).

In these very same years the idea of a systemic therapy with individuals was conceived: if individuals could be seen as systems in themselves, then it was possible to work with individuals considering their position in the relevant systems of their lives, and, at the same time, to "connect the inner and the outer world of the individual". Along those lines, the book *Systemic Therapy with Individuals* (Boscolo & Bertrando, 1996) was written. It maintained a basic Batesonian emphasis, adding to it some narrative, conversational, constructivist, and social constructionist ideas.

In time, we came to realise that this kind of systemic understanding was based on the implicit idea of an inherent order. If we think, like in first-order cybernetics, that the system functions according to embedded rules (Jackson, 1965), in order to maintain its homeostasis (Jackson, 1957), we are also thinking that in the system an immanent order exists that we could—and should—discover. If we think, like in constructivism, that we are superimposing some order according to our internal coordinates, or, like in social constructionism, that some order is created by the dance of social interaction, still we are seeing the world as a place needing order—and, at the same time, we are creating some version of it.

Zygmunt Bauman (1993) proposes a very interesting thesis: modernity tries to create order out of chaos, but it is constantly threatened by chaos. Modernity exists within this tension. If it yields, it finds ambiguity and ambivalence, that become a challenge toward the established order.[1] Ambivalence is the main problem of any definitory activity. When we look for certainty, we bring forth uncertainty: "Problems are created by problem-solving, new areas of chaos are created by ordering activity" (Bauman, 1993, p. 14). Ambivalence is increased by our very attempts to eliminate it. In the early days of the new millennium, the very notion of an inherent order was put into question in ways unheard of, generating new, irreducible forms of ambivalence.

Systemic ideas in a time of crisis

Theories—including therapeutic theories—and social events exist in a circular, rather than linear, relationship. Years of constructivisms and constructionisms taught us that our theories determine our understanding of the context we are embedded in; but we can also say that the context shapes our theories. A change in the context makes it necessary to change our theoretical models, whether we like it or not. Besides reading social change through our theories, we must read—through our theories—the ways in which social change modifies our theories. An exquisitely self-reflexive action. This became even truer in the period when disrupting social change forced us to revise not only social habits and practices, but also our way of framing (living) our own existential reality.

This was not the first time, by the way, that upheavals of this kind happened. To remain in our small world of psychotherapy, it is well-known that Freud, whose theories never showed excessive optimism, emphasised his pessimism after the massacres and deprivation of World War I, arriving to postulate a death instinct previously unseen in his libido-based conceptions (Freud, 1920). That this change was closely related to the war is testified by his most close biographers, such as Max Schur (1972), who had been his personal physician.

When psychoanalysis was exported to the USA, its American version was born, characterised by strong optimism and an emphasis on personal resources, an attitude shared by all other kinds of American psychotherapy. Philip Cushman (1995) connects that attitude to the basic features of (white, patriarchal) American society, including its very geography. Freud's therapy is dominationist—the disruptive potential of the Id must be submitted to the domination of the Ego; it emerged in a Europe overpopulated and compressed by opposing nationalisms. American therapy, instead, is liberationist—any individual is good and positive in herself, and just needs to be liberated by the restraints of society; this reflects an ambient considered as ripe with unlimited possibilities for expansion, at least for white men: the America of the wild frontier.

Through American psychoanalysis, liberationism heavily influenced the original family systems therapy, that showed from the beginning a very similar stance, founded on the scientific optimism of the postwar period, with its basic conviction that any problem could be solved by applying science—in this case, cybernetics—to human problems (Heims, 1991). Antipsychiatry, which would influence the evolution of family therapies in the 1960s, introducing a political and critical stance towards the capitalistic management of mental illness (see Laing, 1965; Laing & Esterson, 1964) was in turn connected to the political activism and critical theories prevailing in those years (Bertrando & Toffanetti, 2000).

Now, we reflected, our problem was: if the world shows us all of its disorder, how can we deal with it without losing our systemic—i.e., order-seeking—approach?

Postmodernism as an answer

Postmodernism was for some time an answer to the crisis of the systemic model, not just for us, but also for many colleagues around the (Western) world. Postmodern thinking is the result of a philosophical tradition dating back to the mid-twentieth century, beginning with the linguistic turn of the second Wittgenstein (1953). The attitude that paved the way to proper postmodernism emerged in the following decade, from Michel Foucault's (2001; 2006) critique, first of psychiatry, then of knowledge itself, and from Berger and Luckmann's (1966) sociology, with their notion of a social construction of reality.

Postmodernism was defined at the dawn of the 1980s in Jean-Francois Lyotard's (1984) book *La condition postmoderne*. According to Lyotard, postmodernism emerged from the enormous amount of knowledge made available to people in the second half of the twentieth century. Under its pressure, we cannot any longer believe in "metanarratives", or *grand récits*, the overarching theories and histories any culture creates, hiding under them most of their contradictions and inconsistencies. The postmodern cultural overload, instead, produces broad scepticism, subjectivism and relativism, a general suspicion of reason and an acute sensitivity to the role of ideology in asserting and maintaining political and economic power (see also Jameson, 1991).

To postmodernists, objective reality and objective knowledge are but illusions, as are truths and moral values: reality, knowledge, and values are constructed by discourses, hence they vary with them. Postmodernism is knowledge without foundation (Rosenau, 1992). All knowledge is local, rather than universal, i.e., it is determined by the political and economic conditions where that knowledge has been created. This is also true for the best modern candidate for objectivity, empirical science. When considered apart from the evidential standards internal to it, science has no greater purchase on the truth than do alternative perspectives (Feyerabend, 1975).

Postmodern ideas were worked through during a long period, but they became really prominent only between 1980 and 1990, and were accepted by the therapeutic community soon after. For systemic therapists, the call toward postmodernism came when Maturana and Varela's (1980) *Autopoiesis and Cognition* and Heinz von Foerster's (1982) *Observing Systems* defined constructivism, a perspective close, albeit not identical, to postmodernism.

Kenneth Gergen, with his book *The Saturated Self* (1991), triumphally introduced postmodern ideas in psychology. His version of postmodernism was social constructionism (Gergen, 1999), focused on cultural and identity issues, all but forgetting those material conditions that were not so prominent in systemic therapy from the beginning (see Lannamann, 1988).[2]

Many therapists soon followed this evolution. With the emergence of social constructionist therapies (McNamee & Gergen, 1992; Hoyt, 1998), postmodernism became the common frame for narrative, conversational, and solution-focused therapies (Bertrando & Toffanetti, 2000). The linguistic turn in therapeutic thinking substituted the original cybernetic description of systems with discourse-based metaphors, such as narratives (White, 1993) or "linguistic systems" (Anderson et al., 1986). Postmodern theory radically criticised the therapist's power and authority, fostering a non-expert, "not knowing" position for the therapist (Anderson & Goolishian, 1992), together with a transparency first outlined by Tom Andersen (1987) in his reflecting team.

Fredric Jameson, as early as 1991, described postmodernism as a specific cultural product of late capitalism. We must remember what was happening in the world when postmodernism emerged and then rose to prominence. These were the years that, in the West, encompass the economic upswing of the postwar era, the transient oil crisis of the 1970s, up to Margaret Thatcher's and Ronald Reagan's first neoliberal period. They were, in other words, probably the most prosperous years that the Western part of the world has lived in all of its history, the peak of the period that Eric Hobsbawm (1994) defined as "the golden age".

The social consequences of such situation are well-known. An unprecedented—and never seen again—richness of workplaces, opportunities, options for personal realisation and profit at the same time, at least for the white, mostly male, affluent enough part of the population. These were the years where the myth of the American dream was perfected: in principle anything is possible for anybody, and limits are either psychological, or linked to contingent issues; what is impossible today will be possible tomorrow, if only we will plan our lives accordingly. This faith in unlimited possibilities is the same we find in postmodern philosophy and therapy.

The heyday of postmodernism coincided with the end of that period. But the sense of that ending was not perceived by Western middle and intellectual classes at the time. The postmodern years were, on the contrary, lived as the beginning of a new era of unlimited prosperity. Under this umbrella, it appeared simply natural to focus on discourses and language: there was no need to change material conditions. Or, at least, this was what most therapists were thinking.

Shortcomings of postmodernism

Returning to us, when we began doing therapy together we immediately felt that the Milan approach we were using was becoming ill-fit for changing times. The old systemic metaphor sounded somewhat mechanistic and cold, and needed something new to revitalise it. We saw postmodernism as a possibility to get rid of the remaining normative assumptions about patients and families, embracing its basic optimism. We were not so sensitive, at the time, to the social and economic issues that conditioned our practice and our lives.

The postmodern turn in psychotherapy (McNamee & Gergen, 1992) had the great merit of shaking the implicit positivism of previous therapeutic theories, introducing a healthy wariness toward psychiatric or developmental categories that were too easily mistaken for objective realities. At the same time, their pretence of explaining—and changing—the whole of reality through language was excessive. Probably many of us forgot that we were clinicians rather than philosophers or sociologists, and we misinterpreted Berger and Luckmann (1966), who basically dealt with the social construction of social realities, rather than of reality as such.

As far as we are concerned, we soon started to doubt at least part of the claims of the postmodern approach to therapy. One of us considered, in that very period, the internal contradictions—the aporias—of postmodernism (Bertrando, 2000), that we can synthesise in the idea that language and discourse actually create the whole of reality. In his apology of social constructionism, Gergen (1999) claimed to have successfully solved problems such as the reality of perception, the relationship between the self and world, the nature of identity, that were inexplicably left unresolved by the best philosophical minds, from Plato and Aristotle to Descartes and Kant and Wittgenstein.

The apostles of social constructionism loved to quote the Proposition 5.6 of Wittgenstein's *Tractatus Logico-Philosophicus*: "*The limits of my language* mean the limits of my world.", or as he next puts it "…the limits of *language* (of that language which alone I understand) mean the limits of *my* world" (Wittgenstein, 1922, 5.6, 5.62). They tended to translate it into the amiable oversimplification ascribed—perhaps apocryphally—to Harry Goolishian: "*Everything is language*". According to most scholars, actually, this statement of Wittgenstein's means exactly the opposite: what we can express in language limits, rather than expanding, our world, and there should be a perfect symmetry between the world we live in and the language that we use to describe it (see Tejedor, 2014). Language does not create worlds.[3]

Postmodern therapy became the triumph of fictional reality. Since any kind of reality is, according to such reading, "socially constructed", we just need to change discourses in order to change realities: Anderson and Goolishian's (1992) celebrated *problem dis-solving*. Now, this may work if we live in a landscape rich in resources and the limits of our choice are only the limits of our imagination. But this perspective is unveiled as inadequate if our hard reality becomes limited and constrictive: we discover that changing discourses does not change bank accounts.

Therapeutic postmodernism, then, was a luxury. It had been possible only in this time, and for the people who could afford it, namely privileged enough people. (A very postmodern-oriented colleague some years ago visited both the Houston Galveston Institute, Mecca of conversationalist therapy, and old Philadelphia Child Guidance Clinic, at the time still faithful to Minuchin's quite modernistic principles. She commented: "In Houston, I saw middle class people, in Philadelphia families of poor migrants. I discovered it was impossible to use in Philadelphia the methods I had learnt in Houston!")

A clean break came with the 2008 financial crisis. The landscape of therapy changed for everybody. In private practice, work issues became a growing part of presenting problems. In many cases, lack of money forced to redefine, and sometime to cancel, therapeutic contracts. In public services, threatened in their very existence, decreasing resources led to expenditure cuts that in turn caused personnel cuts. Insecurity grew, for both therapists and patients. We discovered that both original systemic ideas and later postmodern elaborations were unfit to times of crisis: they became more difficult to maintain—at least in their original, all-encompassing optimism.

The world—or the discourses about the world—shifted from postmodernism to Bauman's (2000) liquid modernity (Chapter 1). We think that what Bauman considers, and Gergen—whom we choose here to represent all major post-modern theorists—does not, are the basic social conditions that underpins both postmodernism and liquid modernity. Gergen focuses on postmodernism as a way of thinking, of seeing and considering reality; Bauman pays attention to what actually happens in society, regardless of what we think about it. Gergen and Bauman agree that individual, rather than collective, agency is the core of the present-day era, but again with a different emphasis: to Gergen, it is an array of possibilities, to Bauman it is an obligation: we have to choose and we must consider ourselves responsible for our choice, even if we did not want to choose in the first place. The postmodern (liquid) condition may well be experienced as an increase of possibilities by privileged enough individuals, whereas the unprivileged ones are subjected to it.

At this point, we felt we needed new ideas to deal with such a scenario. This was when we discovered dialogical theories.

Dialogue in liquid modernity

As our practice evolved we realised that our attitudes toward patients were evolving too. We could not maintain the original position of the systemic therapist, who always had something "unexpected and improbable" (Selvini Palazzoli et al., 1980a, p. 4) to tell patients. Most of all, that attitude did not fit our patients themselves, who felt they had something relevant to say about themselves and the others, and would leap at any opportunity to say it. Dis-agreement on part of the patient became something that we did not try to overcome, but rather respected at all time. In short, we were spontaneously shifting toward a dialogical stance, where the aim of the therapeutic dialogue was not to reach unanimity, harmony, or a final agreement—usually meaning the agreement desired by the therapist. In trying to give some shape to our changing position, we followed suggestions coming from colleagues such as Tom Andersen and Lynn Hoffman, and discovered the work of Mikhail Bakhtin (see Chapter 4).

A philosopher of language and literary theorist who lived in Russia and the USSR for most of the twentieth century, Mikhail Bakhtin was the pro-moter of an approach named dialogism, that entails the acceptance and promotion of a plurality of voices, languages, and perspective within dis-course (Holquist, 2002). Dialogism, in turn, contains two notions, developed at different times: polyphony (Bakhtin, 1984) and pluridiscursivity or het-eroglossia (Bakhtin, 1981). Polyphony refers to the presence of different voices, persons, or characters in dialogue; pluridiscursivity to the co-existence, within it, of different languages, each with its peculiar social and historical connotations.[4]

Bakhtin (1984) developed several of his ideas through an analysis of Dostojevski's "polyphonic novels", where all characters are seen and heard in their free dialogue, without looking for past stories or explanations: they make themselves understood by bringing their own voices into the narrative. Polyphony accepts conflict without attempting to solve it; in a dialogical perspective, nobody has the last word. Everybody keeps their right to reply. The polyphonic author accepts all their characters in their open-endedness, rather than objectifying them: they are neither determined by the author's definition, nor by their social or economic conditions. They are not "types", they do not belong to any typology, they are utterly unpredictable.

At the same time, the polyphonic novel is also pluridiscursive (Bakhtin, 1981). The language spoken within it is manifold, because in it many languages co-exist, each with its specific influences from history and society. A dialogical exchange is the emergence of live meaning generated by live people, interacting through their own physical beings. Bakhtin is interested in the actual world of discourse, rather than the abstract domain of linguistic structure.

Both concepts, albeit differently, imply that real life resembles a cacophony, rather than a more or less pre-established harmony. The immanent order of human facts is a creation of ours. The linguistic world—which, to Bakhtin, means the world in general—is a disordered place, and the idea of order implies the prevalence of a single, authoritarian voice, the one dictating one presumedly "natural" order. Accepting disorder means renouncing, once and for all, to privilege one voice over the others. In dialogue, meaning emerges from a linguistic struggle, where all parties strive to be understood by the others. No viewpoint is final: we are all *in fieri*, building ourselves in relation to the others. And this dialogical relationship constitutes ourselves: only in dialogue with others can we tentatively define our viewpoint.

Dialogue began influencing the field of psychotherapy toward the beginning of the new millennium, exactly the same time when Bauman was defining liquid modernity (Pollard, 2008). Dialogical ideas were easily accepted by postmodern therapists: their emphasis on a non-hierarchical position and on openness in therapy fit dialogical thinking pretty well, so that authors like Tom Andersen (1987) or Peter Rober (2005) began defining themselves as "dialogical". Only one model, however, was entirely based on Bakhtin's ideas: open dialogue, developed by Jaakko Seikkula and his team in Finland (Seikkula & Olson, 2003), an approach that has been fruitfully applied to the treatment of first-episode psychosis (Seikkula et al., 2001).

Open dialogue, actually, descends from the Milan systemic model originally used by the Seikkula team in Finland. Its development, though, distanced them from systemic approaches, to the point of becoming its opposite. Seikkula and Olson (2003) set three basic principles for open dialogue, namely tolerance of uncertainty, dialogism, and polyphony, obviously modelled after Bakhtin's concepts, but also deliberately contrasting the three principles of the original Milan team—hypothesising, circularity, and neutrality (Selvini Palazzoli et al., 1980a).

According to Seikkula and Olson, "tolerance of uncertainty is the counterpart to, in fact, the opposite of, the systemic use of hypothesising or any other kind of assessment tool" (2003, p. 408). As to dialogism, "the Bakhtinian idea of dialogue ... derive[s] from a tradition that sees language and communication as primarily constitutive of social reality. Constructing words and establishing symbolic communication is a voice-making, identity-making, agentic activity occurring jointly 'between people'" (Seikkula & Olson, 2003, p. 409). In the clinical dialogue the therapist should always be, first of all, a listener: asking questions is more important than getting answers; promoting a linguistic exchange more relevant than getting to an ultimate definition. Regarding polyphony, "in contrast to the systemic use of circular questioning, the dialogical emphasis is on generating multiple expressions, with no attempt to uncover a particular truth" (Seikkula & Olson, 2003, p. 410).

In dialogical therapies, Bakhtin sits in the chair that systemic therapists had given to Gregory Bateson. His approach to dialogue is seen as the best possible answer to the new demands brought forward by life in liquid times. Fruitful as they are, his ideas may also generate some problems when applied to therapy. Bakhtin apparently believed dialogue to be positive in itself. In so doing, he did not consider that an unlimited opening can also be bewildering (Emerson, 1997), or hide a reluctance to take definite positions (Bernstein, 1989). We cannot even exclude that, in real life, dialogues can become authoritarian, or even coercive (Fogel, 1985): Bakhtin never clarified whether his concepts are descriptive, implying that any human interaction is necessarily dialogical—in which case no authoritarian dialogue would be possible—or rather prescriptive, exhorting to a discursive practice centred on dialogue rather than monologue—in which case the creation of a proper dialogue would require a consistent effort on the therapist's part (Vice, 1997). Maybe, as Natalia Reed (1999) maintains, Bakhtin's excessive optimism stemmed from treating the (imaginary) dialogues of Dostojevski's novels as true dialogues between actual people. The paradoxical result was to base a theory of embodied dialogue on written fictional examples invented by a novelist. Such considerations led us to use systemic understanding in order to mitigate the shortcomings of a full-fledged dialogical approach.

The book *The Dialogical Therapist* (Bertrando, 2007) represents our first attempt to use Bakhtinian ideas in therapy, especially dialogism and polyphony. Differently from most advocates of dialogical approaches, such as Andersen, Anderson, or Seikkula, we did not dispense with Milan systemic practices altogether (Chapter 4). At the same time, we recovered some of Michel Foucault's ideas. Contrary to most systemic therapists, we had not been introduced to Foucault's work by Michael White, whose narrative therapy (White & Epston, 1991) had extensively adopted a Foucauldian position in relation to power issues. Foucault had been an essential reference point for Italian critical psychiatry, that in turn heavily influenced Italian family therapy (Bertrando & Toffanetti, 2000). We used Foucault's (1977, 1988) ideas about power and technologies of the self in order to go beyond Batesonian abstractions in relation to power relationships (Bertrando, 2007). In subsequent years, Wittgenstein's (1953) work on language games helped us in understanding aspects of language that remained obscure in a pure Bakhtinian perspective.

Around 2010, we deepened our reading of Zygmunt Bauman's sociological writings, after a personal interview with Bauman about therapy in liquid modernity (Bauman et al., 2010), where he offered an interesting suggestion: if original psychoanalysis had been a way to give free rein to the pleasure principle, constrained and suffocated by the reality principle in solid modernity, the task for the therapist in liquid time could be to bring back some reality principle to people (apparently) governed by an unrestrained pleasure principle—a description that could be easily applied to postmodern patients. This led us to become more and more attuned to a critique of the material conditions where we ourselves and our patients lived. This process was also helped by reading another important critic of the postmodern (liquid) world, namely Korean-German philosopher Byung-Chul Han, with his extension and revision of Foucault's ideas, such as biopolitics, that becomes psychopolitics (Han, 2017b) under the pressure of late capitalist forms of life (Han, 2015), and of course the changes brought forth by digital and social media (Han, 2017a).

The contributions of these authors helped us to shape Chapter 1. But our therapeutic practice was also—and possibly even more—influenced by feminist and transfeminist thinking (Chapter 2; Appendix B).

Notes

1 Bauman sees a resemblance (an analogy, a Foucauldian "discourse") between politics and science: both, in order to narrow down their focuses, exclude a group (a group of people, a group of ideas), in order to eradicate ambivalence, uncertainty and doubt. Marginalised people, like blurred, undefined ideas, must be eliminated or neglected.

2 The postmodern emphasis on airy abstractions is visible also in the best intended culture critiques: they tend to address themes of identity and subjugation on a purely cultural level, leaving out the power of neoliberalism to turn everything—including those very critiques—into commodities that can enter the marketplace (see Cangiano, 2024).

3 Such position would be rejected by the "second Wittgenstein" in later years (see Monk, 2005)—but this is another story.

4 A wonderful—and extremely well-written—analysis of pluridiscursivity is, for example, David Foster Wallace's (1999) "Authority and American usage", where the author comments on the existence, within the allegedly unitary American

English, of dialects and "innumerable sub- and subsubdialects" (p. 98), that sometimes have a deep social and cultural impact, like the difficulty for people grown
within Standard Black English to properly manage Standard Written (White) English, thus finding it hard to climb the social ladder to professional and academic
recognition.

References

Andersen, T. (1987). The reflecting team: Dialogue and meta-dialogue in clinical work. *Family Process*, 26 (4): 415–428. DOI:10.1111/j.1545–5300.1987.00415.x.

Anderson, H. & Goolishian, H. (1992). The client is the expert: A not-knowing approach to therapy. In: S. McNamee & K.J. Gergen (Eds.), *Therapy as Social Construction* (pp. 25–39). Sage.

Anderson, H., Goolishian, H., & Winderman, L. (1986). Problem determined systems: Towards transformation in family therapy, *Journal of Strategic and Systemic Therapy*, 5: 1–14. DOI:10.1521/jsst.1986.5.4.1.

Bakhtin, M.M. (1981). Discourse in the novel. In: M. Holquist (Ed.), *The Dialogic Imagination* (pp. 259–422). Texas University Press (original edition 1935).

Bakhtin, M.M. (1984). C. Emerson (Ed.). *Problems of Dostojevski's Poetics*. University of Minnesota Press (original edition 1968).

Bateson, G. (1972). *Steps to an Ecology of Mind*. Chandler Publishing Company.

Bateson, G. (1971). Double Bind, 1969. In: *Steps to an Ecology of Mind* (pp. 271–278). Chandler Publishing Company, 1972.

Bateson, G., Jackson, D.D., Haley, J., & Weakland, J.H. (1956). Toward a theory of schizophrenia. *Behavioral Science*, 1: 251–264. DOI:10.1002/bs.3830010402.

Bauman, Z. (1993). *Postmodern Ethics*. Blackwell Publishing.

Bauman, Z. (2000). *Liquid Modernity*. Polity Press.

Bauman, Z., Bertrando, P., & Hanks, H. (2010). Liquid Ethics – psychotherapy in a time of uncertainty. *Human Systems*, 20 (1): 42–56.

Berger, P. & Luckmann, T. (1966). *The Social Construction of Reality*. Doubleday.

Bernstein, A. (1989). The poetics of ressentiment. In: G. Morson & M. Gardiner (Eds.), *Rethinking Bakhtin: Extensions and Challenges*. NorthWestern University Press.

Bertrando, P. (1997). *Nodi Familiari*. Feltrinelli.

Bertrando, P. (2000). Text and context. Narrative, postmodernism, and cybernetics. *Journal of Family Therapy*, 22 (1): 83–103. DOI:10.1111/1467–6427.00139.

Bertrando, P. (2007). *The Dialogical Therapist*. Karnac.

Bertrando, P. & Toffanetti, D. (2000). *Storia della terapia familiare. Le persone, le idee*. Raffaello Cortina Editore.

Boscolo, L. & Bertrando, P. (1996). *Systemic Therapy with Individuals*. Karnac.

Boscolo, L., Cecchin, G., Hoffman, L., & Penn, P. (1987). *Milan Systemic Family Therapy: Conversations in Theory and Practice*. Basic Books.

Cangiano, M. (2024). *Guerre culturali e neoliberismo*. Nottetempo.

Cecchin, G. (1987). Hypothesizing-circularity-neutrality revisited: An invitation to curiosity, *Family Process*, 26: 405–413. DOI:10.1111/j.1545–5300.1987.00405.x.

Cecchin, G., Lane G., & Ray, W.L. (1992). *Irreverence: A Strategy for Therapists' Survival*. Karnac.

Cushman, P. (1995). *Constructing the Self, Constructing America: A Cultural History of Psychotherapy*. Addison-Wesley Publishing Company.

Emerson, C. (1997). *The First Hundred Years of Mikhail Bakhtin*. Princeton University Press.

Feyerabend, P. (1975). *Against Method: Outline of an Anarchistic Theory of Knowledge*. 4th edition. Verso Books, 2010.

Fogel A. (1985). Coerced speech and the Oedipus dialogue complex. In: G.S. Morson & C. Emerson (Eds.), *Rethinking Bakhtin: Extensions and Challenges*. Northwestern University Press.

Foucault, M. (1977). *Discipline and Punish: The Birth of the Prison* (translated by A. Sheridan). Allen Lane (original edition 1975).

Foucault, M. (2001). *The Order of Things*. Routledge (original edition 1966).

Foucault, M. (1988). Technologies of the self. In: P. Rabinow (Ed.), *Ethics: Essential Works of Foucault 1954–1984, Vol.* 1 (pp. 223–251). Penguin, 2000.

Foucault, M. (2006). *History of Madness*, translated by Jonathan Murphy. Routledge (original edition 1972).

Freud, S. (1920). *Beyond the Pleasure Principle*, English translation by James Strachey. *The Standard Edition of the Complete Psychological Works of Sigmund Freud, Volume XVIII (1920–1922)*: 7–64.

Gergen, K.J. (1991). *The Saturated Self*. Basic Books.

Gergen, K.J. (1999). *An Invitation to Social Construction*. Sage.

Guttman, H. (1991). Systems theory, cybernetics, and epistemology. In: A.S. Gurman & D.P. Kniskern (Eds.), *Handbook of Family Therapy*, Vol. II. Brunner/Mazel.

Haley, J. (1959). The family of the schizophrenic: a model system. *Journal of Nervous and Mental Disease*, 129: 357–374. DOI:10.1097/00005053–195910000–00003.

Haley, J. (1973). *Uncommon Therapy. The Psychiatric Techniques of Milton Erickson, M.D.* Norton.

Han, Byung-Chul (2015). *The Burnout Society*. Stanford University Press (original edition 2010).

Han, Byung-Chul (2017a). *In the Swarm: Digital Prospects*. Transl. by Erik Butler. MIT Press (original edition 2013).

Han, Byung-Chul (2017b). *Psychopolitics: Neoliberalism and New Technologies of Power*. Transl. by Erik Butler. Verso (original edition 2014).

Heims, S.J. (1991). *The Cybernetics Group*. MIT Press.

Hobsbawm, E. (1994). *The Age of Extremes: The Short Twentieth Century, 1914–1991*. Pantheon Books.

Hoffman, L. (1981). *Foundations of Family Therapy*. Basic Books.

Holquist M. (2002). *Dialogism: Bakhtin and His World*. 2nd edition. Routledge.

Hoyt, M.F. (1998). *The Handbook of Constructive Therapies: Innovative Approaches from Leading Practitioners*. Jossey-Bass.

Jackson, D.D. (1957). The question of family homeostasis. *Psychiatric Quarterly Supplement*, 31: 79–90.

Jackson, D.D. (1965). Family rules, the marital quid pro quo. *Archives of General Psychiatry*, 12: 589–594.

Jameson, F. (1991). *Postmodernism or the Cultural Logic of Late Capitalism*. Verso.

Laing, R. (1965). Mystification, confusion and conflict. In: I. Boszormenyi-Nagy & J. K. Framo (Eds.), *Intensive Family Therapy* (pp. 343–363). Harper and Row.

Laing, R. & Esterson, A. (1964). *Sanity, Madness and the Family. Families of Schizo-phrenics.* Tavistock.

Lannamann, J. (1998). Social constructionism and materiality: The limits of inde-terminacy in therapeutic settings. *Family Process,* 37: 393–414. DOI:10.1111/j.1545-5300.1998.00393.x.

Lipset, D. (1980). *Gregory Bateson: The Legacy of a Scientist.* Prentice-Hall.

Lyotard, J.-F. (1984). *The Postmodern Condition: A Report on Knowledge.* English translation by Geoff Bennington and Brian Massuni. University of Minnesota Press (original edition published 1979).

Maturana, H. & Varela, F. (1980). *Autopoiesis and Cognition: The Realisation of the Living.* Reidel Publishing Company.

McNamee, S. & Gergen, K.J. (1992). *Therapy as Social Construction.* Sage.

Minuchin, S. (1974). *Families and Family Therapy.* Harvard University Press.

Minuchin, S., Guerney, B., Rosman, B., & Schumer, F. (1967). *Families of the Slum.* Basic Books.

Monk, R. (2005). *How to Read Wittgenstein.* Granta.

Parsons, T. & Bales, R.T. (1956). *Family Socialization and Interaction Process.* The Free Press.

Pollard, R. (2008). *Dialogue and Desire: Michail Bakhtin and the Linguistic Turn in Psychotherapy.* Karnac.

Reed, N. (1999). The philosophical roots of polyphony: A Dostoevskian reading. In: C. Emerson (Ed.), *Critical Essays on Mikhail Bakhtin.* G. K. Hall.

Rober, P. (2005). The therapist's self in dialogical family therapy: some ideas about not-knowing and the therapist's inner conversation. *Family Process,* 44: 477–495. DOI:10.1111/j.1545–5300.2005.00073.x.

Rosenau, P. (1992). *Post-modernism and the Social Sciences.* Princeton University Press.

Schur, M. (1972). *Freud: Living and Dying.* International Universities Press.

Seikkula, J., Alakare, B., & Aaltonen, J. (2001). Open dialogue in first-episode psy-chosis II: A comparison of good and poor outcome cases. *Journal of Constructivist Psychology,* 14: 267–284.

Seikkula, J. & Olson, M.E. (2003). The open dialogue approach to acute psychosis: its poetics and micropolitics. *Family Process,* 42: 403–418. DOI:10.1111/j.1545–5300.2003.00403.x.

Selvini Palazzoli, M., Boscolo, L., Cecchin, G., & Prata, G. (1978). *Paradox and Counterparadox.* Jason Aronson.

Selvini Palazzoli, M., Boscolo, L., Cecchin, G., & Prata, G. (1980a). Hypothesizing-circularity-neutrality. Three guidelines for the conductor of the session. *Family Process,* 19: 3–12. DOI:10.1111/j.1545–5300.1980.00003.x.

Tejedor, C. (2014). *The Early Wittgenstein on Metaphysics, Natural Science, Language and Value.* Routledge. DOI:10.4324/9781315850245.

Vice, S. (1997). *Introducing Bakhtin.* Manchester: Manchester University Press.

von Foerster, H. (1982). *Observing Systems.* Intersystems Publications.

Von Glasersfeld, E. (1987). *The Construction of Knowledge.* Intersystems Publications.

Wallace, D. F. (1999). Authority and American usage. In: *Consider the Lobster and Other Essays.* Little, Brown & Company, 2006, pp. 66–127.

Watzlawick, P., Weakland, J. H., & Fisch, R. (1974). *Change: The Principles of Pro-blem Formation and Problem Resolution.* W. W. Norton.

White, M. (1989). The externalizing of the problem and the re-authoring of lives and relationship (pp. 3–21). *Dulwich Centre Newsletter* (Summer).

White, M. (1993). Deconstruction and therapy. In S. G. Gilligan & R. Price (Eds.), *Therapeutic Conversations* (pp. 22–61). W. W. Norton & Co. (reprinted from the *Dulwich Centre Newsletter*, 3, 1991, 1–21).

White, M., & Epston, D. (1991). *Narrative Means to Therapeutic Ends*. New York, Norton.

Wittgenstein, L. (1922). *Tractatus Logico-Philosophicus*. (K.G. Ogden, translator.) Routledge and Kegan Paul (original edition 1921).

Wittgenstein, L. (1953). *Philosophical Investigations*. Edited by G.E.M. Anscombe. Wiley-Blackwell.

Appendix B
Feminisms

In Chapter 2 we have detailed how our therapeutic practice changed under the influence of feminist ideas. Here we would like to give an account of the evolution of feminist theory and practice as we understood it.

Feminist waves

Usually, different eras in feminism are described in term of "waves" (Reger, 2017), although this subdivision has been criticised by many. The first wave of feminism dates from the late nineteenth and beginning of the twentieth century (see Tong, 2018). It was mainly centred on civil rights and the fight for women's political power, first of all on their right to vote, which was secured in 1920 in the USA, in 1921 in the UK, and in 1945 in Italy (Johnson Lewis, 2020).

The second wave of feminism emerged in the 1960s, in an era of widespread political upheaval, at least in the Western world. It basically focused on issues such as reproductive rights and the importance of access to birth control and safe and legal abortion, emphasising the importance of women's control of their bodies and reproductive decisions (Izzo, 2002). Mostly a (North) American phenomenon, it was highlighted in the most famous feminist book of the time, Betty Friedan's (1963) *The Feminine Mystique*. The fight for equal pay, nondiscrimination in the workplace, and the redefinition of gender roles was considered too, challenging the notion that female fulfilment is found exclusively in marriage and motherhood (Horowitz, 1996).

Between 1960 and 1980, American radical feminism—radical because it aimed to go to the roots of women's subordination, as well as the conquest of rights and economic independence—defined the gender category: gender began to be intended as the social and cultural construction of the sexes and corresponding roles. This had been envisioned by one of the most important early theorists of feminism, philosopher Simone de Beauvoir, who famously stated: "One is not born, but rather becomes, woman" (de Beauvoir, 2011, p. 330).

DOI: 10.4324/9781003381754-10

According to radical feminists, the biological difference between the sexes had become a difference in roles, which in turn evolved to a hierarchy: men were assigned to production and work, women to reproduction and care. The hierarchisation of differences led to the oppression of men over women and the creation of rigid boundaries between gender identities, with the distancing or non-recognition of those outside the norm. The female gender had been historically defined through difference—beginning from the study of the body in medicine, where the female body was studied as a non-male body (Hamberg, 2008). This means that it has long been impossible to conceive the development of female identity without referring to what happens in the male world. To go beyond these limits, therefore, we should disconnect our identity from the social order, avoiding sexual dualism. The demand for new rights followed: the right of choosing one's sex, the defence of sexual minorities, the right to homosexual marriage and adoption and to have a child.

All in all, this idea of gender—as different from sex—in time began to be applied, besides feminists, by scholars in general, finally arriving to the general public. According to the World Health Organisation:

> Gender refers to the characteristics of women, men, girls and boys that are socially constructed. This includes norms, behaviours and roles associated with being a woman, man, girl or boy, as well as relationships with each other. As a social construct, gender varies from society to society and can change over time.
>
> Gender is hierarchical and produces inequalities that intersect with other social and economic inequalities. Gender-based discrimination intersects with other factors of discrimination, such as ethnicity, socioeconomic status, disability, age, geographic location, gender identity and sexual orientation, among others. This is referred to as intersectionality.
>
> Gender interacts with but is different from sex, which refers to the different biological and physiological characteristics of females, males and intersex persons, such as chromosomes, hormones and reproductive organs. Gender and sex are related to but different from gender identity. Gender identity refers to a person's deeply felt, internal and individual experience of gender, which may or may not correspond to the person's physiology or designated sex at birth.
>
> (World Health Organization, 2021)

By 1980, most feminist—and not only feminist—academic writers had agreed on using gender only for referring to socioculturally adapted traits. In this sense, gender refers to cultural aspects rather than biological differences. This was the final stage of an evolution begun in sociology during the 1950s, later brought on in Lacanian psychoanalysis, then in the work of French psychoanalysts like Julia Kristeva (1986) and Luce Irigaray (1985), culminating in the work of American philosopher Judith Butler (1990). Butler

(1993) even rejected Beauvoir's famous statement. According to it, the body should be considered as pre-discursive, the material basis for any discourse about sex. Butler maintains, instead, that we cannot have a notion of sex and the body without submitting it to some discourse. Bodies are not created by discourses, but we do speak about them, and when they become part of our discourses they lose their foundational value: the relationship between bodies and discourses—between sex and gender—is more complex than we tend to believe: it is actually impossible to tell whether some absolutely "natural" sex actually exists. At the same time, we need some foundation for any discourse about sex and gender, so we are caught in an apparently paradoxical conundrum. All in all, she maintains: "Gender is a complexity whose totality is permanently deferred, never fully what it is at any given juncture in time" (Butler, 1990, p. 21). It does not mean that it is unimportant: the fact is, no final—unambiguous, decontextualised—definition of it is possible. It must vary with the context.

Butler came to regard gender roles as a set of practices, standardised by cultural norm, and then acted upon by women and men. Hence her definition of "performative" practices:

> Gender proves to be performative—that is, constituting the identity it is purported to be. In this sense, gender is always a doing, though not a doing by a subject who might be said to preexist the deed. ... There is no gender identity behind the expressions of gender; that identity is performatively constituted by the very "expressions" that are said to be its results.
>
> (Butler, 1990, pp. 33–34)

Performance, of course, must follow some script. Heterosexual scripts would be transmitted daily by parents, school, friends, books, mass media, films, songs, and we would perpetuate them in our fantasies and in our lives—whether we are attached to them or we resist them.[1] (We can also view gender as a relational category: one is female because somebody else is male. And male and female exist through an act of distinction that we constantly renew.)

The second wave of feminism thus introduced powerful categories, but tended to consider women (gender) issues as disconnected by other aspects of social life—aspects that may be connected to other forms of disadvantage. In the third wave of feminism, between the 1990s and 2000s, Kimberleé Crenshaw (1991), among others, introduced the theory of intersectionality, which addresses the interactions between different forms of oppression and discrimination and emphasises the inhomogeneity of women: significant differences exist between them due to the multiple facets of their identity. Feminists paid growing attention to these issues, with a significant complexification of their thinking and practice. Other variants of third-wave feminism, though, were influenced instead by economic neoliberalism. They maintained, for example, that the success of one woman is the success of all women, presuming that there is no need to change the fabric of neoliberal (patriarchal) society to bring forth women's issues. This position generated the famous metaphor of the "glass ceiling", the invisible barrier that women should break in order to get to proper power positions (Wilson, 2014). As Elizabeth Evans writes:

> The term "third wave feminism" has been interpreted in multiple and often contradictory ways. It has been viewed as both a neoliberal brand of feminism and as a more explicit feminist engagement with global social justice agendas. Some note that third wave feminism seeks to reclaim and subvert traditional notions of femininity whilst others consider it a polemical defence of girliness. It is frequently associated with women of color and intersectionality and yet the dominance of white, middle-class heterosexual voices has also been observed.
>
> (Evans, 2015, p. 15)

Such contradictions may be at least partly explained if we consider one feature common to all these orientations in third-wave feminism: an individualistic focus, that characterises most cultural and political productions of that era, especially the 1990s. While this represented a necessary step beyond the often naive theories of the preceding decades, it also acted as a sort of shift toward an excess of individualism, that had to be trespassed in the following years.

Usually, we place the beginning of the fourth wave of feminism around the year 2000 (Munro, 2013). It generalised the struggles of previous periods against sexual harassment, gender violence, the achievement of equal pay, with the recognition and inclusion of voices of women of different races, ethnicities, sexual orientations and socioeconomic experiences, with particular attention to issues such as consent, empowerment, representation and social justice. There was a strong influence from social media and digital communication, which has allowed the spread of information and activism on a global scale, as in the case of the #MeToo movement, born in 2017 (Ozkazanc-Pan, 2019).

The fourth wave of feminism has seen greater participation and activism of young women, the involvement of men in the fight for gender equality and the visibility and fight for the rights of the LGBTQ+ community, promoting a challenge to stereotypes and to the prejudices often associated with gender identity. "We should all be feminists" can be considered a good synthesis of the fourth wave. A feminist person is a person who believes in political, social and economic equality between the sexes. Gender cannot be a source of discrimination.

In terms of effects on our practice, fourth-wave feminism is today our most important influence, that helped changing many of our basic tenets. Our approach is embedded in the fourth wave.

Feminists and therapy

The feminist critique to family therapy began in 1978 with a fundamental article by Rachel Hare-Mustin (1978), and went on in the 1980s, showing to what extent the (mostly male) founders of systemic and family therapies failed to see how their methods were not based on a supposedly neutral science, but rather reflected prejudices deeply rooted in society.

More or less in the same period, feminist thinking applied to clinical psychology was challenging the psychoanalytic idea of male development as the norm, and of adaptation to the sexual roles of marriage and motherhood as the goal of therapy. That meant going beyond biological determinism to examine the effects of the social context (Miller & Kofsky Scholnick, 2000): if we stop seeing the family as an apolitical, perfect and self-contained machine, we can pay attention to the social context and above all the implicit values transmitted through the family structure itself, which feminists considered inherently patriarchal and anti-feminine. We can say that feminist critique anticipated, in advance of many years, critiques to the excess of abstraction in systemic therapeutic theories.

Also in 1978, the Women's Project of the Ackerman Institute (Betty Carter, Peggy Papp, Olga Silverstein, and Marianne Walters) began questioning the power structure of the institutes of family therapy: the vast majority of therapists were women, yet they occupied few positions of power (see Simon, 1997). They wondered: why cannot I go against men in therapy? What does it mean for a woman therapist to challenge a man who is considered the head of the house? Why do we so often pressure women to change family dynamics? Such reflections brought the Women's Project to publish their influential book *The Invisible Web: Gender Patterns in Family Relationships* (Walters et al., 1988). They aimed at moving the focus of family therapy from a deficit model to a strengths and resources view, depathologising women in therapy first, but all humans in therapy ultimately.

In Deborah Luepnitz's book *The Family Interpreted* (1988), several pioneers of family therapy are considered according to their sensitivity to gender issues. The landscape she depicts, at the end of the 1980s, is somewhat discomforting. Although she can distinguish different degrees of proximity to gender themes, no founding father (or mother) of family therapy takes any explicit position in this respect.

Some of them, actually, present themselves as fully patriarchal and actively opposing female issues. For example, Nathan Ackerman, one of the very first family therapists, is seen as an arch-patriarch, using his own patriarchal persona to re-affirm roles and modes of the traditional American family to the detriment of the women he encounters in his therapies. Murray Bowen, with his insistence on reason and rationality, the Western male attributes *par excellence*, shows no interest in characteristics like emotional sensitivity, traditionally associated with women. Salvador Minuchin, whose therapy is embedded in Talcott Parsons's deeply conservative social functionalism (see Parsons & Bales, 1956), sees the family as a quasi-organic entity tending to integration, thus denying any possibility to change traditional gender roles within it. Most of these therapists, in their actual documented practice, tended to challenge the women in the families and support the men.

Carl Whitaker, the "great original" of family therapy according to Lynn Hoffman (1981), went against the tradition much more frequently, but without explicitly endorsing any feminist view, and with not a few contradictions. Three of the great women of family therapy, Virginia Satir, Chloe Madanes, and Mara Selvini Palazzoli, are criticised not for what they did or said, but for what they failed to do or say: they never took a stance regarding their own being women—not to mention their consideration of women patients—preferring to accept the non-gendered view favoured by systemic thinkers of their time.

As far as the specific systemic field is concerned, a whole chapter deals with a critique of Gregory Bateson's cybernetic epistemology, considered as too abstract, epistemologically weak, gender insensitive, and ahistorical. Bateson's concept of the double bind (Bateson et al., 1956) was, at the beginning, as mother-blaming as most therapeutic ideologies of the 1950s; Bateson himself went beyond that in re-formulating the concept (Bateson, 1971), but neglecting gender altogether: references to gender issues are completely absent from his work. Luepnitz wonders what would have happened if systemic therapy had been based, rather than on Bateson's, on his former wife Margaret Mead's work, given that Mead wrote much more extensively about families and cultures than Bateson himself (see for example Mead, 1935). But probably the deepest criticism concerns the very nature of Bateson's cybernetics: by describing systems as self-regulating, hopefully harmonious wholes, he risks overlooking the importance of conflict and disharmony in human existence. This is coupled with his reluctance, already disapproved by Jay Haley (1976), to conceive systems in terms of power. A neglect that he transmitted to many of his followers.

Strategic therapists—including Haley, despite his long-standing interest in power issues—are criticised, in turn, because they simply pretend that gender issues do not exist, whereas the Milan approach is to blame mostly because of its concepts of circularity and neutrality (see Boscolo et al., 1987): circularity can become a means through which a process of punishment of the victim and legitimation of the persecutor is implemented, neutrality may be mystifying because it makes power roles invisible, and complementarity, a "different but equal" approach, obscures any aspect of inequality. If neutrality in the sense of showing no partiality to individuals within the family can be accepted, neutrality in the sense of not privileging any view over any other, and not trying to influence patients in any manner, becomes a way of not taking position, even when a family seems to be organised in a rather sexist and patriarchal way. The risk, in all these cases, is to accept everything families bring in sessions, including the unacceptable. Moreover, the Milan therapists, although they acknowledged the extent to which individuals and families are influenced by wider systems and context, never extended their consideration to political and gender issues.

In subsequent years, though, the main emphasis in systemic and post-systemic—i.e., narrative, constructive, or conversational—therapies was on discourse and language (see Appendix A). A schism appeared within the field, and feminist therapists and systemic therapists often stood on opposite sides of it. Burck and Daniel wrote in 1995:

> many feminist thinkers and systemic therapists continue to stereotype each other's position. ... Although we think there is now a multiplicity of ways of being a feminist and a systemic therapist, we notice how often feminism is portrayed as holding to a rigid and one-dimensional line. ... Systemic thinking [in turn] has also been stereotyped in feminist writings.
>
> (1995, pp. 3–4)

This gap was mostly bridged after the year 2000, when the fourth wave of feminism appeared. The way in which we tried to contribute to this bridging process is outlined in Chapter 2 of this book.

Notes

1 Butler's definition of gender as performative bears some resemblance to Bateson's notion of premises: premises too are standardised by culture and played out inadvertently according to implicit and unaware social and cultural rules.

References

Bateson, G. (1971). Double Bind, 1969. In: *Steps to an Ecology of Mind* (pp. 271–278). Chandler Publishing Company, 1972.

Bateson, G., Jackson, D.D., Haley, J., & Weakland, J.H. (1956). Toward a theory of schizophrenia. *Behavioral Science*, 1: 251–264. DOI:10.1002/bs.3830010402.

Boscolo, L., Cecchin, G., Hoffman, L., & Penn, P. (1987). *Milan Systemic Family Therapy: Conversations in Theory and Practice*. Basic Books.

Burck, C. & Daniel, G. (1995). *Gender and Family Therapy*. Karnac.

Butler, J.P. (1990). *Gender Trouble: Feminism and the Subversion of Identity*. Routledge.

Butler, J.P. (1993). *Bodies that Matter: On the Discursive Limits of Sex*. Taylor & Francis, 2011.

Crenshaw, K. (1991). Mapping the Margins: Intersectionality, Identity Politics, and Violence against Women of Color. *Stanford Law Review*, 43 (6): 1241–1299. DOI:10.2307/1229039.

de Beauvoir, S. (2011). *The Second Sex* (Engl. Transl. by C. Borde & S. Malovany-Chevallier). Vintage Books (original edition: *Le deuxieme sexe*. Gallimard, 1949).

Evans, E. (2015). Understanding Third Wave Feminisms. In: *Id., The Politics of Third Wave Feminisms. Gender and Politics Series*. Palgrave Macmillan, pp. 19–38. DOI:10.1057/9781137295279_2.

Friedan, B. (1963). *The Feminine Mystique*. Norton.

Haley, J. (1976). Development of a Theory: The History of a Research Project. In: M. Richeport-Haley & J. Carlson (Eds.), *Jay Haley Revisited*. Taylor and Francis, 2010.

Hamberg, K. (2008). Gender Bias in Medicine. *Women's Health*, 4 (3): 237–243. DOI:10.2217/17455057.4.3.237.

Hare-Mustin, R.T. (1978). A feminist approach to family therapy. *Family Process*, 17: 181–194.

Hoffman, L. (1981). *Foundations of Family Therapy*. Basic Books.

Horowitz, D. (1996). Rethinking Betty Friedan and the Feminine Mystique: Labor Union Radicalism and Feminism in Cold War America. *American Quarterly*, 48 (1): 1–42. www.jstor.org/stable/30041520.

Irigaray, L. (1985). *Speculum or the Other Woman* (Engl. trans. by Gillian C. Gill). Cornell University Press (original edition 1974).

Izzo, A. (2002). Outrageous and everyday: The papers of Gloria Steinem. *Journal of Women's History*, 14 (2): 151–153. DOI:10.1353/jowh.2002.0045.

Johnson Lewis, J. (2020). International Women's Suffrage Timeline: 1851-Present. *ThoughtCo*. www.thoughtco.com/international-woman-suffrage-timeline-3530479. Retrieved February 8th, 2024.

Kristeva, J. (1986). *The Kristeva Reader*, ed. Toril Moi. Columbia University Press.

Luepnitz, D.A. (1988). *The Family Interpreted: Psychoanalysis, Feminism, and Family Therapy*. Basic Books.

Mead, M. (1935). *Sex and Temperament in Three Primitive Societies*. Morrow.

Miller, P.H., & Kofsky Scholnick, E. (Eds) (2000). *Toward a Feminist Developmental Psychology*. Routledge.

Munro, E. (2013). Feminism: A Fourth Wave?. *Political Insight*, 4 (2): 22–25. DOI:10.1111/2041-9066.12021. S2CID 142990260.

Ozkazanc-Pan, B. (2019). On agency and empowerment in a #MeToo world. *Gender, Work and Organization*, 26 (8): 1212–1220. DOI:10.1111/gwao.12311.

Parsons, T. & Bales, R.T. (1956). *Family Socialization and Interaction Process*. The Free Press.

Reger, J. (2017). Finding a Place in History: The Discursive Legacy of the Wave Metaphor and Contemporary Feminism. *Feminist Studies*, 43 (1): 193–221. DOI:10.1353/fem.2017.0012.

Simon, R. (1997). Fearless foursome: After 20 years, the Women's Project prepares to pass the torch. *Family Therapy Networker*, 21 (6).

Tong, R. (2018). *Feminist Thought: A More Comprehensive Introduction*. Routledge.

Walters, M., Carter, B., Papp, P., & Silverstein, O. (1988). *The Invisible Web: Gender Patterns in Family Relationships*. Guilford.

World Health Organization (2021). Gender: definitions. www.euro.who.int. Archived from the original on 25 September 2021. Retrieved 12 July 2023.

Wilson, E. (2014). Diversity, culture and the glass ceiling. *Journal of Cultural Diversity*, 21 (3): 83.

Index

For Product Safety Concerns and Information please contact our EU
representative GPSR@taylorandfrancis.com
Taylor & Francis Verlag GmbH, Kaufingerstraße 24, 80331 München, Germany

www.ingramcontent.com/pod-product-compliance
Lightning Source LLC
Chambersburg PA
CBHW050637280326
41932CB00015B/2679